ASE Guide to Primary Science Education

Edited by Wynne Harlen

The **Association**
for **Science Education**

Published by the Association for Science Education
College Lane, Hatfield, Herts AL10 9AA

ISBN 0 86357 405 X (2007: 978 0 86357 405 4)

Executive Editor: Helen Johnson
Design and page layout: Colin Barker
Cover photos (top to bottom): Courtesy of: Vicky Hutchin, Gary Cornford,
Ferris, Sarah Earle.
by Piggott Black Bear Ltd, Cambridge, England

Contents

About the authors

Hilary Asoko is a senior lecturer at the University of Leeds, where she is involved in teacher education programmes and research in science education. Her particular interests are in children's conceptual development in science and how this can be supported in the primary classroom.

Derek Bell is Chief Executive of the Association for Science Education. He has extensive insight into teaching and learning in science through his own teaching, research and experience in teacher education. He maintains contact with a wide range of organisations.

Paul Black, OBE, is Emeritus Professor at King's College London, where he directed the education department from 1976 to1989. He retired in 1995. In the 1980s he helped direct national surveys of school science performance for the Assessment of Performance Unit (APU) and in 1987–1988 he was chair of the Task Group on Assessment and Testing which set out the basis for national testing in England and Wales.

Andrew Clegg is a science education consultant working from the UK and Namibia. He was formerly a science teacher in Yorkshire and Somerset and one-time head of the Department of Mathematics and Science Education at the University of Botswana.

John Dabell is an experienced primary teacher and works as a freelance writer, journalist and education consultant. He works with Brenda Keogh and Stuart Naylor as Millgate House Publishing and Consultancy.

Max de Bóo has been enthusiastically involved in primary and nursery education for many years as a teacher, lecturer and author. She has specialised in primary and early-years education and edited and written books on these subjects including a recent one on the early years for the ASE.

Mick Dunne is Science Education Leader and Programme Manager for all postgraduate Initial Teacher Education courses at Bradford College. He is a member of the Editorial Board of *Primary Science Review* and has a particular interest in environmental education.

Rosemary Feasey is a freelance science education consultant and author. She was the first person from a primary background to become national Chair of the ASE.

Wynne Harlen, OBE, was Professor of Science Education at the University of Liverpool from 1985 to 1990, before becoming Director of the Scottish Council for Research in Education. She is now visiting professor in education at the University of Bristol. She was editor of *Primary Science Review* from 1999 to 2004.

Chris Harrison is a lecturer at King's College London where she leads the Assessment for Learning Research Group whose publications include the 'black box' series. She is a popular speaker at national and international conferences.

Brenda Keogh and **Stuart Naylor** work as writers, researchers, publishers, consultants and professional development providers for teachers, as Millgate House Publishing and Consultancy. They both have extensive experience in teacher education as well as working as teachers and advisory teachers.

Bob Kibble lectures in science education at the University of Edinburgh. His specialist interest is in curriculum development in physics and astronomy. He creates and provides professional development for teachers and, at the time of publication, is Chair of the ASE.

Liz Lakin is Head of Science Education at St Martin's College, Lancaster, where she teaches on both the primary and secondary programmes. She is Reviews Editor for *Primary Science Review* and is the author of several publications on science education.

Liz Lawrence spent 14 years as a primary teacher before becoming advisory teacher for primary science and technology in Barking and Dagenham. She is involved in many local ASE activities and is a member of the Association's Primary Science Committee.

Roger Mitchell is Acting Head Teacher at Ripple Junior School in Barking. He has served on a variety of advisory panels including those for the DfES, QCA and the DTI and is currently Chair of ASE Primary Science Committee. He has particular interests in promoting the effective use of ICT and in developing quality dialogue in primary science lessons.

Alan Peacock edits *Primary Science Review* and formerly ran the Primary Science PGCE Programme at the University of Exeter. He has worked extensively in Africa, and has published research, textbooks and teachers' guides. He is now a consultant in environmental education.

Anne Qualter is Head of Education at the University of Liverpool. She has been active in researching, writing and teaching about primary science for over 25 years, focusing on assessment, children's learning, and how good teachers support and promote excitement for science learning in young children.

Mary Ratcliffe is Professor of Science Education at the University of Southampton and Director of the Science Learning Centre South East. She taught in comprehensive schools in East Anglia and has been Chair of ASE (1996/7). Her research and development interests are in pupils' and teachers' reactions to socio-scientific issues and the development of effective learning and assessment practice.

Michael Reiss is Professor of Science

Education at the Institute of Education, University of London, Chief Executive of Science Learning Centre London, and holds various visiting professorships. He is director of the Salters-Nuffield Advanced Biology Project, a member of the Farm Animal Welfare Council and editor of the journal *Sex Education*.

Ian Richardson, HMI, became the specialist adviser for science in 2003. He has taught science in a wide range of social contexts and worked in Cheshire LEA's Advisory Team. As Professional Officer for Science at the National Curriculum Council he participated in two revisions of the science Orders for England. As an independent consultant he wrote textbooks, worked on the development of KS2 and KS3 national tests and teacher professional development in science and management.

Phil Scott is Professor of Science Education at the University of Leeds. He taught physics and science in high schools for 15 years, becoming a head of science, before starting his university career with the Children's Learning in Science Research Group.

Natasha Serret is one of the main authors of *Let's think through science!* A former primary school teacher, she continues to work with teachers as a primary CASE consultant, researcher and as a member of the primary science PGCE team at the Institute of Education, University of London.

Lynne Symonds works actively with science teachers from many parts of the world to encourage the sharing of ideas. She is currently Chair of the ASE International Committee and of The Commonwealth Association of Science, Technology and Maths Educators.

Lynne Wright is an experienced primary teacher, Ofsted inspector of primary and nursery schools and teacher educator, with expertise in many aspects of science education. She is a member of the ASE Publications Committee.

Introduction

The Association for Science Education published the last *Guide to Primary Science Education* in 1998, at the end of almost a decade of unprecedented change in primary science theory and practice. It might be reasonable to suppose that a steady state had been achieved at the end of the 1990s, but in fact the first years of the 21st century have seen no let up in the pace of change. Both new and familiar topics are discussed in this *Guide*.

The enduring matters that are revisited include the purpose of science education in the early years and through the primary years, the importance of attitudes and values, the nature of children's learning, making provision for continuity and progression, the importance of enabling children to investigate, the role of questions, the use of information and communication technology and the management of science at the school level. These topics remain central to the discussion of primary science, and the chapters relating to them reflect fresh thinking as well as continuity in our understanding of goals and how to achieve them. At the same time, there is now more to say about professional development, particularly with the instigation of the national and regional science learning centres, and more attention is given to transfer from primary to secondary school, to school self-evaluation, to pupil assessment and self-assessment and the formative use of assessment, to talk and dialogue in the classroom and to developing children's thinking skills and creativity. Chapters on these subjects reflect some of the exciting developments that have taken place in the last few years.

Some changes of policy, in England particularly, that have taken place since the publication of the 1998 *Guide* have had a considerable effect on what and how teachers teach. An obvious example is the QCA scheme of work, published too late to be included in the last *Guide* but referred to in several chapters here. The presence or absence of national tests and how the test results are used are also key policy matters that have a considerable impact. It is in relation to policy that differences between countries are greatest. While it is inevitable that some issues specific to England are aired, we have tried to ensure that teachers in other countries in the UK and beyond do not feel excluded. Reference is made to policies and practice in Scotland, Wales and Northern Ireland where these differ from those in England, and indeed a chapter in the first section takes a global view of how science education is practised across the UK and beyond.

One of the interesting changes is the use of the word 'enquiry' which is prevalent in this *Guide*, but hardly featured in the previous one. I see this as more than a change in the way we refer to certain types of investigative experience; rather, it acknowledges the considerable range of experiences that together support children in building their understanding of scientific ideas and processes. These experiences include direct investigation of events and materials but also the use of information and ideas from other sources such as books and the Internet, from their teacher, from argument and debate with other children, from experts who visit or are visited by the children. These are bound together in an approach that sees science as the theories, ideas and processes that are constructed and used to make sense of the natural world, not as a set of facts to be learned.

Organisation of the *Guide*

As an organising framework, the chapters are grouped into four sections. The first section relates to the national level, where matters of overall goals and policies are discussed. The chapters here cover the goals and the criteria of quality to be aimed for and the range of professional development opportunities that can help to raise the standards of provision. The second section groups together chapters relating to policy matters at the school level. This includes decisions about how provision for learning science can extend beyond the classroom and across the whole curriculum. Ways of ensuring continuity from primary to secondary school and ideas for school self-evaluation of all the aspects that affect children's learning in science are also included.

The third section deals with planning at the school level, required to put the school policy into practice. A good deal of this planning falls to the science subject leader, but it generally involves all teachers in agreeing on matters such as the selection of a scheme of work that facilitates progression and continuity and of the materials, resources and ICT that enable plans to be put into practice. Although most of the book is relevant to the education of children across the age range from early years to end of primary, this section includes a chapter giving specific attention to science experiences for 3–5 year-olds.

The fourth and largest section focuses on planning at the classroom level. In keeping with the overall intention of the *Guide*, these chapters illustrate current thinking on these matters rather than providing details of how and what to teach. Help with specific activities can be found in published programmes of classroom materials in book form and, increasingly, online, including many publications of the ASE. In this section there are chapters on making provision for all children according to their needs, planning opportunities for progression in conceptual understanding and thinking skills, and using and encouraging creativity. There are also chapters relating to using questions, dialogue and formative assessment to help learning, including children's self- and peer-assessment.

About half of the chapters contain material that is common with chapters on the same topic in the companion *ASE Guide to Secondary Science Education*, edited by Valerie Wood-Robinson. We believe this common material is helpful in emphasising the continuity in children's science education. In some cases the linked chapters are very similar; in others there are different examples and references to practice in the primary and secondary versions; in others again, more substantial differences in treatment of a topic were seen as appropriate.

Each chapter ends with references and, in most cases, website addresses, where further information can be sought. Some topics lend themselves to more practice-based treatment, whilst others require a more theoretical approach. There are inevitable variations in style among the chapters, reflecting the authors' preferences. Whilst the chapters can be read in any sequence, the sections will hopefully guide readers to their own best starting points and frequent cross-referencing will lead them to other relevant chapters.

All the chapters have been written by members of the ASE who are committed to, and experienced in, developing science education. Notes about the authors can be found on pages v and vi. In general the expertise of the authors ranges across the whole panoply of issues related to primary science but for this *Guide* they have been asked to address just one part of it. Adopting such a focus is quite difficult and, despite editorial intervention, some overlap is inevitable. There will also no doubt be some gaps that are identified, for which I take full responsibility. I am immensely grateful to the authors who willingly agreed to write and did so to quite a tight timetable at times when there were heavy demands on their time.

The future will doubtless bring further developments in primary science practice that will require a new *Guide*. In the meantime, I hope that this book will be found helpful by all involved in primary science education, whether as student teachers, newly qualified or experienced teachers, particularly those with responsibility for leading the subject in their schools.

Wynne Harlen

August 2005

Section 1 National level: Setting the scene

Chapter 1

Primary science education for the 21st century

This first chapter focuses on the most recent practices and trends in primary science education;

Wynne Harlen

however, it is useful to consider these against the backdrop of the continued efforts during the last half century to introduce and improve science as part of the education of young children. So the first part of the chapter looks back briefly at some of the thinking and events that brought us to where we are now. The second part looks ahead, beginning with current views of the goals of school science education as a whole and then looking at what primary school science contributes to this as well as to the overall goals of primary education. Directions of change are towards more attention being paid to understanding the broad ideas of and about science, the development of enquiry skills and reflection on learning, through children's involvement in collaborative first-hand enquiry, dialogue and using assessment to help learning.

Looking back

Throughout the 20th and the latter part of the 19th centuries, attempts were made to ensure a place for science in pre-secondary education. What science education means in practice has changed considerably over the last 150 years, as have the practices of education generally. The changes are reflected in the reports of school inspectors and the writing of education pioneers such as Susan and Nathan Isaacs, John Dewey, Elizabeth Lawrence and Gwen Allen. Accounts of early science lessons have been quoted by Layton (1973) and by Harlen (2001) and Harlen and Simon (2001) in the Association for Science Education journals as part of the commemoration of 100 years of science teaching. There is not space to repeat the story of the development of primary science education here, fascinating though it is, but it is worth pointing out what has stayed the same as well as what has changed.

One rather depressing constant is the contrast between what is advocated and what is practised. For example, whilst in 1890 official reports claimed that:

the formation of accurate habits of observation, of work, of reasoning, and of description were at the early stage of education of far greater moment than the accumulation of facts or the ability to answer examination questions on these facts,

the article went on to point out that for this to happen it was necessary for there to be:

a complete change in the methods of instruction commonly practised and in the attitude of the teacher towards his pupils and his subject.

(quoted in Harlen, 2001, p. 10).

What was happening in classrooms at that time, if anything, was a continuation of the 'object lesson', in which teachers relentlessly taught, and expected children to memorise, facts relating to objects which they were allowed to see, often only as a drawing, but rarely to handle.

Although practice has changed, there is constancy in what pioneers have urged should be achieved through teaching science at the elementary/primary level. For instance, Nathan Isaacs' words at a 1961 conference, quoted in Box 1.1, surely reflect what we hope to achieve today. Isaacs also refers to what is needed as *'scientific literacy'* and argues that *'science in some sense now has claims to form part of the very ABC of education'* (Isaacs, 1962, p. 6). And he points out that this literacy is needed by all, as a means of preventing a *'cultural cleavage'* between the *'scientific community and the non-scientific rest of us'* (p. 7).

> **Box 1.1**
>
> *The school ... can continually offer fresh stimuli and openings for exploration, in various directions; it can provoke questions or expressly invite them; and it can use any that are suitable in order to launch groups of children on their own co-operative quests for the answers. They can be encouraged to consider and discuss, and to put out ideas either by way of actual solutions or at least for next steps. They can be guided and steered, helped over difficulties, and offered hints in the right directions or suggestive leading questions. In all these ways each inquiry that has been set in motion can be carried forward through exciting progress to a successful solution and become an immensely educative experience for all the children who have shared it. For not only have they thus built up by their own efforts some fresh scheme of connected knowledge and understanding, but they have also experienced for themselves some of the typical ways and methods by which such building up can be achieved.*
>
> *A varied series of these co-operative group enquiries carried on week by week, term by term, year by year, on a growing scale, in various main fields which thus become progressively better charted and organised, should take children a long way towards a basic understanding of the meaning of scientific inquiry and of scientific knowledge.*
> (Isaacs, 1962, p. 12)

Implementing the vision

The ideals expressed in Box 1.1 influenced the early curriculum projects of the 1960s – Nuffield Junior Science, the Oxford Primary Science project and Science 5/13 – all of which relied heavily on the ability of teachers to respond to events and to be creative in fostering children's enquiries. But the reports of practice gathered by Inspectors during the 1970s (DES, 1978) showed how far implementation fell short of this ideal. A survey associated with this report showed that only about half of primary classes had any science at all and in only about one in ten was the work developed seriously. Britain was not alone in developing materials that only a small minority could use: in the USA a study in the same year (Weiss, 1978) reported that 70 per cent of school districts did not use any of the materials of the three major projects developed in the 1960s (ESS, SCIS and SAPA).

In response, new curriculum materials, funded variously by local education authorities, the Schools Council, the Nuffield Foundation and by publishers, provided more direct help for teachers to bridge the gap between the aspirations of the primary science enthusiasts and the capacities of the schools to respond to their ideas. Each set of materials made its own selection of content, although they varied less in content than in the extent to which the activities genuinely gave children the chance to use and develop process skills.

The late 1970s also saw the inception of the Assessment of Performance Unit (APU) surveys of science at ages 11, 13 and 15 in England, Wales and Northern Ireland (surveys of a similar nature began in Scotland in 1984 and still continue). In order to develop the assessment programme it was necessary to decide what kinds of achievement should be assessed. This began a discussion that was continued in the development of national curricula at the end of the 1980s. The APU surveys had two further implications. The first was to raise the profile of science in the primary curriculum, putting it by the side of mathematics and English, the only other subjects to be covered systematically in the surveys. The second was to stimulate research into the ideas that children held about the scientific aspects of things around them (Osborne and Freyberg, 1985; SPACE Research Reports, 1990–1998). It was clear from what was found that these ideas could not be ignored because children believed them; they had to be the starting point from which more scientific ideas could be developed.

The place of science in the primary curriculum changed radically as a result of the Education Reform Act of 1988. Not only was the teaching of science required, either by consent as in Scotland, or by statute as in the rest of the UK, but *what* science was taught was also prescribed. Moreover, teachers would have to assess the progress of children's learning in science, an aspect notably missing from earlier work.

Looking ahead

The legacy of the 20th century was that science education could no longer be regarded as starting at secondary school. A key feature of national curricula and guidelines is to identify progression throughout the compulsory years of schooling, with continuity through the primary and secondary years. Chapter 8 describes some of the current initiatives to smooth the transfer from primary to secondary school.

But progression in what? What should we be aiming for at the beginning of the 21st century? What is the role of work at the primary level? Having a national curriculum or national guidelines has not removed the need to ask and answer these questions, for what is learned by children will depend as much on *how* science is taught as on *what* is taught. We can teach children to recite the parts of a plant, if we really want to, or we can engage them in observing and investigating the conditions in which plants grow, learning the names of parts as they need to refer to them, and learning much more as well about plants and about the process of scientific enquiry.

Overall goals of science education

So, before thinking about the learning at primary level, we briefly consider the overall goals of science education. It is not a simple matter because science education in school has to serve two different but equally important purposes. One is preparing future scientists and technologists, and the other is providing all children with sufficient knowledge and understanding of the world around them to enable them to become informed citizens, able to operate effectively and make sensible decisions about science-related issues that affect all our lives. Although in the primary curriculum no distinction is made between these two purposes, there is a tendency for the requirements of later stages of education to bear down on the earlier stages (Millar and Osborne, 2006).

Two influential groups that have considered the nature of 'science for all' in the 21st century have come to similar conclusions: that it is best described as *'scientific literacy'*. One of these groups was of UK science educators who considered *'the form of science education required to prepare young people for life in our society in the next century'* (Millar and Osborne, 1998, p. 2001) and published their findings under the title *Beyond 2000*. The second group was an international group set up by the Organisation for Economic Co-operation and Development (OECD) to advise on the development of tests to assess *'how well students at age 15, and therefore approaching the end of compulsory schooling, are prepared to meet the challenges of today's societies'* (OECD, 2003, p. 9). Both groups expressed the overall aim as enhancing *'scientific literacy'*, meaning a broad understanding of key ideas of science, shown in the ability to apply these ideas to everyday events and phenomena, and an understanding of the strengths and limitations of scientific activity and of the nature of scientific knowledge.

At the secondary level one of the initiatives for achieving these ends is the development of *Twenty First Century Science*. This innovative programme for 14–16 year-olds separates *'the science curriculum into two strands, one designed to promote "scientific literacy" and a second to prepare young people for more advanced study'* (Millar and Osborne, 2006, p. 8).

The goals of primary school science

Looking back at the writing of Nathan Isaacs in Box 1.1 we find consistency with the overall aims of science education today. We also find consistency in overall goals between primary and secondary schools, for scientific literacy is as relevant to young children as to 14–16 year-olds.

In terms of scientific ideas emerging from the content that is taught, there is little contentious about the broad areas to be included. National curricula and guidelines set these out in different ways but all include goals of knowledge and understanding relating to living things and life processes, materials, physical processes, Earth and space, and energy and forces. There is also agreement on the development of process or enquiry skills as a goal. In different ways, curricula implicitly cover question-raising, hypothesising, predicting, using observation, planning and conducting investigations, interpreting evidence and communicating.

A recent concern for reflection on the processes of learning and for motivation for learning – both needed to encourage children to become life-long learners – has added these to the goals of education. Although they are goals of learning in all subject areas, it can be argued that science education has a particularly strong role in working towards them.

Where most changes have taken place, however, and where further change is to be expected, is in how children are helped to achieve these goals. At the primary level in the UK there is a long-established recognition of the importance of first-hand experience and investigation of materials and phenomena of relevance to children's everyday lives. Recent thinking and research evidence have added emphasis on talk, reflection on learning and involvement in self-assessment. How are these likely to feature in primary science as we move further into the 21st century?

First-hand experience

The thinking of young children is characterised by being led by action. In the early years children have to do things to see the effect of their actions, rather than thinking them through. They need to handle and make things change, look at things from different viewpoints, sort and group, and repeat actions again and again (see Chapter 16). As they become older they begin to grasp a series of changes as a whole and to think through familiar actions. They can investigate the effects of changes and make 'fair' comparisons as long as the variables are simple and obvious. In the later primary years they can tackle more complex problems and plan enquiries, but the things they can manipulate mentally are restricted to those that have a concrete reality and relevance for the child. Relevance to daily life experience and reality are key features that facilitate learning at all stages, but what these mean changes across the generations. A piece of coal does not have the same role in the lives of children now as it did, say, 60 years ago. Today, what children see on television, CD-ROMs, and from the Internet can be 'real' for them if linked to everyday experiences. The opportunities provided through these media to see and hear things that expand their experience will only increase in coming years, but they will be no more than fiction if we do not relate them to things and events that are real for the children.

Talk

Talk has a key role in making this link to real life as well as supporting the development of understanding. The seminal work of Douglas Barnes (1978) on speech as communication and as reflection demonstrated how putting ideas and thoughts into words enabled learners to clarify their own thinking and to learn from others. More recent classroom research has further underlined the role of talk in learning and identified dialogue as particularly important. Alexander (2004) identifies a particular approach to teaching called 'dialogic

7

teaching', which aims to engage children and teachers in listening carefully and responding to each other, asking and answering questions, expressing, explaining and evaluating ideas, arguing and justifying. In this process teachers can both gain and use information about how children's learning is progressing. Chapter 20 in this volume expands on these ideas and gives an account of the theoretical arguments that underpin the claims for talk as a tool of learning.

Reflection

Reflection on learning helps to consolidate what has been learned and also to make children aware of the process of learning. This is the first step towards developing metacognitive thinking, where learners can reflect on their reasoning and on how their ideas have changed. Such thinking is necessary in order to develop ideas about science at a later stage in their education. In the past it was generally assumed that primary school children would not be able to stand back from their enquiries and reflect on how they tackled them, and so opportunities for such thinking were not offered. But projects such as *Let's Think* and *Let's Think Through Science* (Adey *et al.*, 2003) have shown that not only do primary children respond to opportunities to talk about their thought processes, but they gain in understanding by doing so (Adey, Robertson and Venville, 2002). Such reflection, prompted by teachers' questions, such as *What have you found out that you did not know before? Have you changed your mind about ...? What made you change your mind?*, may well prevent them slipping back into previous ways of thinking (see Chapter 24). Opportunities of this kind are likely to feature more prominently in the future.

Involvement in self-assessment

Helping children to assess their own learning is a key aspect of learning in which they play an active role in constructing their understanding. When learning is understood in this way, learners are at the centre of the process. It follows that the more learners know about what it is intended should be learned – the learning goals, about where they have reached in relation to these goals, and about what further work needs to be done to reach the goals, the more the learners can direct effort usefully for learning. Chapter 23 provides more discussion on the value of self-assessment and of extending this to peer-assessment. The point to make here is that the benefits include improvement of children's self-esteem, sense of responsibility, self-efficacy (taking ownership) and self-regulation (control over their learning), all of which are positive aspects of motivation for learning. These non-cognitive outcomes of education are increasingly being seen as essential for current and future generations of children, for whom learning in school can no longer provide what they need to prepare them for the rest of their lives.

Conclusion: primary science for the 21st century

What will children be doing in the primary classroom where science for the 21st century is being learned? Putting the above points together helps to provide an answer. This should certainly include:

- being engaged in enquiries that they have helped to formulate;

- working collaboratively in groups towards a shared and agreed understanding of their enquiry and of how to interpret their findings;
- collecting evidence by first-hand observation, with the aid of data-logging where appropriate, and from secondary sources;
- working purposefully, aware of the goals in terms of learning and the quality criteria by which they and others will judge their work;
- presenting their enquiry plans and findings to others and constructively commenting on others' plans and reports;
- using self- and peer-assessment to improve their work.
- recognising what makes an enquiry 'scientific';
- reflecting on what and how they have learned and on what helped their learning.

References

Adey, P., Nagy, F., Robertson, A., Serret, N. and Wadsworth, P. (2003) *Let's Think Through Science!* Windsor: nferNelson.

Adey, P., Robertson, A. and Venville, G. (2002) Effects of a cognitive acceleration programme on year 1 pupils. *British Journal of Educational Psychology*, **72**(1), 1–25.

Alexander, R. (2004) *Towards dialogic teaching: rethinking classroom talk*. York: Dialogos.

Barnes, D. (1978) *From communication to curriculum*. Harmondsworth: Penguin.

DES (1978) *Primary education in England: a survey*. London: HMSO.

Harlen, W. (2001) The rise and fall of peripatetic science demonstrators. *Primary Science Review*, **67**, 9–10.

Harlen, W. and Simon, S. (2001) Elementary school science and the rise and rise of primary science. *School Science Review*, **82**(300), 49–57.

Isaacs, N. (1962) The case for bringing science into the primary school. In *The place of science in primary education*, ed. Perkins, W. H. London: British Association for the Advancement of Science.

Layton, D. (1973) *Science for the people*. London: George Allen & Unwin.

Millar, R. and Osborne, J. (2006) Science education for the 21st century. In *ASE guide to secondary science education*, ed. Wood-Robinson, V. pp. 3–9. Hatfield: Association for Science Education.

Millar, R. and Osborne, J. ed. (1998) *Beyond 2000: science education for the future*. London: King's College London, School of Education.

OECD (2003) *The PISA 2003 assessment framework*. Paris: OECD.

Osborne, R. J. and Freyberg, P. (1985) *Learning in science: the implications of children's science*. Auckland, New Zealand: Heinemann.

SPACE (Science Processes and Concepts Exploration) Research Reports: *Evaporation and condensation* (1990), *Growth* (1990), *Light* (1990), *Sound* (1990), *Electricity* (1991), *Materials* (1991), *Processes of life* (1992), *Rocks, soil and weather* (1993), *Forces* (1998). Liverpool University Press.

Weiss, I. R (1978) *National survey of science, mathematics and social studies education: highlights report*. Document ED152 566. ERIC.

Chapter 2

Taking purposes seriously in science education

It is not inevitable that science be given the high priority that it now enjoys in the school curriculum, or even that it be a subject at all. Its position has to be justified by answering two questions: What contribution can science education make to the general development of children? and What are the purposes that are specific to science education? This chapter focuses mainly on answers to the first question, concentrating on the aim of promoting the intellectual, personal and moral development of children and on those purposes that may be achieved in several subjects but that transcend their individual boundaries. The first section sets out a model to highlight interactions between curriculum, pedagogy and assessment. Subsequent sections deal with the implications for practice of different purposes, by examining in turn the links between curriculum and pedagogy, the pressure of assessment on the curriculum, and the links between pedagogy and assessment. The various threads are then drawn together in the final section.

Paul Black

The triangle

Any commitment to purposes is pointless without a matching commitment to achieving them. Moreover, striving to achieve them may alter the purposes or the way one understands them. A more realistic view of a complex picture may be achieved by close examination of the links between a curriculum and the pedagogy through which it is implemented. This pedagogy is itself powerfully affected by both summative and formative assessment. These purposes of assessment are defined and discussed in Chapter 22. Figure 2.1 represents these three elements and the interactions between them in a simple way.

Two features are central in determining these interactions. For the first, it is

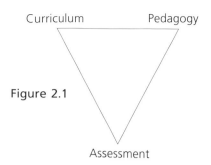

Curriculum   Pedagogy

Figure 2.1

Assessment

obvious that assumptions about how children may learn best will underpin the ways in which those involved develop the interactive links: this will be true whether or not the theories held are made explicit. What is involved here is more than just theories of memory and understanding. The growth in the motivation, self-esteem and self-confidence of children are also powerful factors, and constitute a set of purposes in their own right.

The second feature is the way in which those involved see their own roles, as teachers or as learners. Those teachers who focus on 'delivery' of the curriculum and strive to meet external test requirements will teach very differently from those who see outside prescriptions as constraining their central purpose in striving for the development of the potential of all children. Similarly, children may see themselves as passive recipients or as active and responsible learners.

Changing curriculum, changing pedagogy

Different purposes affect both the approach to teaching, the pedagogy, and assessment. For example, suppose the purpose is to involve children actively in their own investigations in or about science. If this calls for work with equipment, then teachers need, in addition to suitable skills and facilities, the pedagogic skills to handle open-ended practical investigations. The teacher might have to tolerate uncertainty rather than tidy closure, and provide feedback that encourages and guides children's initiatives. This calls for skills and attitudes rather different from those required in teaching other subjects. If the purpose calls for library or Internet research, the pedagogic skills needed are different – more akin to those exercised when teaching English than those usually needed in science. In both possibilities, assessment could hardly be by written test, and would have to be based on teachers' assessments of selected products, combined with inter-teacher moderation.

The challenges are different again if children are engaged in study of the social implications of the achievements of scientists. Such engagement calls for participation in open debate, whereby implicit assumptions and differences in beliefs and values on social and moral issues must come into play. The pedagogic skills then needed may be more akin to those of teaching religion or history. Assessment would involve looking for quality in oral or written argument rather than for correct answers.

Pressures on curriculum and assessment

The need for a national curriculum arose from a culmination of longer-term political and social trends; public and political interest in education continues to be strong. Such interests are heightened by a growing emphasis on the need to expand numbers in tertiary education and by pressures from business, industry and environmentalists. It seems that political control over the curriculum, far from leading to stability, is leading to more questioning of school practices and to temptations to exert power to 'improve' as soon as difficulties are publicised.

Thus, the determination of purposes and priorities for the science curriculum is, like other social issues, an essentially political struggle between competing traditions, perspectives and interests. However, whilst schools are not in full control of specification, they have very strong control over implementation, so that their own priorities, and their views of the priorities of others, will continue to be of outstanding importance.

The instrument that is used to hold schools 'accountable' to the public, the 'bottom line' for most teachers, in England as in some other countries, is the system of tests which are organised outside the control of schools. This could be, in principle, a benign way of reinforcing the implementation of the purposes of the nationally agreed curriculum. However, a study of the effects of the current system of external testing on the work of teachers concluded that:

> As currently constituted external assessment in school science education would appear to have a malign effect on the teaching of science, encouraging teachers to teach by transmission which, in turn, results in negative student attitudes towards school science. Too often assessment in school science supports a practice which sees science as a body of knowledge to be learnt rather than as a way of knowing which has transformed the world in which we live. (Black et al., 2004, p. 2)

Such concerns apply both to written tests, for which the limitations of cost and administration constrain both the testing time and the scope of the aims that they can assess, and, at the secondary level, to teacher-based assessment of practical work.

In technical terms, the accountability system is invalid, that is, it does not measure what it should (see Chapter 22). Added to this is the evidence that short written tests cannot measure with adequate accuracy the limited range of goals that they do measure, that is, they are not sufficiently reliable for their purposes. For example, an analysis of key stage 3 tests shows that it is likely that the proportion of pupils misclassified by at least one level is at least 24 per cent, and might well be over 35 per cent (Wiliam, 2001). Another example concerns the 11-plus selection tests in Northern Ireland, analysed by Gardner and Cowan (2000). Of the 18 000 children tested every year, between 6000 and 7000 succeed; yet analysis of the reliability of the tests shows that about 3000 entrants will be wrongly placed, some gaining places when they should not have, and some failing when they should have succeeded.

The only way to escape the cul-de-sac in which present practice is trapped is to place far more reliance on teachers' own assessments, which some other countries seem able to do. Both Scotland and Wales have policies that are moving in this direction. However, such a system could not command, or deserve, public confidence in England without a large investment in teachers' assessment skills.

Assessment and pedagogy

There are two reasons why pedagogy is relevant to a consideration of the purposes of science education. The obvious one is that it is the means by which the purposes are achieved in practice, so the purposes and the practice have to be moulded to form a consistent relationship. The more subtle purpose is that the way a teacher teaches gives children models of learning, and knowledge of themselves as learners. Enabling children to learn to be effective learners in the future is a central aim of school education, and, in so far as science is one of the powerful modes of learning, becoming effective learners in science is an important aim for all children.

For pedagogy aimed at helping children to develop as learners, formative assessment is central. What is fundamental to it is the development of two-way feedback interactions between children and teachers. Such development requires that children's ideas be elicited with care, that they be encouraged to express these orally and in writing, that teachers respond to what children express by affirmation, challenge and guidance, and that children learn to collaborate with one another and to take responsibility for their own learning. The details of such pedagogy are explored in Chapters 22 and 23. What is important here is that the ways in which teachers interact every day with the children they teach be based on basic principles of learning, namely that effective teachers should:

- start from a learner's existing understanding;
- involve the learner actively in the learning process;
- help the learner to understand the learning aims and the criteria of quality, so enabling self- and peer-assessment;
- support and guide social learning, i.e. learning through discussion.

A pedagogy of science education based on these principles will serve to enhance the general personal and intellectual development of the children. It is through involvement in discussion and dialogue that children may gain experience in using assumptions, models, evidence and argument to reach conclusions. The emphasis on the importance of dialogue in science education is echoed in many studies of learning in general. For example:

> ... in normal human life, communicative activity and individual thinking have a continuous, dynamic influence on each other.

> ... language provides us with a means for thinking together, for jointly creating knowledge and understanding.

> (Mercer, 2000, pp. 9, 15)

Studies of classroom practice in science have shown that it often falls far short of achieving fruitful learning dialogue with and amongst children (see Chapter 20). The following extract from the report of Driver, Newton and Osborne (2000) illustrates this point:

> Our observations and interviews with science teachers suggest that few teachers have the necessary skills to effectively organize group and class discussions and, hence, they lack confidence in their ability to successfully manage sessions devoted to argumentation and discussion in the classroom. Consequently, such activities rarely, if ever, take place. (p. 309)

All of this bears on learning seen only as a cognitive activity. However, there is far more involved. The way in which children are treated in learning has powerful effects on their motivation and self-esteem, which are powerful determinants both in their learning and in other aspects of their personal development. One type of evidence arises from studies of different ways of giving feedback on written work, as discussed further in Chapter 22. From such a study, Butler (1987) concluded that children given feedback as marks are likely to see it as a way to compare themselves with others ('ego-involvement'), while those given only comments see it as helping them to improve ('task-involvement'); the latter group outperform the former.

These differences have important effects on the development of the potential of children to achieve. Extensive research by Butler (1987), Dweck (2000) and others led Dweck to conclusions that can be summed up as follows:

- With ego-involvement, both high- and low-achievers are reluctant to take risks and react badly to new challenges, and failure simply damages self-esteem.
- With task-involvement, learners believe that they can improve by their own effort, are willing to take on new challenges and to learn from failure.

Such issues are far-reaching and fundamental. A school and classroom culture that emphasises competition, by responding more to those quick to answer in classroom dialogue, by highlighting marks and grades for every piece of work, and by giving praise and prominence to those who do best, is creating a culture of winners and losers. Such effects, in common with the practices of setting and streaming, are damaging overall. The winners gain little, whilst the losers come to believe that they are inherently unable to learn and often cease to participate. If schools are to develop the potential of every child, they must replace the culture of competition with one in which all children are encouraged, so putting into effect a principle that everyone can make progress in reaching targets that are appropriately challenging in relation to their progress to date.

Making it happen

As schooling in general and science education in particular are inevitably subject to frequent change, purposes have to be re-examined. In such scrutiny the most important and over-arching purposes must be kept in focus. For primary children, these are the need to develop their power for thoughtful argument and reflection, their developing grasp of the ways in which science contributes to human knowledge, and their enthusiasm for the exploration of science. For secondary children, there should evolve, in addition, a critical understanding of the strengths and limitations of science in guiding personal and social life, and a deepening understanding of science, which might inspire and guide the desire to study it further.

Above all, in the face of well-intentioned but sometimes misguided external pressures, science education must hold on to and amplify its contribution to the personal development and self-confidence of all children, so that all can leave school as competent as possible in their own capacity to learn, and confident that they can always, by their own efforts, develop their understanding of both familiar and new issues.

The continual effort to achieve such purposes ought to be guided by attention to the framework suggested by the triangle model. This implies that attention must be focused on:

- curriculum renewal – and the changes in pedagogy and assessment that such renewal requires;
- renewal of assessment, both in public policies for summative assessment to move from the present negative to more positive effects on pedagogy and on some curriculum aims, and in school practices in formative assessment to help all to become better learners;

- development of teachers' skills so that they can better meet all their curriculum purposes.

The issues that lie at the core of this triangle, and determine the positive interplay between its nodes, are the principles of learning that should underlie all three, and the ways in which both children and teachers understand their roles in the school enterprise. Experience in the development of formative assessment has underlined this issue of role change, both for children (see e.g. Cowie, 2005; Mercer *et al.*, 2004) and for teachers (see Black *et al.*, 2003, Ch. 6). The literature on professional development of teachers shows how difficult and delicate such development can be.

But it must never be forgotten that the underlying value that should be treasured and nurtured in any systemic programme of renewal of purposes is the personal potential and dignity of the children. Such nurture is expressed in the way in which teachers treat those they teach. As Stephen Norris (1997) expressed it:

> *To ask of other human beings that they accept and memorise what the science teacher says, without any concern for the meaning and justification of what is said, is to treat those human beings with disrespect and is to show insufficient care for their welfare.*
>
> *It treats them with a disrespect, because students exist on a moral par with their teachers, and therefore have a right to expect from their teachers, reasons for what the teachers wish them to believe.*
>
> *It shows insufficient care for the welfare of students, because possessing beliefs that one is unable to justify is poor currency when one needs beliefs that can reliably guide action.*
>
> (p. 252)

References

Black, P., Harrison, C., Lee, C., Marshall, B. and Wiliam, D. (2003) *Assessment for learning: putting it into practice.* Maidenhead: Open University Press.

Black, P., Harrison, C., Osborne, J. and Duschl, R. (2004) *Assessment for learning 14–19.* London: Royal Society (www.royalsoc.ac.uk/education).

Butler, R. (1987) Task-involving and ego-involving properties of evaluation: effects of different feedback conditions on motivational perceptions, interest and performance. *Journal of Educational Psychology*, **79**(4), 474–482.

Cowie, B. (2005) Pupil commentary on assessment for learning. *The Curriculum Journal*, **16**(2), 137–151.

Driver, R., Newton, P. and Osborne, J. F. (2000) Establishing the norms of scientific argumentation in science classrooms. *Science Education*, **84**(3), 287–312.

Dweck, C. S. (2000) *Self-theories: their role in motivation, personality and development.* Florence, KY: Psychology Press.

Gardner, J. and Cowan, P. (2000) *Testing the test: a study of the reliability and validity of the Northern Ireland transfer procedure test in enabling the selection of pupils for grammar school places.* Belfast: Queen's University of Belfast.

Mercer, N. (2000) *Words and minds.* London: Routledge.

Mercer, N., Dawes, L., Wegerif, R. and Sams, C. (2004) Reasoning as a scientist: ways of helping children to use language to learn science. *British Educational Research Journal*, **30**(3), 359–377.

Norris, S. P. (1997) Intellectual independence for non-scientists and other content-transcendent goals of science education. *Science Education*, **81**, 239–258.

Wiliam, D. (2001) Reliability, validity, and all that jazz. *Education 3–13*, **29**(3), 17–21.

Chapter 3

What is good science education?

Including science in the primary curriculum is one thing, but providing quality in teaching and learning goes far beyond the requirements of a national programme of study. This chapter draws on the experience and reports of inspectors in discussing the meaning of quality in primary science education, how to improve it, and the extent to which it has indeed changed since 1998. While the evidence is specifically from Ofsted, the points raised are relevant to practice in all countries of the UK and probably beyond.

Ian Richardson

So what is quality?

'Quality hits you in the face' is a memorable phrase used by a science adviser grappling with the issue of standards. The quote is a précis of a view that is certainly pithy but not particularly helpful to those striving for quality. We can become more specific by looking at the reports of inspectors who regularly visit classrooms and evaluate the quality of what they find. High standards and high levels of engagement are seen in lessons where the teacher is enthusiastic and has high expectations of the children. Other key aspects are listed in Box 3.1.

Later, in Box 3.4, we show that the quality of provision has increased since 1998. But it is clear from inspectors' reports that much can still be improved. In the following sections some key areas for improvement are discussed.

Teachers' subject knowledge

When teaching is good, children make good progress and show good attitudes to their work as a result of effective teaching. The teachers' good subject knowledge lends confidence to their teaching styles, which engage children and encourage them to work well independently. Any unsatisfactory behaviour is managed effectively. The level of challenge stretches children without

Box 3.1

Some aspects of good practice

The elements coming together to make science engaging and enjoyable include:
- effective planning
- good subject knowledge
- science enquiry
- clear objectives
- lively and energetic teaching
- good classroom management
- a variety of activities including ICT
- appropriate pace
- challenge and differentiation
- involvement of children in decisions
- effective feedback to children

inhibiting their learning. Based on thorough and accurate assessment that informs children about how to improve, work is closely tailored to the full range of children's needs so that all can succeed. Children are guided to assess their work themselves. Teaching assistants and other classroom helpers are directed well to support learning. Children with additional learning needs have work well matched to their needs, based upon a good diagnosis of them. Good relationships support parents and carers in helping children to succeed.

Science makes high demands on teachers' subject knowledge and in some lessons misunderstandings are evident and children's misconceptions go unchallenged. In primary schools the main weaknesses are associated with areas of the physical sciences such as forces and changing materials, for example gravity, friction and air resistance. Without advice from a specialist subject leader based on the observation of lessons, or specific subject training, it is likely that such weaknesses become entrenched. Schools therefore need to make every effort to identify opportunities for professional development. It is difficult to generate engaging and relevant contexts for science that you have not studied in some depth.

Leadership and management

Leadership and management of science can be evaluated by the impact they have on achievement and standards. Good leadership of science is successfully focused on raising standards and promoting the personal development and wellbeing of children. It also creates a common sense of purpose among staff. In well-managed schools:

- there is effective self-evaluation, which takes account of the views of all major stakeholders, so that subject leaders have a good understanding of strengths and weaknesses and have a good track record of making improvements, including dealing with the issues from the last inspection;
- the inclusion of all learners is central to the school's vision and it is effective in pursuing this and dismantling barriers to engagement;
- the subject is organised well on a day-to-day basis;
- resources are well used, including any extended services, to improve learners' outcomes and to secure good value for money;
- vetting procedures for all adults who work with children are robust;
- good links exist with parents, carers and outside agencies to support the school's work.

The impact of these qualities is seen in good progress made by most children in most areas, in their sense of security and wellbeing, and in the school's deservedly good reputation. The leadership and management provide the subject with a good capacity to improve.

School self-evaluation

It is not the sole prerogative of an inspectorate to use criteria such as those just listed. Teachers are best placed to use the evidence available to them to evaluate standards. Such criteria provide a common 'language' which can be used by teachers, school managers and external inspection agencies. The clear implication of this is that teachers need to take a lead in establishing standards through effective self-evaluation. Standards in science need to be part of professional discussion in schools.

In the early days of Ofsted inspections teachers usually saw being inspected as something that happened *to* them, rather than a process of evaluation in which they were actively involved. Although practice varies across the UK, teachers are increasingly recognising that they have the evidence needed to evaluate standards and quality. It is teachers who are best placed to give an account of the standards in their school. Inspections should begin with the school's self-evaluation and that is now to be the case in both institutional and subject inspection.

Improving management

The importance of leadership and management to promoting effective teaching of science has been commented on in reports from Ofsted. Unsatisfactory and inconsistent teaching is often associated with weaknesses in the management and leadership of the subject. Many science subject leaders have not been encouraged to develop their management and leadership role, which is often restricted to setting out the scheme of work and ensuring appropriate teaching resources are made available to staff. As a consequence they have little direct impact on the quality of science teaching. There are common principles to management in both primary and secondary phases. Attention needs to be given to developing the management role, which might be expected to include the following:

- monitoring teaching and evaluating the standards of children's work and achievement;
- a programme of in-house training, with a focus on those aspects of science that teachers find most problematic;
- the development of a science handbook, which includes guidance on the principles of good teaching and learning, and policy and procedures for assessment to inform planning and target-setting;
- creating a scheme of work with a good range of activities and the systematic development of skills in science investigation.

Improved assessment practice

Symptoms of poorer assessment in primary science are that it is focused almost exclusively on measuring attainment at the end of a teaching sequence, the data produced are inadequately used for analysing areas for improvement in either teaching or learning, and the outcomes of assessment are not well communicated to learners.

In around one primary school in ten the quality of assessment is very good. In these schools staff and children have a clear assessment strategy, which is central to the management of teaching and learning. Box 3.2 provides an example of this practice.

Box 3.2

An example of successful assessment practice

In one school with very effective systems, a range of responses to assessments were made possible and children with different learning styles could be accommodated within this range. Using the idea of a 'buddy', children helped each other to improve, particularly their speaking and writing, which had been identified as significant areas for development in the school. Formative assessment practice was in evidence in all the work seen, with teachers suggesting improvements and children responding, with their progress acknowledged by the teacher. As a consequence, children had a clear understanding of how they had improved and were keen to describe what they had to do to improve further. The school sees further improvement will be made by developing peer-assessment and self-assessment to an even greater extent, with children generating the questions to which others respond.

The most successful assessment is guided by policy and procedures that focus on assessment for learning (see Chapter 22). Another good feature is the extensive use of peer-assessment, with partners marking each other's work, followed by whole-class discussion of the key points. The self-assessment carried out by older learners is based on goals for the end of unit, end of year and end of key stage. On this basis, at regular intervals, learners reflect on their progress, consider their next steps and chart their own progress as a record of these reflections. This understanding of learning and of assessment has put learners in a situation where they can also reflect on their own learning and challenge the provision of suitable materials and activities in lessons.

Children as assessors

My son was awarded 8 out of 10 for his plum crumble in food technology. Setting aside fatherly feelings and partiality, I thought it was a pretty good plum crumble and my son could not explain how he could have got 10/10. The poor lad was commissioned to ask the teacher why 8 out of 10. The answer? Nothing is perfect so we do not give 10/10 and he did not put his spoon away properly. This bizarre reasoning would not have been exposed had he not asked: how would he ever have known about spoon management if his teacher had not been gently challenged? The criteria for success had not been made clear and the assessment was delivered starkly as a verdict but without a rationale.

Assessment needs to be understood by learners if they are to benefit fully from it, and teachers are not the only source of assessment information. When learners are set a particular task they need clarity about the objectives of the activity to do it well. The standard of work that follows can be assessed against the objectives and when these have been clearly expressed and explained children are well able to evaluate the work of others. Chapter 23 discusses learner self- and peer-assessment in more detail.

Planning for scientific enquiry

Scientific enquiry is an aspect of the subject that makes particular demands on teachers' subject knowledge. Schools are, however, adopting a stronger focus on learning through investigative work. This has a very positive impact on children's understanding and enjoyment of science.

The highest standards seen are often in schools where the scheme of work includes well-integrated experiences of scientific enquiry. In these schools, children are involved in planning and carrying out regular science investigations, so that they understand the processes involved. It is this combination of both procedural and conceptual knowledge that promotes effective learning in science. This involvement also promotes enjoyment, as identified in interviews with children on their experiences in science lessons.

Without such regular involvement in scientific enquiry, children are unable to participate and learn actively. For example, where practical work is simply directed by the teacher, without children making their own contribution to the planning, learning is less effective and children show less evidence of developing both their skills and knowledge. Enquiry work can lead to high levels of motivation and engagement, as exemplified in Box 3.3.

Box 3.3

An engaging science activity

In one school the year 2 teacher had introduced the children to magnets and showed how the magnet 'stuck' to a 'tin' box. She set the scene for an investigation where the children were to find as many different objects as possible that the magnet would 'stick' to. She opened up a wide range of ideas and observations, and skilfully passed on ideas by drawing the attention of the children to them. One girl came up with the idea of shape influencing the attraction and this initiated a flurry of activity. The children tried same-shaped objects with different-shaped magnets, looking for some sort of pattern in what they saw, and concluded that shape does not affect magnetic attraction. A boy had very carefully reviewed his work and decided that it was metal things that were magnetic. He then found a pair of 2p pieces, one of which was attracted to the magnet while the other was not. Delighted with his finding, he showed the teacher, who asked him what he thought the difference might be. The boy said *'The magnet is working so the coins must be different'*, a remarkable thought for a year 2 child when looking at two apparently identical 2p pieces.

Engagement and enjoyment

It is a privilege to go into classrooms and see the business of education transacted. It is exhilarating to see children engaged in their work, to hear the buzz of discussion and recognise the satisfaction that comes through understanding and new knowledge.

Box 3.4
Changes since 1998 – an overview based on a review by Ofsted subject inspectors

As shown in Figure 3.1, children's achievement in primary science has improved since 1998. In that time there have been significant gains in teachers' confidence and expertise in science and, as a consequence of improved teaching, while children's achievement in 1998 was good or better in just under half of schools, by 2005 this proportion has risen to three-fifths of schools.

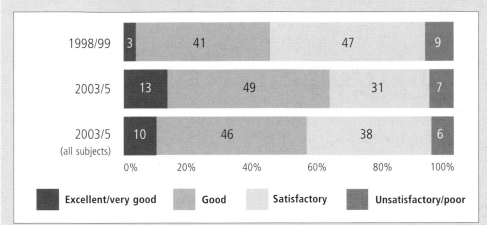

Figure 3.1 **Changes in achievement in science in primary schools, between 1998/99 and 2003/05.**

Data from national tests show the proportion of children achieving the expected level 4 has increased considerably, from 67% in 1998 to 86% in 2004, the latest year for which results are available. Over the same period, the proportion reaching level 5 has risen from 16% to 41%. However, the proportion reaching the expected level 4 has remained approximately the same for the last four years, suggesting that a plateau has been reached. As in 1998, it is teachers' knowledge and understanding of science that needs to be improved if children's achievement is to be raised further.

Teaching has improved since 1998 in both key stages, as shown in Figure 3.2. Teaching is now good or better in around two-thirds of schools, with teaching in key stage 2 being marginally better than in key stage 1. As was the case in 1998, the improvement in teaching is directly related to the increase in teachers' command of the subject: in both cases an increase of 13% in the number of schools judged to be good or better.

Learning has improved in line with improvements in teaching. As was the case in 1998, the best learning takes place where children are fully engaged, taking part in discussions and responding to probing questions that encourage them to talk through their ideas and so develop their understanding. The improvements in teaching and learning have their roots in improvements in planning, choice of teaching methods, and assessment practice.

Assessment practice is good or better in around two-fifths of schools, but it remains much less thorough and constructive than in mathematics and English. As a result of recent

(Continued overleaf)

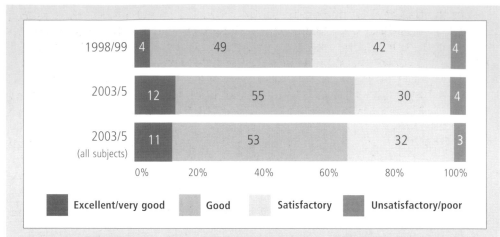

1998/99	4	49	42	4
2003/5	12	55	30	4
2003/5 (all subjects)	11	53	32	3

Excellent/very good   Good   Satisfactory   Unsatisfactory/poor

Figure 3.2 **Changes in quality of teaching of science in primary schools, between 1998/99 and 2003/05.**

uptake of assessment for learning practice and principles there has been a positive impact on children's engagement and their understanding of what they need to do to improve. Teachers have described how much better they are now able to focus on the children's needs and to modify planning appropriately.

Science is still taught in most schools as a separate subject. Research carried out by the Qualifications and Curriculum Authority (QCA) shows that this is so in 64% of schools in years 1 and 2, 77% in years 3 and 4 and 79% in years 5 and 6. However, as teachers have become increasingly confident they have incorporated more cross-curricular elements into their science teaching. For example, around one-quarter more schools now provide spiritual, moral, social and cultural elements in science in a way that is judged good or better and there has been a commensurate increase in the breadth of curriculum opportunities provided to children. There has also been an enrichment of the learning environment through improved resources and a much better use of support staff in science lessons.

In 1998, leadership and management by the science coordinator was identified as one of the strongest influences in the development of science in primary schools. The newness of the subject and the low proportion of teachers with science qualifications meant the coordinator was essential to the development of the subject. The coordination role was initially concerned with the organisation of resources, including practical work. By the time of the 1998 report it was recognised that coordinators were playing a significant role in planning for science across the school. In 2005, although there are very few examples of unsatisfactory management of science, the proportion of schools where management is good, just over half of primary schools, has not increased significantly since 1998.

As shown above, there is some cause for celebration in primary science education. Looking further afield, year 5 children in England performed at the highest levels amongst 25 countries participating in an international survey in 2003. Only two of the 25 outperformed England (see TIMSS website). Despite this favourable comparison it is clear from Ofsted data that performance of primary level children in science has been at a plateau for some years and could be improved.

Since the National Curriculum was introduced, teachers have had the freedom to select appropriate knowledge and understanding from the programme of study. The programme of study has set out the 'what' of science education but not the 'how'. If teachers do not select appropriate work this results in children being taught the same content, often in the same way, as they learned in the previous key stage. This is demotivating for children and is a poor use of teaching resources, not the least of which is time. Demotivation leads to disengagement and to a depressing of standards.

Too often teachers have felt they have to teach didactically to get through the content of programmes of study or awarding body specifications. In the worst cases this is so that they can say they have taught it, regardless of whether the children have understood or learned effectively. In the best practice, teachers use assessment to ascertain how learning is proceeding and use the assessment outcomes to modify planning and to inform children of how they can improve.

Children's involvement is the key to their engaging with science. Group work and class discussion need to be well organised if they are to challenge children sufficiently. The pursuit of scientific enquiry makes a significant contribution to the excitement of science, or it can do. Children need to participate in all aspects of investigation: forming hypotheses, planning, carrying out and evaluating. Those who only carry out instructions from worksheets to complete a practical activity are limited in the ways they can contribute and how they benefit.

Websites

Ofsted: http://www.ofsted.gov.uk
TIMMS (Third International Maths and Science Survey) 2003 report: http://timms.bc.edu/timms2003i/scienceD.html

Chapter 4 Values and ethics in science education

Some teachers may consider that values and ethics are not really a part of science education. Yet every subject, including science, **Mary Ratcliffe** and **Michael Reiss**

is value-laden. If a teacher presents science as a value-free pursuit of objective truth, that in itself is a value position (Layton, 1986) and conveys a particular view of science to children. This chapter examines whether science education should include issues of values and ethics and how teachers of science might explore values and ethics in their lessons.

The meaning of values

In this chapter we adopt a standard working definition of values used by many in the field of values education:

principles, fundamental convictions, ideals, standards or life stances which act as general guides to behaviour or as reference points in decision-making or the evaluation of beliefs or action. (Halstead, 1996, p. 5)

In a classroom where science is being taught, at least three such guides to behaviour might be present:

- How teachers are guided by the values embedded in the science curriculum.
- How teachers are guided by the values of science and how these are conveyed, explicitly or otherwise, and interpreted by children.
- How teachers are guided by the values of individuals and society when considering the implications of science.

Teachers of science have values that relate to their general role as teachers as well as ones that are important in the context of teaching science. There are values embedded in the science curriculum itself. For example, at key stage 2 the current science National Curriculum for England says of children that:

> They begin to think about the positive and negative effects of scientific and technological developments on the environment and in other contexts. (DfEE/QCA, 1999)

However, the focus here is on teachers' actions and the implications for children rather than the nature of the science curriculum.

Values of science

We start by looking at the range of values that could be presented about science and how they relate to contemporary views of the nature of science. Some aspects of terminology related to the nature of science are worth exploring here. Nott and Wellington (1993) developed a useful exercise for teachers to allow them to reflect on their view of the nature of science. In this exercise, agreeing or disagreeing with such statements as 'There is such a thing as a true scientific theory' and 'Human emotion plays no part in the creation of scientific knowledge' allows teachers to draw a profile of their own views to compare with those of others. Underpinning this exercise are a number of dimensions along which teachers position themselves, reflecting some of the terminologies and concepts relevant to the nature of science and its teaching (Figure 4.1).

In reading these dimensions, teachers may reflect on their own position and understanding of the nature of science. Some of the terminology may be very well known; other aspects may be unfamiliar. Although there is no one correct view of the nature of science, some views are widely regarded as having greater validity than others. For example, a mature understanding of the nature of science recognises that while some scientific knowledge is extremely secure, some is more tentative.

A view of the nature of science that is widely held can be summarised thus: science is a creative, collaborative and culturally bound activity in which reliable knowledge is generated through diverse but rigorous methods, albeit knowledge which could be subject to change depending on the collection of further evidence or reinterpretation of evidence (McComas and Olson, 1998; Osborne et al., 2003).

What is not so widely agreed is the extent to which what is accepted as valid scientific knowledge varies from culture to culture. At its simplest, cultures vary in what they expend their scientific efforts on. For example, in the early days of genetic engineering relatively little research was done into the possible harmful ecological consequences of genetically modified (GM) crops. The common assertion from companies involved in these technologies, that GM crops had no harmful effects on the environment, was therefore of little scientific value, since the hypothesis 'GM crops have no harmful effects on the environment' had not been tested. It is worth emphasising that, in this sense, scientific knowledge is produced: it does not simply sit around waiting to be discovered in a straightforward way.

Although the science curriculum has a strong influence on what is taught and how it is taught, the teacher's views on the nature of science and the importance, or otherwise, of ethical aspects will bear on the detail of classroom interactions. Box 4.1 gives an example of a teacher's efforts to focus on the

Positivist
Holds that science is the primary source of truth. The laws and theories generated by experiments are descriptions of patterns in a real, external **objective** world.

Relativist
Holds that judgements as to the truth of scientific theories vary from individual to individual and from one culture to another, i.e. truth is **relative** not absolute.

Inductivist
Holds that scientists generalise from a set of observations to a universal law, inferring from the particular to the general. Scientific knowledge is built by induction from a secure set of observations.

Deductivist
Holds that scientists form hypotheses that are not determined by the empirical data but may be suggested by them. Science then proceeds by testing the observable consequences of these hypotheses, so that observations are theory-laden.

Decontextualist
Holds that scientific knowledge is **independent** of its cultural location and sociological structure.

Contextualist
Holds that the truth of scientific knowledge and processes is **interdependent** with the culture in which the scientists live and in which the science takes place.

Realist
Believes that scientific theories are statements about a world that exists in space and time **independent** of the scientists' perceptions. Correct theories describe things that are really there, independent of the scientists, e.g. atoms.

Instrumentalist
Believes that scientific theories are fine if they work, that is they allow correct predictions to be made. These theories are instruments that we can use but they say nothing about an independent reality or their own truth.

Content is important
Thinks that science is characterised by the **facts and ideas** it has and that the essential part of science education is the acquisition and mastery of this 'body of knowledge'.

Process is important
Sees science as a characteristic set of identifiable **methods/processes**. The learning of these is the essential part of science education.

Figure 4.1 **Some dimensions and terminology relating to the nature of science** (summary from Nott and Wellington, 1993).

nature of science – in this case an experienced teacher, Judith, who participated in a research project to look at the barriers and opportunities in teaching 'ideas-about-science' (Bartholomew, Osborne and Ratcliffe, 2004).

The vignette in Box 4.1 conveys a crucial point in teachers' normal pedagogy when teaching science, seen many times in the research project but illustrated here succinctly. The children had been encouraged to consider their reasoning, but the teacher and class were dominated by the imperative to get 'the right answer'. Judith embraced the research project's aims of explicit teaching of 'ideas-about-science', through evaluation of evidence, and showed a reasonably sophisticated understanding of the nature of science. However, her actions show how strong was her need, whether through long-engrained habit or her underlying values, to arrive at fixed scientific knowledge. This lesson would have conveyed very different messages to children about the nature of science if the reporting back stage had allowed for:

● children to develop their own and challenge each other's ideas;
● the possibility of there being more than one right answer;

Box 4.1

Attempting to focus on the nature of science

Judith set up a lesson in which the learning outcomes were to '*know that scientists often work collaboratively and make hypotheses and predictions*'. She presented pupils with a cube, five sides of which were shown with BAT, CAT, FAT, HAT and MAT on them. Pupils were then asked to work out what they thought was on the sixth (covered) side. (This task was developed by Lederman and Abd-El-Khalick (1998) to support teaching of scientific creativity and pattern-seeking.) The pupils were initially perplexed but once they understood that they had to reason for themselves they engaged in the activity with growing confidence, each group making predictions based on what to them was logical reasoning. The nub of the lesson came when Judith asked about their predictions. The following report is from field notes:

When they report back Judith calls on each group in turn to give their answer and reasoning – though most groups are still discussing and haven't reached consensus. Some groups who were beginning to think about patterns in the alphabet revert to their earlier ideas when reporting back. One pupil explains to the class that she thinks the word is PAT and gives an explanation based on the fact that B and C (BAT and CAT) are next to each other, F and H have one letter between (FAT and HAT), and M and P have two letters between. Judith says that this is the right answer and she goes over it again, explaining that BAT and CAT are opposite each other, FAT and HAT are opposite each other and there is nothing opposite MAT.

- a much greater acknowledgement of the ways in which theories are generated, tested, rejected and refined.

Ethical aspects of science

Whereas science can tell us what we can do, ethics, as a discipline, helps us decide what we ought to do. Just as teachers may have different views on the nature of science, they may also hold views as to whether social and ethical aspects of science should be pursued within the science curriculum (Reiss, 1999). Whatever stance one takes, to ignore the ethical dimension of the pursuit and applications of science is to sell children short in their appreciation of the issues of contemporary science.

There are ethics involved in the *conduct* of science as well as in considering the *implications* of scientific advancements. Every time a child is encouraged to use a ruler to measure the height of a plant, a thermometer to measure the temperature of a liquid or a forcemeter to measure the weight of an object before and after it is immersed in water, that child is being encouraged, through the medium of science, to have a strict regard for evidence. Having a strict regard for evidence is closely allied to having a strict regard for truth (Reiss, 1997).

Many advances in science raise ethical issues in their implications. Ethical issues in ecology and conservation, for example, are increasingly recognised within the science curriculum. But how can teachers, who may have had little or no training in ethics, address ethical issues when teaching science? One response is not to consider ethical issues in science, but rather to restrict teaching about ethics to religious education or other humanities subjects. While this response solves certain problems, we should be aware of the messages it can convey about school science: does it reinforce a view that school science is remote and irrelevant to everyday life?

Lack of discussion of socio-scientific issues in science classrooms could lead children to ignore the scientific evidence behind a problem and see science as a sterile pursuit unconnected with modern societal issues. Many societal issues arise precisely because of advances in scientific knowledge. If children were the ones who determined the content of the science curriculum, social and ethical issues would definitely be included as they are seen to be important for their future and very motivating (Cerini, Murray and Reiss, 2003; Haste, 2004).

However, consideration of socio-scientific problems can raise issues for the teacher. From a year-long study of classroom discussions of socio-scientific issues (Ratcliffe and Grace, 2003), we recount in Box 4.2 one particular interaction which shows the dilemmas for teachers.

The exchange in Box 4.2 shows, perhaps unsurprisingly, that these boys are very egocentric. It also illustrates the dilemma in which teachers of science can find themselves. Should this teacher persist with exploring the environmental impact arising from consumer choice? Should he try to impose his own views? Should he act as devil's advocate or as neutral chair? Should he spend time clarifying the individual and societal values that impact on such decision-making?

Of course, social science lessons thrive on discussion, exchange of opinion and evaluation of evidence – clarification of values being a strong feature. And here's the paradox: despite science being an evidence-based discipline, at the frontiers full of controversy about competing theories and models, school science

---

Box 4.2

An ethical teaching dilemma

The lesson was about what material you would use for replacement window frames – and it could just be done from the point of view of examining the advantages and disadvantages of the properties of softwood, aluminium, hardwood and uPVC as materials. However, the teacher gave the pupils opportunities to clarify their views on the issue. This extract is from his summary at the end of the lesson:

Liam: *Well, we thought we'd go for uPVC 'cos it's quality and if you buy the softwood you've got to keep up the maintenance. It would cost more and you'd probably end up paying as much as you'd pay for the uPVC anyway – so you might as well buy that.*

Teacher: *Did the environmental effects have any bearing on your decision?*

Mike: *A little bit.*

Keith: *Yeh, a little bit, [very quiet] just a tad.*

Teacher: *So that helped sway you away from hardwood?*

Keith: *Oh yeh, but we still think just cutting down one more tree for our bedroom window's not going to make that much difference.*

Teacher: *OK. Do you all agree with that?*

Liam: *Yeh.*

At this point the teacher does not pursue the conversation further.

does not normally involve discussion and argument, either of scientific controversies or of socio-scientific issues. This seems to be mainly because for so long school science has been seen as a body of accepted knowledge – which of course *most* of it is; but a body of accepted knowledge to be learnt and regurgitated in exams, not to be interrogated for its evidence base. Teachers who see their role entirely as helping children to understand the way the natural world works may not wish to engage in value-laden discussions.

Given the dilemmas teachers of science may face in dealing with socio-scientific issues in the classroom, what guidance is available to them? The Crick Report (Advisory Group on Citizenship, 1998, p. 59) acknowledges three general approaches adopted by teachers in handling controversial issues: the 'neutral chair', the 'balanced' and the 'stated commitment' approach:

- In the role of **neutral chair** the teacher acts as facilitator in encouraging children to explore the issue and express their opinions fully. Teachers do not declare their own views.

- The **balanced** approach assumes that teachers will ensure that all different aspects and views are covered. They will discourage discussions which only concentrate on one particular viewpoint, acting as 'devil's advocate', if necessary, to counter one-sided arguments.

- In the **stated commitment** approach the teacher declares his or her own views at the outset, encouraging children to disagree or agree on the basis of their own reasoning.

Each of these three perspectives has advantages and disadvantages. The 'stated commitment' approach allows children to recognise teachers as authentic beings with their own perspectives on an issue, yet *'carries the risk that teachers who use it may well be accused of bias and attempting to indoctrinate those whom they are teaching'* (Advisory Group on Citizenship, 1998, p. 59). The reality that individual teachers hold views is ignored in the 'neutral chair' and 'balanced' approaches, though these approaches have the advantage of encouraging open discussion. However, the plurality of views encouraged by both these approaches may prevent children from developing the critical skills needed to judge the worth and validity of different solutions. The teacher in the extract in Box 4.2 is, to a certain extent, combining elements of these three perspectives in a commonsense approach – a stance that is encouraged by the Crick Report to dispel fears of indoctrination and insensitivity.

Whichever approach is taken, a great deal can be achieved by teachers encouraging children to reflect on the reasons for the ethical views they hold. At its simplest, gently asking *'Why do you think that?'* can be effective. The next step is encouraging children to think about the implications of their views for others as well as for themselves. And 'others' doesn't just mean 'other humans': it can mean other animals and even the environment.

References
Advisory Group on Citizenship (1998) *Education for citizenship and the teaching of democracy in schools: final report* (The Crick Report). London: The Stationery Office.

Bartholomew, H., Osborne, J. and Ratcliffe, M. (2004) Teaching students 'ideas-about-science': five dimensions of effective practice. *Science Education*, **88**, 655–682.

Cerini, B., Murray, I. and Reiss, M. (2003) *Student review of the science curriculum: major findings*. London: Planet Science. www.planet-science.com/sciteach/review/findings.pdf (accessed 24 May 2005).

DfEE/QCA (1999) *Science: the National Curriculum for England*. London: Qualifications and Curriculum Authority.

Halstead, J. M. (1996) Values and values education in schools. In *Values in education and education in values*, ed. Halstead, J. M. and Taylor, M. J. pp. 3–14. Lewes: Falmer Press.

Haste, H. (2004) *Science in my future: a study of values and beliefs in relation to science and technology amongst 11–21 year olds*. London: Nestlé Social Research Programme.

Layton, D. (1986) Revaluing science education. In *Values across the curriculum*, ed. Tomlinson, P. and Quinton, M. pp. 158–178. London: Falmer Press.

Lederman, N. and Abd-El-Khalick, F. (1998) Avoiding de-natured science: activities that promote understandings of the nature of science. In *The nature of science in science education*, ed. McComas, W. F. pp. 83–126. Dordrecht: Kluwer.

McComas, W. F. and Olson, J. K. (1998) The nature of science in international science education standards documents. In *The nature of science in science education: rationales and strategies*, ed. McComas, W. F. pp. 41–52. Dordrecht: Kluwer.

Nott, M. and Wellington, J. (1993) Your nature of science profile: an activity for science teachers. *School Science Review*, **75**(270), 109–112.

Osborne, J., Ratcliffe, M., Collins, S., Millar, R. and Duschl, R. (2003) What 'ideas-about-science' should be taught in school science? A Delphi study of the 'expert' community. *Journal of Research in Science Teaching*, **40**, 692–720.

Ratcliffe, M. and Grace, M. (2003) *Science education for citizenship: teaching socio-scientific issues*. Maidenhead: Open University Press.

Reiss, M. J. (1997) Seeking values in science. *Questions of Maths and Science*, **4**, 28–30.

Reiss, M. J. (1999) Teaching ethics in science. *Studies in Science Education*, **34**, 115–140.

Chapter 5

Continuing professional development: enhancing professional expertise

Derek Bell

The nature of teaching in all subjects, but particularly in science, changes constantly, bringing a continuing need for teachers to update their subject knowledge, understanding of learning and application of new approaches and technologies in teaching. This chapter considers what we mean by continuing professional development (CPD), provides an overview of the variety of CPD opportunities that exist to enhance professional expertise, and sets out some of the initiatives that are being put in place to improve access to and recognition of CPD for teachers of science. It also discusses some of the tensions that exist for teachers of science in trying to enhance their professional expertise and ensure their own professional development.

Why do we need CPD?

Without question teaching is a complex process. We only have to look at the standards that have been produced to provide benchmarks for gaining qualified status (such as those for England and Wales by the TTA/DfES – see website) to appreciate the wide variety of skills, knowledge and understanding required. However, we all know that a newly qualified teacher still has much to learn and that becoming a good teacher is more than simply ticking off a series of tasks or achievements. Furthermore, we recognise that the subject matter we teach has moved on, that understanding of approaches to teaching, learning and assessment has developed, and that the curriculum and the context in which we work have changed. In other words, we realise that 'what we learnt in initial training' is not enough. We need to keep updating our skills, knowledge and understanding if we are to teach effectively in order to continue providing high-quality learning opportunities for children. Also, for our own benefit and interest, we need to keep learning, exploring and enhancing our own expertise and enthusiasm.

There is clearly a need for all teachers, regardless of their subject discipline or phase, to keep up to date. For teachers of science, however, there is a particular imperative to do this for three key reasons. The first is the need for updating of subject knowledge in order to help keep abreast of at least some of the new developments and levels of understanding in science. The second relates to the demand for new teaching approaches to accommodate different learning styles, not only to meet the needs of those pupils who will continue to study sciences through to university but also to develop young people's scientific literacy to enable them to engage with issues they will meet in their lives. Finally, there is a need to be able to apply principles of formative assessment in science lessons and to use information and communication technology effectively to enhance the teaching of science.

What do we mean by CPD?

CPD is a term widely used in a variety of contexts but often referring to different things. In some situations it relates to courses; in others it means engaging in research, reading articles and books; in yet others it refers to attending conferences and in others to a variety of informal means of gaining new ideas. More recently, use of the World-Wide Web and the Internet for gathering information, contributing to electronic discussion groups and engaging in on-line courses has added yet another area of activity that is referred to as CPD. In fact, CPD is not any of these individual things but is a complex amalgam of them all, plus others that have not been mentioned. Thus, finding a definition of CPD is not a straightforward task. Rather we need to build up a model or concept of CPD that is applicable to a range of circumstances but at the same time sets out key features of what it means both generally and with specific reference to the teaching of science.

In a recent study, Leaton Gray (2005) reported that the term CPD is said to have been coined in the mid-1970s in relation to training for the building profession because 'it did not differentiate between learning from courses and learning "on the job" ' (p. 5). In her short review of research relating to CPD, Leaton Gray highlights the positive benefits of sustained collaborative professional development (see EPPI, 2003) and the potential impact of longer award-bearing schemes with a subject focus (see Soulsby and Swain, 2003). Leaton Gray also notes the change in terminology from In-service Training (INSET) to CPD which, she argues, 'signifies a shift in emphasis away from the provider and/or employer, towards the individual. In other words, the individual is now responsible for his or her lifelong career development, under the umbrella of the school or schools that employ the teacher' (Leaton Gray, 2005, p. 5).

This shift reflects a much wider debate about CPD, both in the UK and internationally, that is trying to address the question 'What do we mean by

CPD?' and, importantly, how to embed CPD into the culture of schools, colleges and the profession more widely. In its deliberations to develop its remit the Training and Development Agency (formerly The Teacher Training Agency, TTA) for England and Wales proposed that the term CPD should be used to refer to:

a planned and sustained series of activities, designed to improve a teacher's knowledge and skills. In this usage, CPD is not to be viewed as a 'bolt-on' or a short-term experience, but as a continuous exercise in addressing individual teacher's needs and in supporting improvements in their professional practice over time. (TTA, 2005a p. 5)

A wide range of activities can contribute to professional development. These include accredited and non-accredited courses, studied at centres or on-line, school-based courses, action research, mentoring, exchanges, placements, sabbaticals, award schemes and peer networks. There are also a large number of sources that might provide training, help, advice and guidance. These include local education authorities or boards, higher education institutions, national strategies, small and large independent providers, professional bodies and, of course, subject associations such as the Association for Science Education (ASE). Some of the activities take place in-house while others require time to be spent off-site. The important thing is that provision for CPD needs to be relevant and build on existing understanding, knowledge and skills so that it can be used to enhance practice. Principally this should be related to teaching and learning but it will also include other aspects of professional expertise such as interpersonal, leadership and management skills.

Provision of CPD

Frameworks for professional development

In recent years the interest in CPD has increased significantly and extensive advice and materials are available. In particular, the General Teaching Councils for England, Scotland and Wales (GTCE, GTCS, GTCW) have each identified it as a priority. In England, the Training and Development Agency (TTA, 2005b) is now responsible for, among other things, developing, coordinating and putting in place standards for CPD. Importantly there is recognition that CPD is not separate from initial training so that already there are mechanisms in place for improving support for individuals in their first year of teaching. These include career entry profiles and entitlements for induction (TTA, 2005c). Further developments are being undertaken to provide improved continuity and coherence to the overall framework of professional development for teachers in the UK.

However, these approaches are generic and need to be placed in the context of both the subject and the phase in which the teaching is taking place. In relation to science there has been a great deal of development work which helps to provide a framework in which professional development for teachers of science can take place.

ASE Certificate of Continuing Professional Development

One such framework is provided by the ASE Certificate of Continuing Professional Development, which is equally applicable to both primary (see Haigh, 2003a) and secondary (see Haigh, 2003b; Haigh and Reece, 2003) teachers. Originally aimed at individuals in the early years of their teaching career, this approach has been found to be relevant at any stage in a career. The approach is firmly based on the needs of individual teachers and their schools and encourages them to explore seven areas of development:

- Subject knowledge and understanding.
- Pedagogical content knowledge: how to present the subject matter to different learners.
- Development of teaching and assessment skills.
- Understanding teaching and learning.
- The wider curriculum and other changes affecting teaching.
- Management skills: managing people.
- Management skills: managing yourself and your professional development.

The process involves an audit and self-review against these elements which contribute to professional expertise and then the identification of a programme that ensures academic, pedagogic and professional rigour. Support and monitoring of progress involve a mentor and tutor providing advice and encouragement. An important element of this process is the need to think about how different activities (e.g. attending courses, making presentations to colleagues, writing schemes of work and personal reading and research) can all contribute to professional development in a focused and coherent manner. Importantly, this involves evaluating the impact that there has been on practice.

National network of Science Learning Centres

The issue of CPD for teachers of science has been under discussion for some time in the UK and several reports have been published (e.g. Dillon *et al.*, 2000; Roberts, 2002), which have all argued for the need to strengthen subject-focused CPD and culminated in recommending that Government should be involved in improving CPD opportunities for teachers of science.

This resulted in the announcement in October 2003 of the setting up a network of Science Learning Centres as a joint initiative funded by The Wellcome Trust and the Department for Education and Skills. The purpose of the national network of Science Learning Centres is to offer high-quality professional development principally for those involved in science education including primary, secondary and post-16 science teachers, technicians and teaching assistants. The overall aim is to improve science teaching, raise morale in the teaching profession and through their teachers to inspire pupils with a more exciting, intellectually stimulating and relevant science education, enabling them to gain the knowledge and the understanding they need – both as the citizens and as the scientists of the future.

The network is made up of nine regional centres in England (see Figure 5.1) and the National Science Learning Centre based in York, which has a remit to cover the whole of the UK. Discussions are taking place to develop ways of providing complementary provision in Wales, Scotland and Northern Ireland, linking with the National Centre. Each of the centres is run by a consortium of partners, but with its own identity, and is working to develop programmes to meet the needs of the teachers, technicians and teaching assistants around its

1.National Centre: University of York	
Regional Centres	*Main location*
2. North East:	Framwellgate School, Durham
3. North West:	Manchester Metropolitan University
4. Yorkshire and the Humber:	Sheffield Hallam University
5. East Midlands:	University of Leicester
6. West Midlands:	University of Keele
7. East:	University of Hertfordshire
8. London:	Institute of Education, University of London
9. South East:	University of Southampton
10. South West:	@Bristol, Bristol

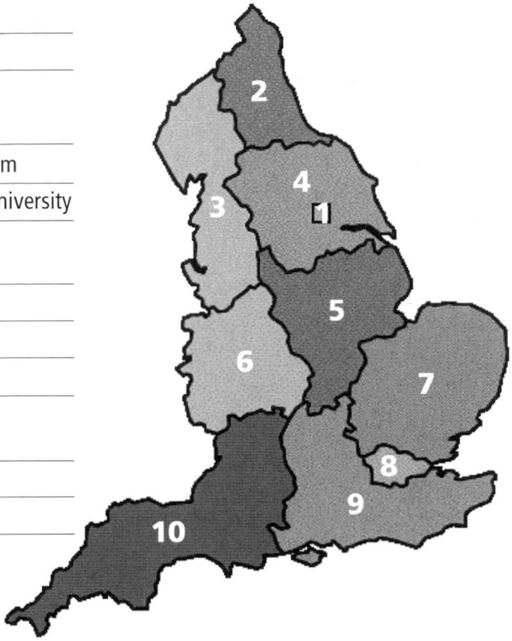

Website: www.sciencelearningcentres.org.uk

Figure 5.1 **National network of Science Learning Centres in England.**

region, although you do not have to live in a particular region to attend a course.

Although each centre has its own character, by working together the synergies in expertise and facilities promise to make the impact of the network greater than the sum of its parts. Together with all their partners, which include the ASE, the centres are aiming to make available CPD that is:

- relevant to individual career development needs yet contributes to meeting the school priorities;
- up to date, reflecting new developments in scientific knowledge and tackling the moral and ethical issues that arise in contemporary society;
- practical, providing ideas that can be implemented in the classroom or laboratory yet give time to think more deeply about underpinning research and other evidence;
- of high quality, in both the standards of the provision and the environment in which it takes places;
- reflective, providing time and opportunities to learn from other colleagues but with provision for personal follow-up and support.

Science Learning Centres Web portal

A particularly exciting aspect of the national network is the development of the Science Learning Centres Web portal (SLC, 2005, see websites), which will provide not just details of the programmes and activities available with on-line booking, but on-going support for CPD. By building up a collection of materials for courses and other forms of advice and support this Web-based resource will be central to the way in which the Science Learning Centres support CPD for teachers and technicians. A key element is the facility for each individual to have his or her own electronic CPD portfolio and web-space to store and record evidence of CPD activity, regardless of where it has been undertaken. Access to the portfolio is restricted to the individual, who has the power to make parts of it available to other people or to simply maintain it for personal use.

CPD recognition and reward

One of the issues that the Science Learning Centres, along with others, have been grappling with is how to acknowledge that someone has undertaken some CPD and, perhaps more importantly, how to give recognition to individuals who have continued to keep up to date. There are programmes available, mainly through higher education institutions, that give credit or qualifications for particular courses or research activity, but recognition for a wider range of activities is more difficult to achieve. The GTC in England (GTCE) has developed the Teacher Learning Academy, which provides a framework for recognising CPD. The GTC in Scotland (GTCS) has also developed a process by which teachers gain recognition for their CPD (see websites). Throughout the UK, the increased emphasis in performance appraisals on the quality of teaching and learning and their links with salary arrangements underline not only the need for teachers to engage in CPD but also for them to be able to demonstrate their commitment and have it recognised.

Having looked at other professions, some years ago ASE started exploring the possibility of gaining a Royal Charter, which could allow the Association to offer a chartered designation for science teachers. The outcome of the discussions between the Science Council (an independent body acting for the Professional Institutions and Learned Societies across the breadth of science in the UK – see websites) and the ASE is the development of a new designation of Chartered Science Teacher (CSciTeach). The ASE was successful in being awarded its Royal Charter in November 2004 (see Roberts, 2005; Bell, 2005; Lawrey, 2005) and is currently working with the Science Council to agree the detailed arrangements for CSciTeach.

The CSciTeach designation aims to recognise the unique combination of knowledge, skills and qualities demonstrated by good science teachers, who also show their commitment to maintaining their high-quality expertise through ongoing CPD. Apart from setting quality standards, a key feature of CSciTeach will be the requirement for it to be renewed every five years, thus ensuring that claims that individual's expertise is up to date can be substantiated in line with practice in other professions. Although the details have still to be agreed, the setting up of this charter designation is timely and, in the context of wider developments, provides a major opportunity for science teachers to enjoy recognition, and possibly reward, for their professional status. Further information will be posted on the ASE website (see websites) as and when it becomes available.

CPD entitlement and responsibility

For the most part the argument about the importance of CPD has been won and, as outlined above, much progress has been made in developing CPD specifically for teachers of science. There also seems to be willingness at all levels of government and throughout the profession to try to make this work. However, the practicalities can get in the way of turning all the theory and good intentions into reality. Inevitably there will be difficulties, but with appropriate leadership and careful management at all levels much can be achieved.

From the perspective of the individual, which in this context is probably the most important, there needs to be scope for negotiation with head teachers, subject leaders and colleagues in order to work towards gaining an overall balance of professional development. Developing appropriate transparent mechanisms for identifying and meeting CPD needs is fundamental to reducing the tensions, as is a common understanding of entitlements and responsibilities.

Few people would disagree with the idea that CPD should be an entitlement for all teachers and should be planned with personal and organisational needs in mind. Hand in hand with the idea of entitlement goes the matter of responsibility of both the organisation and the individual. The organisation has a responsibility for making sure that CPD opportunities are available for individuals and teams so that they are able to develop their own professional expertise, which contributes to school improvement. The organisation is also responsible for ensuring that any specific entitlements (e.g. the arrangements for support, guidance and funding for teachers in their induction year) are provided. Individuals have responsibility for keeping themselves up to date, developing new skills and maintaining the highest possible professional standards in everything they do. This includes thinking ahead to possible future developments and preparing for them in appropriate ways.

A third dimension to the area of responsibility is that to the profession, ensuring that science teaching generally is of the best possible quality and contributing to raising the status of the profession as a whole. Although it may not be a day-to-day priority, the way in which science teaching is perceived in the wider community makes an important contribution to the confidence that parents, industry, business and government have in the science education available to our young people.

References

Bell, D. (2005) Achieving chartered status. *Education in Science*, **211**, 10.

Dillon, J., Osborne, J., Fairbrother, R. and Kurina. L. (2000) *A study into the views and needs of science teachers in primary and secondary state schools in England. Final Report to the Council for Science and Technology.* London: King's College London. Summary available at: www.cst.gov.uk

Haigh, G. (2003a) The ASE's continuing professional development programme. *Primary Science Review*, **79**, 11–12.

Haigh, G. (2003b) The focus of teachers' in-service training. *Education in Science*, **202**, 24–25.

Haigh, G. and Reece, M. (2003) Integrating CPD into your practice: linking the ASE cCPD and developments at key stage 3. *Education in Science*, **205**, 24–25.

Lawrey, K. (2005) Incorporation by Royal Charter: value, significance and responsibility. *Education in Science*, **211**, 11.

Leaton Gray, S. (2005) *An enquiry into continuing professional development for teachers.* London: Esmée Fairbairn Foundation. Available at: http://www.esmeefairbairn.org.uk/grants_reports.html

Roberts, G. (2002) *SET for success: the supply of people with science, technology, engineering and mathematics skills.* London: HM Treasury. Available at: www.hm-treasury.gov.uk

Roberts, G. (2005) SET for success: a key role for Chartered Science Teachers. *Education in Science*, **211**, 8–9.

Soulsby, D. and Swain, D. (2003) *A report on the award-bearing INSET scheme*. Available at: http://www.teachernet.gov.uk/docbank/index.cfm?id=4129

Websites

ASE (The Association for Science Education): www.ase.org.uk

EPPI (Evidence for Policy and Practice Information and Co-ordinating Centre) (2003) *The impact of collaborative CPD on classroom teaching and learning. How does collaborative continuing professional development (CPD) for teachers of the 5–16 age range affect teaching and learning?* Available at: http://eppi.ioe.ac.uk/EPPIWeb/home.aspx?page=/reel/reviews.htm

GTCE (General Teaching Council for England). Continuing professional development: http://www.gtce.org.uk/cpd_home/

GTCS (General Teaching Council for Scotland). Continuing professional development: http://www.gtcs.org.uk/gtcs/cpd.aspx?MenuItemID=111&selection=5

GTCW (General Teaching Council for Wales). Continuing professional development: http://www.gtcw.org.uk/cpd/information.html

Science Council: www.sciencecouncil.org

SLC (Science Learning Centres) (2005) Web portal: http://www.sciencelearningcentres.org.uk/

TTA (Teacher Training Agency) (2005a) TTA's expanded CPD remit: response from the TTA to the Secretary of State; covering letter (MS *Word* file 30 KB) and detailed report (MS *Word* file 78 KB). Available at: http://www.tta.gov.uk/php/read.php?sectionid=371&articleid=2385

TTA (2005b) *Expanded remit for the Teacher Training Agency*. Available at: http://www.tta.gov.uk/php/read.php?sectionid=284&articleid=1945

TTA (2005c) *Induction for newly qualified teachers* (NQTs). Available at: http://www.tta.gov.uk/php/read.php?sectionid=188&articleid=1311

TTA/DfES (2002) *Qualifying to teach: professional standards for qualified teacher status and requirements for initial teacher training*. London: Teacher Training Agency. Available at: http://www.tta.gov.uk/php/read.php?sectionid=108&articleid=456

Chapter 6

Science education across and beyond the United Kingdom

When teachers spend time teaching in schools overseas, their most common response is that they have learned more about

Alan Peacock, Lynne Symonds and Andrew Clegg

Alan Peacock, Lynne Symonds and Andrew Clegg

our own system in the UK through having to make comparisons and to think about why we do things the way we do. This chapter looks at how some issues relating to the teaching of science are dealt with in some different regions of the globe. It begins near to home with the differences across the countries of the UK and then gives a glimpse of what is going on in Europe, North America, Africa, India and China. Finally, some points are brought out that show what we have to learn from taking a wider perspective of ways of implementing science education.

Science, globalisation and environmental awareness

The ease with which we can now link with other countries has the potential to affect science education throughout the world. For science teachers in Britain, it presents a rich, exciting and ever-changing menu of resources, ideas, inspiration and learning opportunities. Opportunities to develop a global perspective include school linking, teacher exchange, project sharing, collaborating through the Association for Science Education's *Science Across the World* website (see websites) and considering the current realities of science education in societies that, at least on the surface, are different from our own. We can benefit from this global perspective by identifying international trends, relating these to our thinking, and acknowledging what we can learn from other ways of doing things.

Variations in practice within the UK

We first need to look at differences within the UK, notably what distinguishes England from Wales, Scotland and Northern Ireland. Recent developments in these countries demonstrate that, in the primary phase, each is moving away from the heavily structured content focus that characterised the early years of the National Curriculum in England towards more generic thinking and learning skills within a 'real world' context. The Scottish Executive has National Guidelines for the 5–14 age range, of which one subject area is Environmental Studies, incorporating Society, Science and Technology (see website). This immediately sets science within an integrated approach that *'brings together the main ways in which pupils learn about the world'*, rather than seeing it as a subject with a separate identity. An important difference from the National Curriculum in England is that these guidelines are not mandatory: almost all teachers use them, but they do not have the statutory force experienced south of the border. Skills development focuses on the strands of *preparing* for tasks, *carrying out* tasks and *reviewing and reporting* tasks; this categorisation runs across the Environmental Studies framework, and is not specific to science. Science shares many learning outcomes with history and geography and, like these subjects, embraces the importance of *'active citizenship, the central concept of equity'*.

In Northern Ireland, science is part of a curriculum area called *The World Around Us*, which incorporates science and technology, history and geography. Changes to the assessment system proposed by the Council for Curriculum Examinations and Assessment (CCEA, see website) will increase the emphasis on teacher reporting; as in Scotland, science is not formally tested. In Wales, too, there has been a movement towards active teacher assessment using skill profiles and away from formal testing, in the hope that, as in Scotland and Northern Ireland, these moves will help free up the science curriculum for more creative teaching and learning. So far England has not been willing to abandon National Curriculum tests at ages 11 and 14.

Across the UK, there have been attempts, so far less effective in England than in the rest of the UK, to change the post-14 science examinations and curricula. The aim is to combat the decline in candidates choosing science, through such initiatives as *Twenty First Century Science* (see Chapter 1), offering shared and coordinated teaching approaches across GCSE science subjects, with new options such as *Environmental and land-based science*, a wholly e-assessed qualification offering units in agriculture, horticulture and conservation. The intention is to cater for those who want to work or study in a wider range of fields, rather than becoming 'academic' scientists post-16.

Trends in Europe

Science education tends to reflect the educational priorities of a country. However, at the same time, representatives from different systems are increasingly coming together to share and cooperate in a desire to improve the attractiveness of school science and tackle the universal problem of the rejection of science by adolescents as a preferred field of study. In the recent past, science teaching in secondary schools across Europe tended to be didactic and theoretical, whilst at the same time, in many countries, science hardly existed at all as a subject in the primary phase. What science there was at primary level tended to be subsumed within study of the natural environment – weather, local habitats, conservation, pollution, the earth, living things. There was a marked absence of emphasis on the 'big ideas' of science, such as energy, forces, photosynthesis, particle theory or chemistry concepts, in the primary phase. As a consequence, learners in many countries experience a relatively abrupt transition on first encountering science in high school, as examples below will demonstrate.

In Europe, projects such as SCIENCEDUC (see website) have brought together teachers and trainers from various countries as the basis for a wider collaboration in the future. Initially, the countries involved were Estonia, France, Hungary, Portugal, Sweden, Germany and Italy. The programme was seen as contributing to a reduction in inequality through science education by combining the rich diversity of European tempers, education styles and innovations. Several European countries have been following such guidelines to improve science teaching across the primary and lower secondary age ranges. Where implemented, they allow children to use thinking skills, ask questions, make hypotheses and conduct experiments to verify them, while learning how to work in groups and respect each other, thus preparing for active citizenship in the future.

Science educators in many countries, therefore, are no longer concerned with simply getting some 'real' science into the primary curriculum but with the quality of science learning. This often means setting up systems to provide professional development and other support to ensure initiatives that have been successfully implemented in particular localities can be 'scaled up' to take root nationally. In France, for example, teachers are progressively implementing such hands-on principles in their classes. *La Main à la Pâte* (see website) sets out to improve science teaching in primary schools through a focus on experimentation, observation and questioning. It promotes school twinning through e-learning, around shared scientific and technological projects. Several countries are also adopting *Science and Technology for Children* (STC), a structured enquiry-based programme originating in the USA (see below), for example Sweden, where it is known as *Science and Technology for All*.

Developments in the USA and Canada

Increasingly in the USA the Internet is being used to give wider access to materials both for the classroom, as in the WISE (Web-based Integrated Science Environment) project, and for professional development (see website). The STC approach has also led on to a matched version for middle schools (STC/MS, see website). These programmes are tightly structured by UK standards, although they do promote progression in scientific skills and processes as well as ideas. Transition to middle school in the US (at grade 6, age 12) is well managed in this scheme: the curriculum focuses on life and earth sciences on the one hand, and physical science and technology on the other. But it is important to remember that, beyond this stage, many states do not have mandatory national curricula for science, and science is frequently taught in high schools as separate disciplines, and often in separate years, thus limiting continuity and integration.

Canadian science education exemplifies some of the points emerging above. Provincial curricula vary widely: in Ontario, for example, primary science (grades 1–8, ages 6–14) is based on five themes (life systems, matter and materials, energy and control, structures and mechanisms, and earth and space). Grades 9–10 (ages 15–16) then focus on ecosystems, matter and energy, the universe and electricity, as 'academic' and 'applied' strands. From grade 11 (age 17), the curriculum reverts to conventional biology, chemistry and physics. In Quebec, however, the curriculum is structured very differently. At primary level, science and technology is one 'subject area' required to link with 'broad areas of learning' including 'environmental awareness and responsibilities', through 'cross-curricular competences' which cover many skill areas. From grade 9 onwards, however, the curriculum is structured into life sciences, chemistry, physics, and earth and space sciences. In both provinces, applications have been given as much emphasis as the subject matter of science.

So a key question raised by the above is: Does a skills-based, integrated approach in primary schools prepare children for specialisation in the secondary phase? Should it? Or should the post-primary sector build on the strengths of the primary approach, to overcome the decline in pupils' interest in science?

Africa – the problems and progress

Science Teacher Associations in Africa report problems associated with enormous populations of often poorly trained teachers lacking access to information or professional development. The main problems facing teachers of science relate to the lack of adequate funds and materials, overcrowded classrooms, administrative failings, low salaries and consequent lack of teacher motivation, overloaded curricula, and the pressures of recall-focused testing systems. Yet changes and improvements are taking place.

Southern Africa (Botswana, Lesotho, Mozambique Namibia, South Africa and Swaziland) can be taken as an example. Schooling tends to be divided into four phases: lower primary (3 years), upper primary (4 years), junior secondary (2 years) and senior secondary (2 years). Access to junior secondary schools varies from mandatory (Botswana) to less than 20 per cent in some other countries. Science is not compulsory in senior secondary in most of these countries, but is likely to become so within the next few years. None, however, has yet embarked on the development of appropriate science curricula for senior secondary schooling. Science is taught as a single subject in most countries in primary schools: via the mother tongue in lower primary, and then in English at upper primary level. It is then split into two subjects (in Namibia and South Africa) for junior secondary: in other countries the split comes at senior secondary, usually into the three traditional subjects. Science curricula at all levels tend to be conventional, reflecting closely their colonial predecessors that catered to a selective minority. Most have statements regarding the acquisition of skills as well as knowledge and understanding, but these are not yet reflected in teaching.

Throughout the region, science lessons rarely include practical work; there is widespread evidence that simply placing equipment in schools does little to bring about a change in science teaching. Despite many African children's early involvement in real practical activity in the home and farm, with first-hand experience of collecting water, animal care, gardening, cleaning, preparing food and cooking, there is little tradition in schools of using everyday equipment to teach science. Nor is it often realised that using everyday items in this way is actually quite a high-level skill, for which most teachers have to be trained. Similarly, little opportunity has been taken to develop an environmental science focus based on children's experiences. The main problem is that teachers are often conditioned to value a traditionally 'academic' science curriculum aimed at test success and therefore do not enable children to see the significance of science in relation to their daily lives.

One positive feature of science education in the region is the rise in both quantity and quality of the research and development that is being carried out in the tertiary institutions (mainly in South Africa), a good deal of which is finding its way into science teacher education programmes. The Southern African Association for Research in Maths, Science and Technology Education (SAARMSTE) is in a healthy state and holds a large annual meeting.

An increasing minority of secondary schools in the region have computers: data-logging equipment exists in the region but as yet is used rarely, as most science teachers are not yet computer literate. All this is beginning to change dramatically throughout the region, by circumventing software licence costs through the use of Open Source software, negotiating favourable educational Virtual Private Network (VPN) rates, and wireless Internet connections for schools without 'phone lines. There is a lack of good local e-learning materials in science but this issue too is being addressed.

A recent study of promising practices in science education across Africa has shown that the key element in improving practice has been teachers' professional development. In French-speaking West Africa, for example, the use of an Internet-based support system that involves several countries has diminished science teachers' sense of isolation, and enabled them to learn from each other through sharing of ideas and attending distance-learning seminars, supported by materials and tuition provided in collaboration with a university in France (see RESAFAD website).

Health education forms a significant part of basic science education, particularly HIV/AIDS education. The Science Teachers' Associations of Nigeria and Ghana work together and with the ASE and CASTME (Commonwealth Association of Science, Technology and Mathematics Educators) to improve their capacity for reciprocal learning. Science teachers from Cameroon and Gambia have carried out some effective work in HIV/AIDS education, extending far beyond the schools.

Developments in China

Basic science is part of Chinese children's primary school studies, but often they do not realise that this is science. The curriculum includes the study of 'Nature and Work', which includes simple biology, as well as measuring shadows, simple circuits, etc. In primary school, the teachers focus on identifying strengths, so that children are 'selected into science' on the basis of internal tests. Many schools still have very large classes, where the teaching approach is characterised by the teacher reading from the text, then demonstrating an activity and finally testing children's recall. There is, however, a strong emphasis on the environment: teachers take children out of the classroom to make observations, for example to study insects in their habitats. After primary school, however, science becomes much more prominent in the curriculum, being taught as separate subjects or as combined science, depending on location. Whilst science equipment itself is sparse, ICT provision is definitely generous, even in the large schools of central China, where computer suites are standard. Video is also often used as part of lessons. There seems also to be a relatively smooth transition from primary to secondary science programmes, something not well achieved in most other parts of the world.

India

In India, textbook content is still very Eurocentric, despite the large contribution of India to scientific knowledge. Teachers and learners perceive science as imported ready-made knowledge, and science is presented in an authoritative manner in the classroom, so that learners take the role of passive receiver rather than creator of knowledge. A new approach to the curriculum developed by the National Council for Educational Research and Training (NCERT) sets out to encourage the teaching of science in such a way that students acquire scientific and technological literacy and understand how basic scientific principles are applied in finding solutions to problems in agriculture, weather, energy, health/nutrition, industry, defence, etc. The curriculum also stresses that science teaching should focus on processes such as experimentation, observation, data collection, classification, analysis, making hypotheses, drawing inferences and arriving at conclusions for objective truth (see NCERT website).

Disparities between states are still great. Despite all the difficulties, with often only a poorly surfaced chalkboard and at best a few textbooks as resources in overcrowded classrooms, an impressively high degree of attentive learning still takes place. Children are often keen to learn, listening carefully, valuing their lessons and their teacher. They work hard for their exams, and families must budget carefully to pay the exam fees. In much of Africa and Asia science is seen as a good thing, beneficial to society and enabling progress in many fields.

Implications and ways forward

It would seem that for many years, teachers in many parts of the world have not been at ease with science, especially in the primary phase. They fear to say 'I don't know' to children, when being 'stuck' is often the starting-point for real science. They are often reluctant to do practical work, and are discouraged by obstacles that are put in their way, such as punitive inspections, endless tests, rapidly changing administrative requirements, health and safety directives and the introduction of new technologies. One effect of this has been to discourage teachers from working not only outside the assessed curriculum but also outside the classroom, in the everyday world of learners. Fieldwork is harder and harder to justify, teachers say; hence the environmental awareness that many curricula emphasise is harder and harder to achieve.

Yet this glimpse of science in some other countries indicates not only that things are improving in many areas, but also that we can learn from how science is taught in other countries. Botswana, whose main exports are diamonds and cattle, has built agriculture and earth sciences into the secondary curriculum, and has led the way in tackling AIDS education in primary schools. Kenya has done a great deal of work on identifying the pre-vocational skills needed by school leavers in the informal and tourist sectors of their economy, such as in food preparation, hairdressing, stone carving or metalworking, and has begun to redevelop the science curriculum to incorporate these. Some highly creative and successful teachers, who take problem-solving literally and organise their curriculum around it, are to be found in rural schools in Kenya. It may not be appropriate for UK children to design and build windmills to saw wood, or to collect, test and identify insects causing skin lesions amongst children, for instance, but we should value the skill and confidence of those teachers who are prepared to take greater ownership of what and how they teach, in order to meet their pupils' needs. In many ways, we in England do things differently; but we often fall short of what we hope to achieve, particularly in the way we manage such matters as the impact of testing, the use of published materials, generating a sense of purpose and relevance for young learners, and the transition from primary to secondary science.

So how might we, as part of the international science education community, contribute to the improvement not only of science education but also of its image, which is currently a fairly negative one among learners in many countries? One key way would be to sustain and develop even further the international perspective of our publications, journals and web-based materials such as *Science Across the World*, and to find ways to make these more widely available. Another would be to use publications and web-based professional development to encourage and support teachers and children working practically outside the classroom, so that they can become confident and skilled in 'making science real', in order to develop greater environmental awareness. A third focus might be on the way different countries manage the link between primary and secondary science, where there is still a hiatus that affects children's positive image of the subject by turning it into something that seems no longer to have relevance to their lives. And finally, we might look for ways of helping less well-resourced countries to develop their own materials that reflect the needs, cultures and languages of their children, materials that teachers will have the confidence to allow children to use themselves. Nothing less, in the end, will be effective.

Websites

ASE (Association for Science Education) *Science Across the World*: www.scienceacross.org
CCEA (Northern Ireland Council for Curriculum Examinations and Assessment): www.ccea.org.uk
La Main à la Pâte: www.inrp.fr/lamap/-
NCERT (National Council for Educational Research and Training): http://www.ncert.nic.in/sites/publication/schoolcurriculum/ncfr.htm
RESAFAD (Réseau Africain de Formation à Distance): www.sn.resafad.org
SCIENCEDUC: www.cienciaviva.pt/projectos/scienceduc.asp?accao=changelang&lang=en
Scottish 5–14 guidelines: http://www.ltscotland.org.uk/5to14/guidelines/index.asp
STC/MS (Middle Schools Science Technology for Children): www.carolina.com/stc/
WISE (Web-based Integrated Science Environment): http://wise.berkely.edu

Section 2 School level: Policy matters

Chapter 7 Science in the whole curriculum

This chapter looks at the position of science within the wider curriculum. There are two main reasons for exploring this broader perspective. One is that there are some common skills and it may be efficient to take advantage of this. The other is that the relevance and interest of science content is helped by linking it with other contexts relating to the subject or to everyday life. The first part of the chapter considers the relevance of enquiry skills in all areas of the curriculum, particularly mathematics, language and ICT. The second part points out that science provides a context for the development of other skills, particularly in literacy and mathematics. The need for enquiry skills to be used and developed in relation to science content so that they help children in their understanding of science concepts is discussed in the third part. It is important not to isolate science from other subjects, however, so the fourth part looks at establishing and maintaining links with other subjects and with everyday life. This leads to the conclusion that to implement science so that it is enjoyable and relevant to children, schools might seize the opportunity to create programmes of study that bring together various areas of the curriculum.

Liz Lakin

Cross-curricular skills

As suggested in Chapter 1, although there are different ways of expressing them, the process or enquiry skills in most curricula implicitly cover questioning, hypothesising, predicting, using observation, planning and conducting investigations, interpreting evidence and communicating. These skills are not unique to science; they appear across the curriculum, popping up in all manner of subject areas. The ability of children to transfer these skills from one

Figure 7.1 **Equipment set up for simulating huddling of bees and monitoring the temperature in the huddle.**

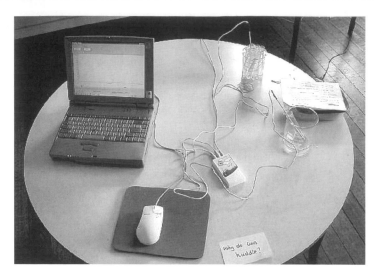

curriculum area to another needs to be developed and enhanced. For example, problem-solving and data-handling form part of the English National Curriculum for mathematics, and specific reference is made to science in terms of the selection and use of data-handling skills when problem-solving (DfEE/QCA 1999, p. 73).

Similarly, the headings in the information and communication technology (ICT) programme of study for both key stages 1 and 2 echo the skills identified above. Although these relate directly to developing competence in ICT, we should not miss the opportunities to develop these generic skills through science. Gathering, storing and retrieving information from a variety of sources is fundamental to science. Developing these research skills provides an ideal opportunity to use ICT as a tool, in the form of CD-ROMs and Internet sites, as well as reference books. As an example, while exploring adaptation in science a link can be made between penguin and bee behaviour through a modelling activity in which temperature is monitored via a data-logger. Both bee and penguin colonies 'huddle'; populations as a mass slowly rotate with a spiralling motion. Organisms on the colder outside get slowly drawn into the warmer central mass of the huddle. During this process they keep themselves and each other warm. This can be simulated and monitored using the equipment in Figure 7.1.

Variation in light levels, humidity and temperature can all be readily monitored using simple data-logging equipment, leaving children to concentrate on other scientific skills such as planning and data-interpretation when exploring the factors that affect plant growth. Equipment such as data-loggers, digital cameras and other ICT appliances needs to be used to enhance the teaching and learning of science where other methods would be inappropriate or not as effective. This is recognised by Feasey and Gallear (2000a) who emphasise that without a science context the skills acquired remain generic and caught up within the enthusiasm of using the new technology. At the forefront of the teacher's mind when planning should be the question, *'Are we using ICT for ICT's sake or for science's sake?'* This idea underpins all cross-curricular involvement.

Science as a context for developing literacy and mathematics skills

Skills of organisation and communication of information feature throughout the curriculum. Whether through drawings or prose, modelling or using ICT, the skills needed to communicate ideas, knowledge and understanding from one person to another are fundamental to human existence and central to science and the scientific community. The communication of scientific ideas and findings can be notoriously dull, but by drawing on the expertise and opportunities developed in the teaching of literacy, the process can be enriched and enlivened (see Feasey, 1999). Indeed, for children to develop into informed citizens, able to participate in the ever-changing dialogue of the 21st century, they need a sound science background and appropriate literacy skills. As with all skills, these need time and opportunity for development. Box 7.1 gives some suggestions for developing different kinds of literacy skill in science.

Having the skills to communicate effectively is one thing, but to engage fully in modern-day society an individual requires the skills of a numerate person. Feasey and Gallear (2000b, p. v) point out that *Number is central to science; it allows people to access patterns and trends, to make comparisons and draw conclusions.* To appreciate and make sense of the world around us, such as the regular pattern on a snail's shell, the swift movement of a spider scurrying across the floor, the tessellation of soap bubbles forming alongside each other as we soak in the bath, or the light and flexible yet strong giant structure of the biomes at the Eden Project in Cornwall, we need an understanding of science

---

Box 7.1

Forms of communication in science might include:

- **Recount** – where children retell events: *How a plant grew over several weeks, or what happened when the teacher slowly warmed a piece of chocolate.*

- **Report** – where children describe the way things are: *The parts of a plant, different features of animals, the parts of a food chain, or the properties of a material.*

- **Explain** – where children explain processes or how something works: *Explaining how we can see through a periscope, how sound reaches our ears, why a plastic saucepan handle may be better than a metal one, or why crazy things like paper or wax-kettles don't work!*

- **Instructions** – where children state how something should be done through a series of sequenced steps: *Plan investigations before carrying them out, and write out the order in which they will do things.*

- **Persuasion** – where children argue the case for what they have done in a positive and constructive way: *That their way of separating dirt from water is best or that it would be very sensible not to start smoking at all.*

- **Discussion** – where children present arguments and information from different viewpoints: *Describing the benefits and drawbacks of micro-organisms, or presenting the reasons for and against wind power.*

Figure 7.2 **Shape and symmetry underpin adaptation and survival in the biological world, but also inform structure and flexibility in the physical world, as evident in this bridge.**

and an appreciation of number. Shape and space, symmetry and scale, measurement and graphical representation – all part of the mathematics curriculum – feature significantly in science and the world around us. Shape and symmetry underpin adaptation and survival in the biological world, but also inform structure and flexibility in the physical world, as evident in the bridge in Figure 7.2.

Using enquiry skills to develop scientific understanding

So can we develop science process or enquiry skills just through the way we teach other subjects? The answer must certainly be '*no*' because when skills are used in relation to a particular context domain they are helping the development of concepts within that domain. That is, if the skill of interpretation, for instance, is used in relation to patterns in mathematics then the concepts developed are mathematical ones. Sometimes it may look like science, but miss the opportunity to develop science understanding. For example, some 11-year-olds were investigating adaptation as part of the science session and were exploring the relationship between the surface area of an organism, its volume and overall heat loss. This is a high-level concept area in both science and mathematics, but rather than spending time exploring the science ideas involved, trying to understand why this relationship is important and to apply it to various organisms (a bulky organism such as an elephant and a lean organism such as a giraffe), time was spent working out the mathematics involved.

By using the skills to develop their understanding, children begin to recognise how scientific ideas are created and to appreciate the nature of scientific knowledge. This is an important aim of science education, as suggested in Chapter 1. So attention to developing enquiry skills in relation to scientific content is essential. Teachers of 5–7 year-olds readily introduce the 'cars down the ramp' investigation. The aim is to examine the relationship between the height of the ramp and the distance travelled by the car. Children very quickly work out the connection and are keen to move on to the next part. This often involves changing the surface of the ramp, thereby introducing a new idea: friction. But this is a concept better introduced later and suffers from overemphasis early on. What has been overlooked is the opportunity at an early stage to develop the skills of enquiry and procedure that are so fundamental to more in-depth science introduced later in the curriculum. These skills, although generic across the subjects, need to be developed and honed within the context of science so that the learner can apply them effectively and skilfully as their science knowledge and experiences become more challenging and complex.

But this is not the same as saying the science should be separated from other areas of experience; quite the contrary. Unless these ideas have relevance for the learner they become isolated and their significance obscured. Gillard (2005, p. 7) explains that if we envisaged *science as a body of facts and truths to be learned and memorised, then it would be possible to teach science in an objective way and carry out practical work to prove things*. She goes on to state that if *'science is perceived as a great exploration in which we endeavour to understand the world we live in, then we open up the possibility of thinking creatively about our world'*. Through the processes of discussion and communication, science becomes a social activity that infiltrates the very fabric of our lives. Indeed, to avoid children seeing school science as a form of fantasy and distinct from everyday life, we must ensure that the content of the science session means something to them. It must be relevant and connected to their lives beyond its timetable allocation. This view is echoed in the 'Breadth of study' section of the English National Curriculum for science, which states that science knowledge, skills and understanding should be taught through familiar contexts and linked with other areas of the curriculum. Setting science within a real-life context makes the knowledge gained relevant and meaningful, and likely to spark children's interest and motivation (see Box 7.2).

Box 7.2

Setting science within a real-life context

A teacher with a mixed class of 5–6 year-olds was introducing an investigation into the effect of sunlight on different things. The session began with the children examining a collage of shapes stuck on to a piece of black sugar-paper that had been left in the sunshine for the previous three weeks. The children noticed with interest how the exposed paper had faded when compared with that hidden beneath the shapes. A discussion developed centred around their explanatory suggestions. It was an extremely hot day and the discussion soon changed emphasis to incorporate sun-block and suntans. On leaving the classroom at break time, one astute 5-year-old offered his friends some of his suntan cream to protect them against the sun whilst in the playground.

Maintaining links to real life as ideas become more abstract

As children progress through school the concepts and issues they are exposed to become more abstract and complex: notions of electricity and friction, pollination and fertilisation, the rock cycle and particle theory, for instance.

The risk of isolation and irrelevance increases and the need for everyday contexts becomes ever more important. The child may not be ready to make this conceptual leap, but the use of models and simulations, analogies and associations invariably helps. We can act out the parts of a circuit or the process of pollination and draw analogies between the structure of an apple cut in half and the make-up of planet Earth. We can stand back with glee and watch as we simulate an erupting volcano by adding just enough vinegar to bicarbonate of soda. These strategies all work to some degree but have their limitations and run the risk of introducing misconceptions. By using these in parallel with the real-life context – observing insects visiting flowers, going to a power station and experiencing the enormity of electricity generation and distribution, watching a video of an erupting volcano, identifying the effect of plate movements on rocky outcrops – these abstract ideas become real.

Sometimes it may be more effective to explore scientific ideas and issues through the vehicle of other areas of the curriculum. Environmental topics, so often debated and discussed during a science session, can be animated through drama and role-play (Littledyke, Ross and Lakin, 2000, p. 56). Once the underpinning science has been explored, role-play can be used to give a realistic feel to the issues arising from a real-life scenario such as meeting the increasing demand for electricity. A mock enquiry featuring representatives from all sides of the community can enable children to begin to appreciate the complexity and emotive nature of the situation.

The art of skilful and effective debate, however, does not just happen: it needs to be developed. By drawing on strategies used within personal, social and health education (PSHE), such as 'diamond ranking', opportunities can be created for children to exercise and explore their own and others' perspectives on some of science's more challenging issues. These might include, for example, the tension between biodiversity and deforestation or between organic and intensive farming. Statements relating to the issues are printed on a selection of cards and presented to the children. They arrange the statements in a diamond shape, putting the statement with which they agree most at the top and working down to the one they agree with least. This approach allows the children to externalise their own ideas and to listen and discuss each other's. The debate develops as the statements are arranged and rearranged until a general consensus emerges.

Environmental issues are often revisited during PSHE and citizenship education, and the underlying principles of these issues are often science-related. By combining the two areas of the curriculum, some effective and progressive teaching and learning can take place, as the example in Box 7.3 shows.

Conclusion

In this chapter we have explored the importance and significance of science process skills and the need to make science relevant, whether through the cross-curricular approach or within an everyday-life context. Running counter to this is the danger of disintegration: of children acquiring disjointed, disconnected and potentially meaningless information. This is a particular danger with a potentially abstract and inaccessible subject such as science. Within the Scottish curriculum, science, technology and issues of society are incorporated within an overarching theme entitled Environmental Studies 5–14

Box 7.3

Food choices

As part of citizenship education a year 5 class was considering food and farming within their local community. The children visited a local farm and afterwards, back at school, they discussed several of their experiences (Lakin, Lipington and Pask, 2004). One product produced and used by the farm was an organic fertiliser made from the breakdown of comfrey

Figure 7.3 **Children make choices about food items they would buy and justify their decisions in the 'shopping bag game'.**

leaves. Back at school the process was repeated and set the scene for investigation of modern farming methods. The children learnt about the legislation associated with intensive farming and explored the difference between this and organic methods. Children mind-mapped issues concerned with animal welfare that can arise from different farming systems and explored consumer choice in terms of food production and 'food miles' – the distance a product has travelled from production to purchase. This was drawn together by the 'shopping bag game', whereby they were asked to make choices about food items they would buy and justify their decisions (Figure 7.3). They used knowledge gained from previous sessions and pondered over the choices they had to make. Despite tasting several of the items, the majority of children opted for the cheaper, highly processed products they knew they liked. The activity did however go some way to encouraging the children to think about why they do things and what influences their decisions.

(LTS, 2000). This sets science within an integrated approach that *'brings together the main ways that children learn about the world'*, rather than it being a separate subject with its own identity. While all teachers may not have the luxury of such an integrated curriculum, they do have the potential to step beyond the constraints of a common programme of study and take ownership of the curriculum. In England the Primary Strategy urges teachers to enrich the learning experience by building learning skills across the curriculum and to be more proactive in deciding what, when and how they teach (DfES, 2003, p. 3). This renewed sense of ownership should bring back enjoyment, motivation and enthusiasm into teaching, thereby engaging children and instilling in them a desire to know and understand more about their world.

References

DfEE/QCA (1999) *The National Curriculum handbook for primary teachers in England.* London: Qualifications and Curriculum Authority.

DfES (2003) *Excellence and enjoyment: a strategy for primary schools.* London: Department for Education and Skills.

Feasey, R. (1999) *Primary science and literacy.* Hatfield: Association for Science Education.

Feasey, R. and Gallear, B. (2000a) *Primary science and ICT*. Hatfield: Association for Science Education.

Feasey, R. and Gallear, B. (2000b) *Primary science and numeracy*. Hatfield: Association for Science Education.

Gillard, L. (2005) *Science knowledge for primary teachers*. London: David Fulton.

Lakin, L., Lipington, L. and Pask, P. (2004) How can science be creative? *Primary Science Review*, **81**, 4–6.

Littledyke, M., Ross, K. and Lakin, L. (2000) *Science knowledge and the environment: a guide for students and teachers in primary education*. London: David Fulton.

LTS (Learning and Teaching Scotland) (2000) *Environmental Studies – science, society and technology 5–14*. Edinburgh: Scottish Executive.

Chapter 8 Effective primary/ secondary transfer

Discontinuity in educational experiences as children move from primary to secondary school has

Roger Mitchell

been blamed for the dip in achievement and in enjoyment of school that is often found in the year after transfer. In the past more attention has been given to easing children's social passage, but now a number of initiatives also address the curriculum and pedagogic issues at this important stage. This chapter aims to show that, although there are very real challenges, there are many ways in which they can be met. It identifies the problems that schools face and provides some examples of ways in which the essential mutual understanding between primary and secondary teachers can be achieved, transfer smoothed and continuity in children's experiences facilitated in some science-specific structured projects.

The challenges

Regardless of the setting, it is important that we think of the apparent barriers to successful transfer as 'challenges' rather than 'problems' or 'dilemmas'. Once this is established it is easier to think about 'strategies' and 'solutions'. It is useful to establish a working group of colleagues from both phases and to brainstorm all the perceived challenges in a particular setting. Some of the most common challenges that have been identified are listed in Box 8.1.

Once the list of challenges has been compiled it needs to be refined by identifying any factors that teachers cannot influence and those where it is possible to provide strategies that will have the most positive impact. This refined list will provide the working group members with a coherent set of

Box 8.1

Challenges to effective transfer

- Providing a time and venue for all parties involved to be present, which is more challenging the more schools there are involved in the process.

- Knowing (and trusting) the experiences that children have had previously.

- Being aware of the expectations of the school and phase to and from which the children are transferring.

- Deciding how much information is to be passed on, what type of information, and how useful it is.

- Reaching agreement in the teacher assessments of the children's abilities and levels of attainment.

- Implementing planned transfer projects, e.g. visits by teachers and children, teacher exchanges, curriculum-based bridging or transition units, joint activity planning.

criteria on which to base their judgements of the best way forward.

Although the main focus will inevitably be identified as those year groups that directly border the transfer point, the outcomes of such discussions should also take account of the bigger picture. Embedding the transfer process in the culture of the whole school will allow the good practice identified to be disseminated to a wider staff group. For example, the nature of science concept acquisition allows us to operate a spiral curriculum (see Chapter 13). Enquiry skills and areas of knowledge and understanding are revisited at appropriate levels throughout a child's education. So if we are looking at a specific skill or area as the focus for a transfer project that will feed through from primary to secondary, it is worth considering building directly on work undertaken by children in earlier years – and being explicit about this with both colleagues and children. This will give the transition unit greater value and provide opportunities for all teachers involved to become more aware of the expectations at different levels of education.

Strategies for success

Once partner schools have established their requirements in relation to primary/ secondary transfer they need to think about how these requirements can best be met. There are no hard and fast rules. However, two key factors will influence the success of any emerging projects. Firstly, it is important that the head teachers of all partner schools are committed to the project, as this level of leadership will be necessary for sustainability. Secondly, the schools involved should try to use existing structures to facilitate their work. For example, an established cluster group of schools may have regular meetings programmed into their academic cycle. It would be prudent and appropriate to use such established structures to promote any new partnership projects. Other actions for primary schools that have been identified as contributing to successful primary/secondary transfer are listed in Box 8.2 (note that school years are identified here in terms of the English education system, where year 6 is the final year in primary education).

Box 8.2

Actions to facilitate smooth transfer

- Regular meetings between head teachers from partner schools.
- Activity days for all year 5 and 6 (or equivalent) children to introduce them to their next school.
- Development of a transfer document in collaboration with the partner secondary school for key information about each year 6 child to be sent on to the secondary school well before the end of the school year.
- The use of transfer data to ensure well-balanced tutor groups of mixed ability and a good social mix.
- Early visits to primary schools by relevant secondary school staff including the special educational needs coordinator.
- Special visits to their new secondary school for year 6 children identified as being vulnerable.
- A year 6 induction day with secondary form-tutors near the end of the school year, followed by a parents' event on the evening of the same day.
- Use of ICT for transfer of pupil data.
- Exchange visits between primary and secondary teaching staff involving collaborative planning, team-teaching, etc.
- Use of structured transition units in years 6 and 7 in the core subjects, supported by some year 6 lessons undertaken in the secondary school and visits to year 6 lessons by year 7 teachers.

Developing mutual understanding

It was mentioned earlier that common challenges affecting successful transfer are, on the part of secondary schools, knowing (and trusting) the experiences that the children have had previously, and, on the part of primary schools, being aware of the expectations of the school and phase to which the children are transferring. It is also important to develop consensus in respect of teachers' assessments of the children's attainment. Some activities that can be undertaken by schools to assist in developing the mutual understanding needed for meeting these challenges are now outlined.

Agreeing the course of progression

Many clusters of feeder schools and their secondary school put aside one of their annual in-service training days for a joint event. This is the perfect opportunity to develop a better mutual understanding among colleagues from all schools and phases involved in transfer. Box 8.3 gives an outline of one activity that can be useful in breaking the ice and promoting relevant discussion.

The same type of task as in Box 8.3 can be undertaken with respect to enquiry skills, using the same materials or using the progression of enquiry

Box 8.3

Developing mutual understanding

Units from the QCA schemes of work for key stages 1 and 2 (years 1–6) and for key stage 3 (years 7–9) (see websites) for a particular area of science can be presented to mixed groups of teachers from different key stages. For example, a group could look at the theme of electricity in year 2 (unit 2F – *Using electricity*), year 4 (unit 4F – *Circuits and conductors*), year 6 (unit 6G – *Changing circuits*) and year 7 (unit 7J – *Electrical circuits*). Key questions should be provided for the groups to consider, such as:

● What do you notice about the pupil expectations for each unit?

● What do you notice about the expected level of scientific vocabulary for each unit?

● How do you think this contributes to continuity and progression in the teaching of this area of science?

● Is there anything that surprises you about the content of the units?

● Is there anything that doesn't surprise you about the content of the units?

This may appear to be a fairly low-key task, but such units are often used in isolation, with no reference to the other linked units within the same key stage, and seldom with any reference to the linked units from other key stages. This may be the first opportunity that colleagues have had to get a full picture of this area of science in such a holistic way. Consequently, the feedback will often be very enlightening.

skills in the primary years suggested in books such as Goldsworthy and Feasey (1997) and Harlen and Qualter (2004). The expectation for enquiry skill development across the primary phase can be used as a starting point for discussion as to how this development is extended in secondary science.

Developing consensus on assessment

The use of children's work in science, annotated with the age of the child and the key learning objective, can also be helpful when working in cross-phase groups. Such 'agreement trialling' leads to a better understanding of criteria used in teacher assessment. For instance, it is often the case that a piece of work that primary teachers identify as achieving a particular level is marked lower by secondary teachers. At some levels this difference appears to be because work that primary teachers see as providing a good *explanation* of a scientific concept is viewed by secondary teachers as providing a good *description* of that concept. It is these sorts of differences of viewpoint that need to be addressed if the teacher assessments that are transferred to secondary schools are to be trusted by those who receive them.

Structured transition projects

Although there are several transition projects available to schools, none will suit every circumstance. In undertaking such projects it is vital that the schools involved identify their unique needs and adapt materials and strategies to suit their specific requirements. This will allow the most relevant work to be undertaken and, more importantly, facilitate a greater ownership of the project for all those involved.

The Key Stage 3 Strategy requires all schools in England to address issues of transfer between key stages 2 and 3. Consequently, many regional and local education authority (LEA) Strategy coordinators initiated transfer schemes or adopted and promoted existing schemes. For example, the 'Bubbles' scheme, which originated in Cheshire (Cheshire LEA, 1997) several years prior to the Key Stage 3 Strategy, was taken up by other LEAs. The DfES Standards website (see websites) has a number of case studies of transition projects in science and other curriculum areas, including a successful science project based in South Gloucestershire and Bristol LEAs (McMahon, see websites).

The Welsh Qualifications and Curriculum Authority (ACCAC) has published a booklet, also available on their website, called *Bridging the gap* (see website). The booklet provides several examples of developing and using bridging units to support transfer between key stages 2 and 3, including some examples from science. Box 8.4 gives one of these.

Although there is no doubt that the activities in Box 8.4 were of great value, opportunities may have been missed here with regard to fuller collaboration, for example team-planning and team-teaching by teachers from both phases in all of the investigations. In another cluster, primary and secondary teachers

---

Box 8.4

A Welsh example of bridging work

One group of primary schools and their secondary school has produced together a scheme of bridging work linking investigative work and practical skills in science.

The aims are:

- *To introduce pupils to methods of investigation through planning, obtaining evidence, conducting and evaluating.*

- *To teach measuring skills relating to length, mass, volume, time and temperature.*

Two investigations are designed to meet these aims:

- *How does insulation make a difference?*

- *How does a spring stretch?*

The practical equipment was supplied by the secondary school and secondary teachers visited the primary schools to observe and support investigative lessons.

These lessons were followed up with pupils in Y7 starting science with the chapter on 'Investigations' in a published scheme. At the end of the first term, pupils carried out an investigation 'Which crisp has the most energy?' This included the use of ICT for data-logging and producing graphs. Primary teachers visited the secondary school to observe pupils carrying out this investigation and talked to them about their findings. This provided a good basis for future discussion about transition work.

(Quoted from ACCAC *Bridging the gap* website)

realised from their discussions that they had different ways of undertaking investigations. The teachers worked together to agree a common investigative approach and introduced this across both phases. This is a good example of how collaboration can aid continuity for children in the transfer process.

The Science Transition in Scotland Project (see website) also aims to support teachers to help children's science education through the transfer from primary to secondary school. This web-based resource provides materials for use by clusters of partner schools. Every month a new experiment and newsletter are posted. The site provides resources that are easily adapted to suit particular clusters of schools. It also contains information and advice for cluster activities as well as case studies from successful projects. The Case Study Library is a useful forum for teachers to share experiences and information.

Much of the most significant work on primary/secondary transition projects has had major external funding. For example, starting in 2001, STAY (Science Transition AstraZeneca Science Teaching Trust York) was a three-year project of the AstraZeneca Science Teaching Trust, in partnership with York University, City of York LEA and 13 partner schools (Braund, 2004). The project developed bridging units in scientific enquiry based on two investigations, 'Fizzy drinks' and 'Bread'. Children were taught the year 6 part of the unit in the second half of the summer term, and the linked year 7 component when they transferred to secondary school in September. Lesson plans focused on the component skills of scientific enquiry, teaching these specifically and progressively. The project was disseminated to, and adopted by, all York schools in 2002. In 2003 the bridging units were used in East Yorkshire LEA, and to date there has been training and licensing of the project in over 50 LEAs and school clusters.

One of the most recent transition projects is the North Yorkshire AstraZeneca Science Pedagogy and Progression Project (NYASPP, see website). Prompted by discussions of the need to concentrate on curriculum and pedagogical aspects in transfer work, the project is focused on teaching the process skills of scientific enquiry as this is work that underpins the science that children do either side of transfer, irrespective of the topic studied. This project built on earlier work which found that:

- *pupils in KS3 often repeat practical work that they have done before in primary school without any additional challenge. They find this boring and demotivating;*
- *teachers value an improved understanding of the ways in which each other work including how the language of teaching and learning can be made more contiguous;*
- *there has been a very significant and serious reduction in the amount of practical work done in Y6 classes and this is widening the gap between Y6 and Y7 teaching;*
- *there is a great need for continued professional development of teachers in the area of scientific enquiry, particularly in teaching about ideas and evidence;*
- *teachers in both phases are looking for ways of linking good quality opportunities for a range of types of scientific enquiry to their current schemes of work and to QCA units.*

- *Additionally teachers in both key stages are being focused on progressing pupils' learning from scientific enquiry by the changes in SAT questions in KS2 and KS3 papers in 2003.* (NYASPP website)

The NYASPP project addresses these issues through the development and teaching of pairs of practical tasks – one to be taught in year 5 or 6 in primary school and the other to be taught at some stage in key stage 3. Four such tasks have been produced which use pedagogical approaches that clearly show teachers and children the expected progression in knowledge, skills and challenge as they move from primary to secondary work. Key stage 2 teachers are encouraged to communicate to children how the work will be developed in the secondary school, and key stage 3 teachers are encouraged to recognise and build on children's previous achievements in the primary school. The NYASPP approach is the latest major project to provide support for primary/ secondary transition work in science. Its flexible approach means that it is easily adaptable to the needs of different cluster groups.

Science Passport

Finally, the ASE/Science Year *Science Passport* is described in Box 8.5. For the *Science Passport* to be of greatest impact, partnership schools need to work closely and look for opportunities to collaborate in both planning and teaching

---

Box 8.5

Science Passport

Developed as part of the ASE/Science Year CD-ROM initiative, the *Science Passport* is a template for successful bridging projects between primary and secondary schools. It is designed to resemble a real passport. There are six A4 pages that fold into an A5 booklet. Children have a section for a passport photograph and details about themselves, including primary and secondary school information. A personal section introduces the idea of inherited characteristics and there is space for information about investigations in years 6 and 7.

There is a choice of investigations with structured teacher notes as well as activity support sheets for children. The investigations are:

- **Looking at habitats and adaptations** – in which communication, group work and literacy are highlighted at different points in the activity.

- **Solutions** – which uses dissolving jelly as a focus for developing investigative and practical skills, including prediction, analysis and evaluation.

- **Golden ratio** – where the children focus on their faces and collect variation data that draws them into the world of the ancient Greek golden ratio. Numeracy is highlighted in the calculation of simple ratios.

Throughout these activities children can collect visas for skills and investigations to carry forward into key stage 3. These build for the children a reassuring link between schools. There is also an apparatus checklist, a vocabulary page and a final section where the children record the science centres they have visited. As a record of children's achievements at key stage 2, the passport provides tangible information to key stage 3 teachers on which to build.

with the materials. The *Science Passport* and its associated support materials are available to download free (see website). Further information about the *Science Passport* and its successful application in a transition project can be found in the case study 'Using the *Science Passport* for transition' (see website).

References

Braund, M. (2004) Bridging work in science: what's in it for primary schools? *Primary Science Review*, **82**, 24–27. Available to ASE members at: http://www.ase.org.uk/htm/members_area/journals/psr/pdf/psr_82/pg-24-28.pdf

Cheshire LEA (1997) *Bridging the gap, KS2/3 liaison – Bubbles*. Winsford: Cheshire County Council.

Goldsworthy, A. and Feasey, R. (1997) *Making sense of primary science investigations*. Hatfield: Association for Science Education.

Harlen, W. and Qualter. A. (2004) *The teaching of science in primary schools*. London: David Fulton.

Websites

ACCAC. *Bridging the gap*: http://www.accac.org.uk/uploads/documents/1515.pdf

DfES Standards site: http://www.standards.dfes.gov.uk/keystage3/casestudies/cs_sc_transition

McMahon, K. *Transition in science – South Gloucestershire LEA and Bristol LEA*: http://www.standards.dfes.gov.uk/keystage3/downloads/cs_sc_transition.doc

NYASPP (North Yorkshire AstraZeneca Science Pedagogy and Progression project): http://www.york.ac.uk/depts/educ/projs/STAY/NYASPPNov04.htm

QCA Key stage 3 Scheme of work for science: http://www.qca.org.uk/9906_13181.html

QCA Key stage 2 Scheme of work for science: http://www.qca.org.uk/9907_13180.html

QCA Key stage 1 Scheme of work for science: http://www.qca.org.uk/9908_13179.html

Science Passport: http://www.sycd.co.uk/who_am_i/passport/activity.htm

Science Transition in Scotland Project: http://www.sciencetransitionscotland.org.uk/

Using the Science Passport for Transition: http://www.standards.dfes.gov.uk/keystage3/casestudies/cs_sc_transition_pass

Chapter 9

Learning science outside the classroom

Several organisations concerned with helping children to learn outside the classroom are expressing concern that this is **Alan Peacock** and **Mick Dunne**

not happening as often as they consider it should. This is especially worrying as children seem to 'play out' less when they are not at school than used to be the case. This chapter begins by expanding on the reasons for making provision for children to spend some time learning outside the classroom. It then looks at opportunities available to schools in their own grounds and in places children can visit. There follow some examples of schemes for providing out-of-school learning activities, some 'dos and don'ts' based on evaluation of visits outside the classroom and hints on heath and safety.

A rationale

Many reasons are advanced for the decline in what can loosely be called 'fieldwork': cost, health and safety, risk of litigation, time involved, pressures on teachers and the sense of being 'snowed under'. At the same time, many agencies are doing a great deal to encourage teachers to get out more and take advantage of the resources available in the immediate locality of the school and further afield. For example, the Real World Learning campaign is a movement by a consortium of major environmental agencies to foster more out-of-school learning (see Field Studies Council website). Other agencies, such as the Countryside Agency, English Nature and the Soil Association, are also working closely with schools to this end. Schools have encouragement for this kind of activity in official documents; for instance the Primary National Strategy (DfES, 2003) in England encourages schools to be more flexible, to take more control of their curriculum and to give children these kinds of experiences.

Why take children out of school to do science? Box 9.1 lists some justifications for working outside the classroom.

65

Box 9.1

Why go out of school?

Working outside the classroom:

- provides first-hand experience of processes such as focused observation and recording;
- lets children use play to explore science ideas in a safe context;
- provides experience of the physical, social, environmental and ecological aspects of the real world;
- provides opportunities for novel, unique and exciting learning experiences;
- embeds science learning in meaningful contexts;
- provides practice in and application of skills used in the classroom;
- can expand the science curriculum and give it purpose;
- builds closer relationships between children and teachers, as well as between children and other 'expert' adults;
- provides stimulation and motivation;
- gives opportunities to develop children's autonomy which encourages important attitudes such as respect;
- helps develop a child's identity.

Opportunities in the locality

Wherever a school is situated there will be opportunities to work outside, starting with the school grounds, which will include both natural and built environments. Even if there are only a few bushes around the school, a teacher can still use these to provide valid activities for children, such as the following 'caterpillars' activity, which develops the idea of camouflage. Cut different-coloured pieces of wool each into 10 strips, about caterpillar length, and scatter them in the bush. The children 'become birds', and are given one minute to find as many caterpillars as possible. They will find the brightly coloured ones, but not the green/brown/yellowy ones! Or use school buildings and walls to study materials and their properties, investigate habitats, weeds, the best places to grow pot plants, forensic science (whose footprint is that?!).

Beyond the immediate locality

Going slightly further afield, there will probably be a wildlife trust, wetland centre, city farm, museum or similar, not too far away. These are usually staffed by experts, many with a teaching background, who are very keen to receive school groups. They will have a wide repertoire of good activities for children and will be able to help teachers by suggesting ideas for enquiries and explorations in locations near schools: a wood, pond, farm, disused quarry, hillside, stream, canal, seashore, or even a shopping mall. For younger children, science is first and foremost about learning to observe phenomena more and

Box 9.2

National centres providing experiences and activities for learning science

- Science Museum and the Natural History Museum (London)
- National Space Centre (Leicester)
- Magna (Rotherham)
- Eureka! (Halifax)
- Museum of Science and Industry (Manchester)
- Dynamic Earth (Edinburgh)
- At-Bristol (Bristol)
- Techniquest (Cardiff)
- Eden Project (Cornwall)

All of these have websites that allow teachers and children to download materials, link the visit to the curriculum, plan a visit and support follow-up work. They, and others throughout the UK, can be accessed from the *24 Hour Museum* website (see websites).

more closely with all the senses in order to gather evidence. Any kind of scientific investigation depends on children seeing the need for evidence, and almost anywhere novel is good for this as it raises new questions to investigate.

There is now a rapidly expanding network of major science learning centres across the UK, established deliberately with education in mind (see Box 9.2).

Finally, there are national agencies offering partnerships with schools that take children out to work in the environment at venues such as National Trust properties (the National Trust Guardianship scheme, see Box 9.3) and organic farms (through the Soil Association and Farming and Countryside Education, see website); the Royal Society for the Protection of Birds, and events like 'Countryside Live!' sponsored by the Countryside Agency. Local authorities often run their own schemes such as the Somerset Waste Action Programme (SWAP), which allows schools to visit a working landfill site and recycling centre (Vrdlovçova, 2005). Recent evaluations of these (see below) show a striking success in terms of harnessing children's enthusiasm for science learning, and improving their behaviour, language and inter-personal skills at the same time.

Examples of successful out-of-school science learning

Boxes 9.3 and 9.4 give two brief examples of how schools have developed their science outside school.

Many other locations are appropriate for science, such as supermarkets, hospitals, manufacturing enterprises of various kinds, building sites, ports and harbours, opticians; whatever is available in the school locality. Once a visit has been planned and the safety issues sorted out, a good starting point is usually children's own questions. For example, they may well wonder what

Box 9.3

National Trust Guardianship scheme

The National Trust Guardianship scheme involves partnerships between schools and properties in which children become involved in stewardship and conservation activity through regular visits to a particular site. Over 120 such partnerships exist around the country (see National Trust website). Studland Bay in Dorset is one such long-established scheme: the children from St Mary's First School, Swanage, have a well-defined area of heathland behind the dunes, which they manage through removal of bracken and birch and by carrying out a long-term study of heather species on site. The area is also home to important populations of lizards and snakes, for which children have helped create suitable habitats (Gadstone and Kemp, 2004). Over many years, these young children have developed a bank of research data which is not only valuable in itself, but also shows the development of science research skills at an early age. Their work is also communicated on site to the public through leaflets.

Box 9.4

Farm visits

The Soil Association supports workshops on organic farms, which develop children's understanding of food, farming and environmental skills.

At Low Luckens Organic Resource Centre based at a farm in Cumbria, children from urban schools in Carlisle come for whole days to feed and tend animals (pigs, cattle, ponies), make fences, identify pond life, find out how people used to live, excavate old wells, and generally do what one child described as *'real men's work'*! Integral to the children's day is also a great deal of careful scientific observation and questioning, for example, about the wind turbine and rain-water collection systems (see Low Luckens website).

At Ashlyn's Farm in Essex, children from multi-ethnic inner-London schools feed animals they have never seen before, and learn a great deal about reproduction, growth, seasons and many other science ideas.

happens to all those bottles placed in the bottle bank. Every year many children visit one of the most modern glass treatment works in Europe, managed by Rockware Glass (a subsidiary of British Glass) at Knottingley, West Yorkshire. They are able to use a purpose-built education unit that overlooks the factory site and engage in a variety of educational tasks and activities suitable for both younger and older primary children for science and other subjects. Available resources include hands-on work with a mock-up of the recycling process, with opportunities to test different materials, video, interactive quizzes, a viewing platform and a site visit (see Rockware Glass website).

Lessons learned: some 'dos and don'ts'

Context and purpose

Despite many opportunities to engage in science education beyond the classroom, it is likely that the majority of schools and nurseries do not maximise their educational potential. Learning possibilities of a venue or activity must be specifically identified as part of the normal planning processes: context is crucial and preparation essential. Of critical importance is the match between the desired learning outcomes (the teacher's reasons for going in the first place) and contextual considerations for the learning, such as issues of timing, group sizes, the use of activity sheets and so on. At some centres, specialists are available (wardens, guides, explainers, farmers, education officers) who provide planning support as part of their general provision; this is most effective when there is liaison with, and guidance from, the teacher. Centre staff see many different school groups: they rely on teachers to help them respond to specific needs, rather than providing an 'off the shelf' programme.

Teachers must also be very clear about their science objectives. For example, if the children are going to engage in a pond-dipping activity, should they concentrate on identifying and counting the plants and animals, on simple relationships, on the production of food chains and even food webs, or on adaptation? Only the teacher knows what is appropriate for the children and must not be afraid of setting the agenda. Where no on-site assistance is available because of the nature of the venue then teachers must make a preliminary visit to devise tasks and activities. Not only do these need to be designed to meet specific learning outcomes, but they must also be do-able on the day, which will depend on seasons, weather, time, and so on.

One-off or serial visits?

Of the100-plus primary schools using an Education Bradford environmental centre, only a couple visited more than once in a single academic year. The same would be true of venues such as the Eden Project, where cost of travel can be a major factor. Excursions to such places are frequently seen by children as a 'day out' rather than being particularly relevant to identified learning experiences. Multiple, linked visits, say once a term or half-term, can be more expensive but their educational capacity is likely to be much greater than disconnected trips. Taking smaller groups regularly by minibus can end up being more cost effective. A pattern of serial visits offers progressive and fascinating insights into change over time, for example by observing and recording seasonal changes or life cycles; yet evidence suggests that visits are rarely organised with these objectives in mind. Regular visits also enable children to establish relationships with adult experts, as in the National Trust Guardianship scheme, which in turn helps these adults to target their provision for the children more appropriately.

Preparation and follow-up

It is essential that adequate preparations are made for visits, and that they are followed up back in the classroom. Many of the specialist centres provide a menu of science activities, differentiated by age range, that teachers are able to choose from and which are delivered by the specialist centre staff. However, this does not obviate the need for preparation; otherwise work started by the children during the trip is likely to remain incomplete and not used to develop the children's knowledge and understanding when back in school. That out-of-school visits motivate and stimulate the vast majority of children is without question; but whether they are being taken to a local supermarket to look at a range of food types, to the local tip to identify different forms of waste or to a zoo, considerable effort is required before the visit, during the visit and after the visit in order to maximise the effectiveness of the learning experiences. The 'trip mentality', which encourages children to spend more time thinking about ice-creams, lunch breaks and the shop than about the purpose of the visit, needs to be played down. By not having any food or drink for sale on site, for example, the 'Countryside Live!' days proved very successful in this respect.

Making visits effective

Preparation involves not only preparation for the children but also for all adults involved. They have a key mediation role during the visit, so it needs to be made clear beforehand what accompanying adults are expected to do: what will they need to focus children's attention on? what kinds of questions are appropriate? Often, accompanying adults are preoccupied with behaviour management rather than with learning so it is important to stress their role in learning.

Another important planning decision relates to the use of resources, both those provided by the centre and those teachers prepare themselves. All evaluations suggest that the use of activity sheets on site is not helpful; they distract children from using their senses, and the dreaded clipboard becomes a physical handicap. There is nothing more discouraging to a small child than lugging a clipboard round all day, along with a rucksack full of food and drink, an outdoor coat, and the rest. It is best to leave the clipboard at school, and complete the worksheets, if relevant, when they get back.

Follow-up activities can take many forms and it is not unusual to see literacy considerations outweighing those of science. The class display, with word-processed 'newspaper articles' on 'our visit' may look good, but often the science ideas and skills (and positive attitudes) can be lost as a consequence. Here again, serial work scores highly, as children can see that they are taking part in a longitudinal investigation that is accruing scientific evidence, as well as actively creating things, growing plants and conserving habitats. The pride that children take in talking about this kind of work far outweighs the value of writing pinned on the wall. Some organisations not only provide web-based materials to assist with this kind of follow-up, but also offer outreach support, where their staff will visit schools to provide ongoing input. A powerful example of the success of this approach is the SWAP programme mentioned earlier (Vrdlovçova, 2005).

Health and safety

Appropriate management of health and safety is a major concern to those practitioners who recognise the huge educational potential of working beyond the classroom. Publication of *Health and safety of pupils on educational visits* (DfEE, 2000) has addressed many concerns but largely ignores children within the foundation stage. Specialist venues contribute to alleviating health and safety pressures on schools by providing comprehensive activity-specific risk assessments. The *Management of Health & Safety at Work Regulations* (1992) require employers to produce risk assessments and demonstrate how risk is managed. There is a duty on all teachers, therefore, to inform their employers of 'identified risks' – ignorance of this responsibility is no excuse! A complete risk assessment needs to be completed before the visit takes place. Multiple copies of *Health and safety of pupils on educational visits* (DfEE, 2000) are available free from DfES Publications and from the DfES website, which provides links to other relevant documents including: *Standards for adventures, Handbook for group leaders, Group safety at water margins* and *Health and safety: responsibilities and powers*.

Parental concerns need to be addressed by schools. Many specialist centres produce videos that are specifically designed to support schools in tackling this issue. Children and parents who attended the same trip during the previous year provide useful advocates.

Assessing the learning

Inspectors have frequently praised the quality of schools' science work outside the classroom, particularly as it appears to enhance children's language and social skills as well as their science attitudes. But how best to assess this without spoiling the enjoyment and sense of achievement that children experience?

Children operating outside the classroom love to show others what they have learned and quickly adapt to alternative methods of recording. They are more likely to use reporting in groups, role-play, digital cameras and minidisk recorders, mapping techniques, cartoon strips, poster presentations or oral presentations. Evaluations of visits have also indicated that children have many more misconceptions about the environments they encounter than we imagine.

It is best to avoid too much of the kind of assessment that identifies the out-of-class work with testing and formal assessment. Using such work as a vehicle for extended writing should not be discouraged; but the danger is that through redrafting, marking and display of such work, children can easily learn that the literacy objectives matter more than the scientific attitudes and skills being developed. On the other hand, a display of photographs of children working outdoors, with examples of artefacts produced or used, can communicate very effectively the sense of achievement they experience. Learning with known and trusted adults helps develop those valuable one-to-one conversations that are important in the development and assessment of children's ideas.

Conclusion: the benefits of working in the environment

If we genuinely want children to make sense of their world, then working on science outside the classroom is essential. Learners' experiences become embedded in authentic contexts so science can become more meaningful and real. Experience in a wide range of contexts shows that the vast majority of children are enthusiastic about such ventures and apply themselves fully to this work. The educational benefits are huge, but there is a cost. There is a need for careful and focused planning to maximise learning and to consider

71

serial visits rather than 'one-offs' to take full advantage of these experiences. Health and safety, financial and time considerations can be dominant factors in the decision-making process, but there is a wealth of information, guidance and even financial support available, often from the centres visited, to assist teachers. The question perhaps is not, *What do we gain by going outside the classroom?* but *What science are children missing by not having these experiences?*

References

DfEE (2000) *Health and safety of pupils on educational visits.* DfES Publications (see DfES website).

DfES (2003) *Excellence and enjoyment: a strategy for primary schools.* London: Department for Education and Skills.

Gadstone, M. and Kemp, D. (2004) Goodies, baddies, and quoits. *Primary Science Review*, **83**, 24–26.

Vrdlovçova, J. (2005) Waking up to waste. *Primary Science Review*, **86**, 8–11.

Websites

24 Hour Museum: http://www.24hourmusem.org.uk

DfES Health and Safety publications: http://www.teachernet.gov.uk/wholeschool/healthandsafety/visits/

Farming and Countryside Education: http://www.face-online.org.uk

Field Studies Council: http://www.field-studies-council.org/campaigns/rwl/index.aspx

Low Luckens Organic Resource Centre: www.lowluckensfarm.co.uk/

National Trust Guardianship: www.nationaltrust.org.uk/.../learning/guardianship/

Rockware Glass: www.glassforever.co.uk

Chapter 10
School self-evaluation of teaching and learning science

Lynne Wright

School improvement is now a permanent feature of school life, and there are tremendous pressures on schools, from many directions, to do ever better. This is one reason why the school development plan (SDP) is now often called the school improvement plan (SIP). This chapter is about what schools can do to evaluate their performance in relation to provision for science education. The first part concerns what can be learned from analysing children's performance. This is followed by consideration of the importance of evaluation of teaching with some suggestions about how to do this. Subsequent sections concern self-evaluation of the curriculum, how children are supported in taking responsibility for their learning, the relationship with parents and others outside the school, and matters relating to health and safety.

Why school improvement? Who is it for?

It has been many years since schools could be regarded as 'islands' within their communities, remaining largely unaccountable to them and to wider society. There is an increasing expectation that schools will share their philosophy, aims and approaches with the outside community. Although accountability to a wide range of stakeholders continues to put schools under pressure, it is right that they should demonstrate how well they are doing in helping each child to do his or her best.

To this end, it is most important that schools have as full a picture as possible of children's standards of *attainment* in science, as indicated by school and external tests and other performance data. Crucially, schools need some measure of the *progress* children are making in science as they move through the school. However, accountability requires a much broader picture than this. It is necessary to look beyond the most easily measurable outcomes in order to gauge the effectiveness of science teaching in improving not only standards and achievement but children's attitudes to science and the school's partnership with parents and the community.

In England, external inspection seems to be a permanent feature of school life and has evolved through many manifestations, from 'we will tell you how well you are doing' to a more shared approach based on a school's own evaluation (see Chapter 3). Whilst external inspections are becoming shorter and more focused, crucially they are increasingly based on a school's own rigorous analysis of its data, both quantitative and qualitative (Ofsted, 2003). Even without this external pressure, it is in a school's best interest that its own analysis is ruthlessly honest and accurate. School self-assessment at any level, and for any aspect or subject, relies upon evidence collected by the school in a measured and planned way, rather than on assertions, expectations or hope! The National Advisers and Inspectors Group for Science (NAIGS) has produced a helpful checklist, *Writing a subject evaluation that works*, in the same format as the self-evaluation form required for Ofsted inspections in England – see NAIGS website.

Evaluating achievement

It is possible, but time consuming without a computer program, to analyse school data to build up a picture of the attainment and achievement of individuals or groups. Happily, there is an increasingly sophisticated array of software programs available to help senior managers and science subject leaders to do this. Such analyses need to be very objective. Looking for reasons for particularly good performance is a positive experience, but it is less comfortable when there has been no, or only slight, improvement or even a downturn in performance. In these instances it is even more important to establish reasons for the results, rather than to provide excuses. Honest and objective explanations help to inform the next stage of the SIP so that the strategic plan guides the actions of all concerned in the teaching of science within the school, particularly the action plan of the subject leader. This plan must also take into account national and local priorities, as this is ultimately what schools are judged against.

What to analyse, and why?

It is important to look in depth at the attainment of different groups within a cohort (see Ofsted, 2005). Do boys outperform girls, or vice versa? Does this reflect the national trend? Is there a reason for this and is the school doing anything to redress the balance? How well are children doing who have special educational needs or are in the early stages of learning English (or whatever language science is taught in)? Is there any significant difference in cohorts of younger children between the attainment of those born earlier or later in the academic year? Are children new to the school doing better, as well as, or worse than they did in their previous school(s)? Is there a clear and detailed picture of the attainment of children of different minority ethnic groups? Is the attainment gap wider for one group than another? If so, how does the school plan to narrow the gap? Is an increasing proportion of children achieving at higher levels? The answers to these questions give clear indications of the next steps in self-evaluation, and in the subject leader's action plan.

Monitoring progress

Having found out the standards the children are reaching, it is essential that schools look at what progress groups and individuals are making in their science learning. Schools need to find out which children are making the expected progress, those who are achieving beyond what is expected of them and those who are not doing as well as anticipated against individual targets set for the end of each significant stage in their education. Targets for attainment in science need to reflect teachers' knowledge of individual children, taking into account the impact of teaching and any planned intervention strategies during the key stage. The progress of those with special educational needs may be judged against special needs performance criteria and those in their individual education plans, if specified. The expectation is that schools should be able to share information about the projected progress in science of individual children from year to year and when they move to another school.

Although progress and achievement can be judged in a global way by comparing test scores year on year this does not help the subject leader to pinpoint any areas of specific success or difficulty, which may highlight areas of good or weaker teaching in science. It is necessary to look beyond test scores to find out the detail of children's progress, both as a cohort and as individuals. How well are they applying their science knowledge and understanding to new learning in new contexts? Do children use an increasing range of science terms correctly and with understanding? Do they conduct investigations in an increasingly well-organised and logical way and choose the most appropriate method of recording and displaying the results using increasingly precise measurements? How well do they make predictions based on their science knowledge and explain their findings in relation to their initial hypotheses?

This level of analysis will enable the subject leader to identify any areas in the science teaching that need to become a priority in the science action plan. It will identify where professional development is needed to increase an individual teacher's knowledge and expertise. It will also help class teachers to identify which parts of the learning programme are posing difficulties for individual children, so that science teaching plans can be amended to give extra support. Any such analysis will also indicate particularly strong areas of science teaching, or which teachers can provide good role models. Teaching plans can be adapted to provide extra challenge for children achieving above the average.

Evaluating teaching and learning and children's attitudes to science

Although there is not necessarily a direct link between achievement and the quality of teaching, achievement that is below expectation requires investigation. One explanation might be very young children entering school with very restricted life experiences and little idea of why they are at school. In these instances, the children initially tend to be passive recipients of teaching and it takes much skill, knowledge and enthusiasm on the part of the teacher to instil the idea that the children have to participate in learning.

To establish effective self-review the senior management team and science subject leader need to have a clear picture of standards in teaching across the school and how these link both to standards of attainment and achievement and to progress in learning. One of the most reliable ways of doing this is to monitor science teaching. In a small school this is not easy to organise as it often relies upon other staff releasing a head teacher with teaching responsibilities or a classroom-based subject leader to carry out the observations. To do this objectively, and to provide the most useful information, the focus of the observation needs to be understood by, and shared with, all participants.

It may be impossible to carry out lesson observations because release time cannot be found, or other subjects take priority. However, it is still important to maintain an overview, or to address a specific problem that has arisen and needs explanation. In this case, looking at children's work in science can give a lot of valuable information. One of the best ways of establishing children's attitudes to science and the effectiveness of teaching and learning is talking to them! This can be done both formally through individual reviews or informally in small-group discussions. Box 10.1 lists some questions that can guide the self-evaluation of teaching.

Observing science teaching also gives the subject leader a good idea of children's attitudes to science and science lessons. It will enable a picture to emerge of whether they are enthusiastic learners or passive recipients of teaching and how much scientific curiosity they display. The sorts of questions they ask and their intellectual independence in pursuing scientific enquiry are also good indicators. Their ability to work cooperatively, to organise themselves and to behave well under all circumstances is not only another indicator of their attitudes but further evidence of the quality of teaching. There is a very strong link between good teaching in science and children's positive attitudes and enjoyment. All these are an integral part of self-evaluation.

How effective is the science curriculum?

It is also necessary to evaluate the quality of the science curriculum from time to time. Even if test results and teaching evaluations are good or improving, it is important to know why this is a positive area of the school's work so that the good features can be built on and, perhaps, transferred to other curriculum areas.

If children enjoy science lessons, work hard and generally record their work accurately and with care it is a reasonable, albeit subjective, indicator of a lively and relevant science curriculum. Schools where this is particularly noticeable have quickly adapted their curriculum to the context of their own school environment. Some schools adopt a commercial scheme of work wholeheartedly. While this often produces thorough teaching to build up well-developed science concepts, it can lack the excitement of teaching and learning science that is found in the best schools. (See Chapter 12.)

Box 10.1

Self-evaluation of teaching

- Is the content of a lesson scientifically accurate?
- Has the teacher enough personal science knowledge and understanding to lead the learning of all groups of children forward at a good rate?
- Do teachers' plans provide for progress of all groups of children and those who need individual support?
- Do teachers share the objectives of each lesson with the children so that they have a clear idea of what they are expected to learn?
- Is a range of teaching styles deployed within a lesson or a topic sufficient to suit the preferred learning styles of all children?
- Are different methods of teaching, and of children's recording of their science learning, appropriate to the science content being taught?
- Are children given enough opportunity and time to think through, explain and explore their own science ideas using enquiry, investigation, research and discussion?
- Is marking regular and consistent?
- Is the school's marking policy followed?
- Does marking concentrate on what was planned for the children to learn?
- Does marking correct misconceptions and inaccurate use of science terminology?
- Does the teacher ask questions which develop children's thinking in science?

Most importantly in evaluating the science curriculum, or scheme of work, the subject leader needs to check that it stems from the school's mission statement which should, in turn, link to the main aims of the school science policy. The existence of such a statement signals the intention of providing equality for all children, but the crucial thing is how far this aim is reflected in practice throughout the school. It is vital that the contexts for teaching science should be of interest to both boys and girls and to children of all abilities. The choice of these contexts also needs to take account of the experiences of children of different ages and the cultural experiences of different ethnic groups. Other factors, including local events and interests, such as a new school pond or building work in the community, give the science curriculum the added interest that makes it relevant to the children in a particular school. All these elements should appear in a school's year and term plans and so should present little problem for the subject leader in monitoring them. Planning at each key stage should also ensure that science skills, knowledge and understanding are taught in such a way that key early science concepts are introduced at the right level and built on in further teaching throughout the school. An evaluation should also check that sufficient time is given to the teaching of science to enable quality teaching and learning.

Supporting children in their science learning

Since children are partners in the learning process, it is sensible to evaluate how well they are supported in this. Support can only be really effective if there is consistency of teachers' judgements within a school and, even better, over a wider range of schools. This is why the moderation and standardisation of the assessment of children's work is such an important process, and why portfolios of assessed and moderated science work are so useful. These exemplify to children and teachers different pieces of work of a particular standard. Once criteria are agreed and understood, children can be involved regularly in assessing their own work. The teachers' diagnostic comments, if they are sharply focused, help the children to see how they can improve. The children are better able to judge how well they are doing and, with practice, identify what they need to do to improve their work (see Chapter 23).

Central to this are discussions with children in order to find out whether they know and use effectively the assessment criteria for their work. Discussion, however informal, can also establish whether they understand their next steps and what they have to do to take them.

In the face of the many pressures schools are under, the effectiveness of this level of individual self-evaluation within the whole-school self-evaluation process is often overlooked. Through evaluating the level of support children are given in their science learning, senior managers and the science subject leader are well placed to be even more accurate in their evaluation of the effectiveness of science teaching and its impact on standards and achievement.

Partnership with parents/carers, other schools and the community

Many adults' memories of their own science learning are very different from what goes on today, and some will not have been taught science at primary school. Parents/carers are very important partners in the education of children and schools need to evaluate how successful they are in promoting effective and mutually supportive relationships. At its most basic level, this means ensuring that parents/carers get regular information about how well their children are doing in science. To be really helpful, regular information should also outline the main areas of science learning over a set period, including the topic or theme, with suggestions of how parents/carers can support their children and the school. This might include, for example, interesting websites to explore with their children or suggestions for shared activities such as blowing bubbles, or places to visit, such as a museum to look at dinosaur skeletons.

If a school makes a practice of asking parents and carers for their views, the focus of one questionnaire could be how well the school's provision in science is helping develop their children's interest and curiosity, and their desire to do well. In order that parents and carers can give informed views, some schools run science evenings so that they can experience the school's approach to teaching science at first hand. This is an 'eye-opener' for many parents/carers, who realise that not only can science be interesting and fun but it requires the learner to develop and use a wide range of skills in different contexts. Parents and carers are introduced to different styles of teaching and learning, all of which promotes a closer partnership based on shared understanding and aims. In this way, a school's self-evaluation of its effectiveness is beginning to look beyond itself and widen the circle of the school community.

The partnership that the school has with other schools and the use it makes of the wider community is a further area for self-evaluation. It is important not only to arrange for visits and visitors to extend children's science experiences, but to gather evidence of their impact on learning by asking questions such as these. Are the resources of the local community used as contexts for developing science ideas and skills? Do visitors enthuse the children so that they gain a clearer understanding of what it means to work scientifically? Is there a fruitful partnership with other schools that provides a supportive network of professional development for teachers? Are scarce resources shared between schools so that all aspects of science can be taught to the required levels?

Ensuring the health and safety of pupils

In England it is the responsibility of the school's governing body to ensure that children are working in a safe environment; in other countries the responsibility is delegated to the head teacher. However, the science subject leader also has a key role in this respect. The science scheme of work needs to highlight where particular safety precautions should be taken and check that all members of staff have read any local and national guidance on safety in science. Any accidents need to be logged so that possible action can be taken to avoid a similar accident happening again. The subject leader needs evidence that teachers are following the safety guidelines. Although this is difficult to do at first hand, it can be part of the subject leader's planned overview of topic and lesson plans, so that safety is a proactive feature rather than a reactive one.

Conclusion

A school's evaluation of its own effectiveness is a critical process in helping it to develop and improve, however high its standards are currently. The resulting document not only gives judgements on how well the school is doing, but also provides solid evidence of the contributory factors across the whole range of its work. It is a living document that, when reviewed and updated regularly, gives the school the basis for its improvement plan so that all children have the best possible chances to do their very best.

References

NAIGS (2005) *Writing a subject evaluation that works*. Available from QCA website at: http://www.qca.org.uk/15173.html

Ofsted (Office for Standards in Education) (2003) *Handbook for inspecting nursery and primary schools*. Document reference number: HMI 1359.

Ofsted (Office for Standards in Education) (2005) *Interpreting data* (CD). London: Ofsted.

Section 3 School level: Programme planning

Chapter 11

The science subject leader's role

This chapter is concerned with the leadership and management of science in the primary school. In the majority of schools this is delegated to a named teacher with the job title of science coordinator or science subject leader; in other cases the role is shared between several individuals either taking on different aspects of the role separately or operating as a team with one or more subject responsibilities. But, whatever the job title or organisational structure, there are certain functions that must be carried out in order to sustain and improve the teaching and learning of science in a primary school. The functions and the knowledge, skills and qualities required to carry them out effectively are discussed and illustrated here.

Liz Lawrence

Purpose of the subject leader role

The TTA *National standards for subject leadership* (1998) identify the core purpose of subject leadership as being to:

> *provide professional leadership and management for a subject to secure high quality teaching, effective use of resources and improved standards of learning and achievement for all pupils.* (TTA, 1998, p. 4)

This short definition contains both the primary purpose of subject leadership – a direct and positive impact on standards – and the means by which it will be achieved: the dual role of manager and leader. It emphasises the leadership and management role rather than pedagogical or subject knowledge. However, an effective subject leader requires subject-specific knowledge in addition to generic leadership and management skills and a thorough understanding of the school-specific context.

Roles and responsibilities

The TTA standards set out the key outcomes of subject leadership. These, appropriately, begin with the impact on the children, who are expected to:

show sustained improvement in their subject knowledge, understanding and skills in relation to prior attainment; understand the key ideas in the subject at a level appropriate to their age and stage of development; show improvement in their literacy, numeracy and information technology skills; know the purpose and sequence of activities; [be] well prepared for any tests and examinations in the subject; [be] enthusiastic about the subject and highly motivated to continue with their studies; through their attitudes and behaviour, contribute to the maintenance of a purposeful working environment... (TTA, 1998, p. 5)

An effective subject leader also informs, involves, supports, motivates and develops other teachers, ensures good communication with parents/carers and other adults in the school community, enabling them to support the learning of the children, and provides a clear perspective on the subject to heads and other senior managers, enabling them to make well-informed decisions. The key outcomes make it clear that the achievement of the children is at the heart of everything the subject leader does.

As the example in Box 11.1 shows, a clear focus on children's achievement involves a subject leader putting into place, reviewing and updating systems that ensure that teachers know:

● what to teach and to what depth or level of detail;

● how it will be taught;

● what the children will do;

● what the expectations are;

● how attainment will be assessed;

● what action will be taken as a consequence of the information from assessments.

The subject leader is required to demonstrate good practice in using these systems and to support colleagues in making them work. It is also vital that they are monitored and reviewed. The subject leader will need to have mastered a range of management skills but will also require enough pedagogical and subject knowledge to be clear about the curriculum, teaching methods, assessment criteria and standards.

One context in which subject-specific knowledge is particularly important is health and safety. Primary science is statistically very safe but the subject leaders will still need to take responsibility for keeping their knowledge and reference sources up to date. They will also need to ensure that health and safety procedures feature in policy documents, risk assessments are known about and adhered to, and colleagues are aware both of sources of advice – e.g. *Be safe!* (ASE, 2001), CLEAPSS and SSERC (see websites), local authority advisers – and situations in which that advice should be sought. As with other aspects of the job, systems and monitoring of them are required.

Box 11.1

Good subject leader practice

The experienced subject leader, working in a structured and effective school, is able to make a significant contribution to children's progress and achievement.

Emma is the science subject leader in a large infant school. She has responsibility for resource provision but ordering and organising of resources is delegated to support staff. There is a detailed scheme of work linked to clear assessment and record-keeping. The school has a planned programme of monitoring during which subject leaders carry out book scrutinies and lesson observations. As part of each monitoring cycle Emma is expected to use monitoring and assessment data to produce a report for the head teacher and governors identifying strengths and areas for development. She delivers this report in person, answering questions on it, and uses it to prepare her input to the school improvement plan. The head teacher has been very supportive of her professional development and she is able to take on the full responsibilities of effective subject leadership.

Functions of the subject leader

Various models are used to categorise the functions of subject leadership. One approach found useful in training subject leaders groups them under the headings of provider/administrator, impact maker and communicator.

Provider/administrator

The tasks that fall under this heading, although time-consuming, can usually be carried out without being released from teaching. They include:

- auditing, budgeting for, selecting and deploying resources, including people, accommodation and expertise (see Box 11.2) (previously ordering and organising resources would also have been listed but these tasks are no longer required of teachers in England);

Box 11.2

Making good use of resources

The subject leader in an urban primary school has identified a need for better provision for environmental science. She involves colleagues, the school council, parents/carers, governors and outside agencies in planning the creation of an outdoor classroom with a variety of habitats, wild and cultivated plants (including vegetables) and animals. The whole school is involved in developing and maintaining it and its continued use is ensured by embedding activities such as growing plants, raising butterflies and chickens and studying the range of habitats in the curriculum for different year groups. Children have ownership of this resource and treat the whole environment of the school with care and respect. All staff value the contribution it makes to science and to the creative and community ethos of the school.

- supporting colleagues, including providing or identifying opportunities for professional development (see Box 11.3);
- informing and advising colleagues informally or through documentation such as the policy, scheme of work, health and safety advice and other guidance.

This list has many similarities with the role of the coordinator in the past. Although necessary, these often-reactive functions alone will be of limited effectiveness.

> **Box 11.3**
>
> **Supporting colleagues**
>
> The subject leader has identified specific areas of weakness in her colleagues' subject knowledge and requested LEA support. Workshops and demonstration lessons are used to develop understanding of specific areas of physical science and how they can be taught. All teachers in the year group observe and discuss the demonstration lessons. The subject leader then supports the teachers in delivering the lesson to the remaining classes in that year group. The teachers modify the plans to offer guidance appropriate to the class.

Impact maker

In order to achieve a sustained improvement in standards the subject leader needs to take on a more proactive role. Some aspects of this require the subject leader to work with colleagues during lesson time; thus the school as well as the individual must be committed to developing the role of the subject leader. Through a rigorous cyclic process of self-evaluation and improvement, coupled with a vision of what high-quality science education in the school will look like, an impact-making subject leader can build on existing provision, embed good practice and drive standards upwards. The impact-maker role involves:

- establishing and reviewing standards (see Box 11.4);
- monitoring (see Chapter 10), making judgements and analysing;
- prioritising, planning and developing;
- providing a role model, mentoring and coaching.

Becoming a role model can be daunting for a new subject leader and it is important to distinguish between the all-knowing expert (a rare creature indeed) and the subject leader who models aspects of good practice and also recognises and draws on the expertise of others, modelling the equally important role of learner, as in the example in Box 11.5.

Communicator

Effective subject leaders must be able to communicate information and expectations clearly and, importantly, their own enthusiasm for the subject. Their ability to communicate with adults, discuss and share good practice and help all to move forward together enables the school to be a learning community. This aspect of the role encompasses some of the motivational aspect of leadership, ensuring that everyone is able to contribute to common goals and

Box 11.4

Establishing and reviewing standards

Effective use of data ensures that high standards are expected and children are supported in achieving them.

A large junior school has rigorous tracking and support procedures which involve the experienced subject leader working with other members of the senior leadership team. The subject leader uses her expertise to identify assessment opportunities and ensure that all teachers are aware of the required standards. Internal assessment data are used to identify children who are underachieving. For younger children this is addressed through the usual teaching programme; year 6 children receive 'booster' provision taught by the deputy, a science specialist. Analysis of national test data allows the school to identify and address weaknesses in its provision.

Box 11.5

The subject leader as learner

The subject leader who is not yet experienced enough to take on the full role is initially given responsibility for provision and administration. She begins by auditing where the school is before implementing any changes. The impact-making role remains with senior colleagues who support development towards meeting the TTA standards.

Rajini is the newly promoted science subject leader in a primary school. She has only been teaching for a few years. This is her first position of responsibility and, although enthusiastic about science, she has concerns about her subject knowledge and her lack of experience of the whole primary age range. Initially her role consists of auditing, replenishing and organising resources and ensuring that colleagues have copies of planning documents. She attends courses to improve her subject knowledge and, through network meetings with other subject leaders, begins to develop ideas for raising standards in her school. Informal discussions and usage of resources suggest that teaching is not consistent across year groups, does not always follow the plans and makes too little use of practical and investigative activities. Monitoring of books and planning confirms this, and Rajini implements a programme of planning support and staff meetings with a focus on scientific enquiry. Planning folders are collected, and out-of-date worksheets and lesson plans are replaced by new resources which are matched to the units in the scheme of work. She organises a science week to raise the profile of problem-solving and investigative science. Senior colleagues retain all responsibility for data collection and analysis, monitoring and evaluating; the subject leader plays some part in development planning and takes the lead on implementing changes. The school has identified monitoring teaching as the next step in Rajini's development as a subject leader and she has also expressed an interest in becoming more involved in data analysis and target setting.

recognise the successes along the way. Box 11.6 gives an example of the role of subject leader being shared among a team of teachers who meet regularly to discuss progress and actions that need to be taken. A small school may need a different responsibility allocation when there are too few teachers to have a separate leader for each subject. Box 11.7 illustrates a solution to this problem.

Box 11.6

Subject management by collaborative teams

At Brindishe School, a one-form entry primary school, subject coordinators have been replaced by team leaders. The team leader for science and technology has responsibility for '*the management, organisation and development of science teaching and learning, for strategic thinking and planning and for the improvement of children's standards of achievement*', an apparently similar role to that of subject leader. The difference is that the team leader is supported in this by teachers and teaching assistants with an interest and/or expertise in the subject. Regular meetings allow the whole team to plan, allocate tasks and responsibilities, check progress against success criteria and time limits and review achievements. The ability to share tasks, ideas, perspectives and expertise makes the team very effective; the range of members and collective enthusiasm carry the impact quickly across the school. Although the team leader retains overall responsibility and is accountable for any drop in standards the team approach has formalised the contributions of other people, improving efficiency and effectiveness.

(Adapted from an article by Keith Barr, 2003)

Box 11.7

School leadership and subject leadership interwoven

The small two-form entry, very successful urban infant school where Paul is deputy head has a structure that does not involve traditional subject coordinators. Named people are responsible for resources but they do not take a lead on developing the subjects. Vision and direction are provided by the head teacher and Paul (who is not class-based); they also monitor teaching and learning and track children's progress in all the core subjects. They regularly teach classes, in order to release the teachers in each year group to plan together. This helps them to establish a clear picture of standards across the school. The scheme of work, developed by Paul, provides teachers with objectives and clear assessment criteria; teachers have the freedom to plan and sequence activities to meet these objectives and to link with other areas, particularly ICT, where the school is a centre for development and innovation. Teachers have a variety of interests and expertise and the management structures within the school promote sharing of ideas across and between year groups. Although the head and deputy sit at the centre of the structure and have responsibility for the strategic direction and standards, subject and pedagogical knowledge in science (and other subjects) are generally not seen as residing in any one individual.

The role in practice

The role of the science subject leader will of course require all the functions identified above. The standards identified by the TTA (1998) in England provide a detailed and ambitious checklist of tasks, outcomes and competences relating to the role of the subject leader. However, as the examples of practice given here show, schools use many different models and structures in order to achieve the central aim of high-quality teaching and learning in science. The newly appointed or inexperienced subject leader will have different priorities and needs from an experienced and senior one. The demands a school with deficiencies in its basic provision makes on its subject leader will be different from those of a successful, stable school with a history of strong subject leadership. The knowledge, skills, experience and qualities of the available personnel, the management structure and leadership style favoured by the head teacher, and other circumstances affecting the school will all influence the way in which the tasks and responsibilities of subject leadership are allocated.

Looking to the future

At a time of change in education it is reasonable to assume that the role of the subject leader will not remain static. In many schools subject leaders are assuming an important role in self-evaluation. The self-evaluation procedures required by the new inspection framework in England are clear about the need to make judgements when monitoring, to make evidence-based statements rather than vague assertions and to have clear plans for developing areas of concern. This is not a new definition of effective leadership but it provides an additional model reinforcing good practice.

The changing emphasis in professional development away from a dependency model to one built around the school as a learning community, with colleagues sharing their expertise and moving forward together, and networks of schools working in partnership, is reliant on strong subject leadership, particularly in the areas of staff development and teaching and learning. Communication with other subject leaders can enable the science subject leader to build a view that goes beyond their own school and subject area. The ability to manage change, both externally imposed and as a response to internally identified issues, will also continue to be important. Any future developments in the role will be both positive and empowering if the emphasis continues to move from managing science to supporting high-quality teaching and learning.

References

ASE (2001) *Be safe! Health and safety in primary school science and technology*. Hatfield: Association for Science Education.

Barr, K. (2003) Managing science and technology: one school's approach. *Primary Science Review*, **79**, 4–7.

TTA (1998) *National standards for subject leaders*. London: Teacher Training Agency. Also available at: www.tta.gov.uk/

Websites

CLEAPSS: http://www.CLEAPSS.org.uk
SSERC: http://www.SSERC.org.uk

Chapter 12

Selection of materials, programmes and schemes of work

In common with other subjects science must compete with a range of demands on the time

Anne Qualter

and energies of teachers. Pressures on the curriculum have resulted from the spotlight being trained, for example, on information and communication technology, on literacy and numeracy, on the early-years curriculum, on creativity and on communication skills and citizenship. None of these areas conflict with the requirements of science education, but all these changes in the wider curriculum must impact on, and so inform changes in, the school's scheme of work for science. This chapter addresses the question of what informs or drives changes to the school's scheme of work or the materials required to support a high-quality, relevant and fresh science curriculum. It begins with four case studies, which are amalgamations based on interviews in 12 primary schools. These are then used to discuss in more detail the principles that guide the decisions about how best to provide for children's learning in science.

Four case studies

It has been argued that too much prescription has served to narrow the curriculum. This has been identified as an issue in Scotland where changes began in 2004 for implementation in 2007 to:

> remove unnecessary detail from existing 5–14 guidelines in curriculum areas such as Expressive Arts and Environmental Studies to allow teachers more flexibility and scope to provide rich and varied experiences, and reduce the time spent on assessment. (Ministerial Response, SEED, 2004, see website)

90

Box 12.1

Case study 1: Bryn Fellin

Bryn Fellin is a two-form entry primary school in a small industrial town in Wales where science is taught in the medium of English with Welsh as a separate curriculum subject. Anna became science subject leader in 2000 just as a revised curriculum was introduced. She decided to use this as an opportunity to initiate a whole-school review of science in which teachers' views were sought of what was really important. Teachers identified three areas for development. They wanted to:

Use what teachers believe is important.

- build in more enrichment by looking to opportunities outside school, particularly the local country park, the education authority's coastal education centre and local business;

- enrich the curriculum in school by keeping up with new ideas and making use of new technology;

- extend and develop work on healthy living, and integrate sex education into the curriculum rather than seeing it as a separate issue.

Teachers need to feel confident that the scheme of work forms the basis for sound medium- and short-term planning.

Although some schools in Wales use the QCA scheme of work (DfES, 1998) to check content coverage, the staff decided against this. They wanted to be more flexible in their planning and were confident in their knowledge of the attainment targets in the curriculum document, and how to use them to inform their planning. They wanted to include a number of topic weeks such as a 'Healthy week' to involve the whole school, and to include more visits to local industry, to Techniquest (the interactive science centre in Cardiff) and the countryside. Partly as a result of attendance at a 10-day course for new science subject leaders, Anna decided to evaluate each of these changes whilst keeping to a mainly subject-based approach for the older children and a themed approach for the 5–7 year-olds.

Build in evaluation; expect to continually change and improve.

Keeping links with other science coordinators, and attending regional meetings of the Association for Science Education helps to keep the curriculum fresh. The school makes use of concept cartoons (Naylor and Keogh, 2003) and assessment for learning (Goldsworthy, 2000), in making sure that their teaching continues to develop and improve.

Box 12.2

Case study 2: Fosketts

There are many sources of resources as long as the school has a strong vision of where it is going.

Fosketts is a small non-selective private village school of 120 3–11 year-olds in England. The school day is longer than normal, starting at 8.30 am and running to 3.30 pm for younger or 4.00 pm for the older children. The National Curriculum for science is followed, but not slavishly. The children take the national tests and teachers use all the National Curriculum resources available. The school chose to adopt a published scheme of work based on the prescribed curriculum to provide a solid basis for shared planning.

A published scheme can give confidence and coherence whilst allowing teachers to do things their own way.

New IT equipment can open up a whole array of new possibilities.

The key to how science is approached is the commitment of the staff to science in the local environment. Thus, for example, a project looking at endangered species involved surveys of stag beetles (local but endangered) to provide data for a real scientist's study. In order to maximise the potential resources and relevance of projects, links are often made with special national 'weeks'. Thus National Tree Week became the focus of work by the youngest classes in the school. This provided a range of opportunities to obtain useful resources and use lively websites. To boost funding for resources, various sources are often approached. Data-logging equipment was provided as a result of a bid to the Royal Society (indeed funding for further stag beetle work came from this source too). Use of the science CREST (see website) awards for 11-year-olds and involvement in numerous competitions keep the children excited and the school well resourced.

Changes in emphasis in the national tests for 11-year-olds led to more work being done on investigations, including using the new electronic whiteboards to work through planning experiments beforehand so that ideas and knowledge can be shared. The science subject leader finds that this approach raises performance by making the children really think about the science they are doing.

Box 12.3
Case study 3: Greston Primary

Greston Primary is in a deprived inner-city, dockside setting with many children who struggle to learn. The school had extremely low scores on national tests despite improved and indeed positive inspection reports. The curriculum had become closely focused on the core subjects, especially literacy and numeracy, but still followed the curriculum guidelines for science. However, improvements were hard to make.

The prescribed curriculum must not get in the way of learning by taking the focus away from the child's needs.

The head teacher, with the encouragement of advisers, decided to take what felt like a radical step, to shift the focus to a cross-curricular approach for some classes in the school. This aimed to give greater emphasis to providing an enriched and highly relevant curriculum through working with topics such as 'Shopping', 'The three bears', 'Ships coming in' and 'Fit and healthy'. The staff felt that the prescribed curriculum was letting the children down, but at the same time believed that the rigour and broad content of the National Curriculum should not be lost.

Where children live is an important source of inspiration, even in the most disadvantaged areas.

They therefore felt strongly that they should continue to follow the QCA scheme of work broadly, but should modify and reorganise it to fit in with cross-curricular topics. Teachers believed that they could maximise their time by making use of lesson plans available on the Internet (such as *Science Web*, see website), which could be modified to suit the theme and allow easier use of other resources such as BBC *Science Clips* (see website) for the whiteboards, as they tend to be designed to fit the QCA scheme. It was felt important that the school scheme should provide a supportive framework in which to plan creatively.

Teachers need to feel confident that they are meeting national requirements.

Teachers do not have to invent everything for themselves, but make use of websites and lesson plans, etc.; a clear view of where they are going is key.

93

Whenever new ideas come into school they will influence our thinking about science.

The scheme of work as it is taught never stays still; it must be constantly monitored.

The curriculum is not only what is taught in school – it is what is learned. Where parents as educators are valued, that is part of the scheme or the school programme.

Box 12.4

Case study 4: St John's

St John's Parish School is in a fairly affluent urban area where most children have parents or carers who expect them to do well. However, teachers were concerned that they needed to get back to the pleasure of learning and to bring the children's parents along with them. The staff had been involved in a project on emotional intelligence; they were focusing on the use of puppets to help children express themselves and explore ideas, not simply in relation to how they felt but also to help them explore ideas in science and other subject areas.

The school had adopted a cross-curricular approach with a focus on creativity long before the Primary Strategy *Excellence and enjoyment* was published (DfES, 2003, see website). They saw no real need to change the science scheme of work that had been in place for a few years. However, it had become clear that some parents were questioning the approach, worrying that the children were playing too much and working too little. The question was how to extend the children's learning by involving parents and carers. The staff decided to devise role-play boxes where each box would take a theme (such as 'inventions', 'owls', 'growing'). Boxes contained a book to share, some websites to visit, equipment (e.g. seeds, a trowel, etc.) to support role-play, a game, and opportunities to make something. Children had a big box for a week once each half term. Parents and children completed the evaluation book and parents expressed real pleasure in the opportunity to learn with their children and to see science learning (along with other subjects) as such fun.

Of course, the whole exercise of putting the boxes together, identifying resources (using the school's good selection of published schemes and textbooks) and designing games and role-plays acted as a catalyst as teachers discussed their ideas, which in turn helped to inform further changes to the school scheme of work for the following year.

A well-planned scheme is not a static one, but changes as we learn and as new ideas come through.

The intention is to clarify the purposes and intended outcomes of education while leaving teachers more freedom to decide how to achieve these ends.

Similarly, in England, the Primary National Strategy states that to improve primary education:

> one of the best ways will be to look to primary schools to take more of the initiative – for teachers to be able to lead improvement themselves, through their own professional abilities. We want schools to feel freer to take control, and to use that freedom to:
>
> • Take a fresh look at their curriculum, their timetable and the organisation of the school day and week, and think actively about how they would like to develop and enrich the experience they offer their children. They should take account of the individual needs of all children in the school, the local context, the particular skills and enthusiasm of the staff, the distinctive ethos of the school, the resources available in the wider community, and also their knowledge of good practice and of what delivers results.
>
> (National Primary Strategy, Executive Summary, DfES, 2003, see website)

With this freedom comes the responsibility to make the best decisions for the children in the context of the particular conditions and environment of each school. Naturally these vary considerably and so it is useful to preface general discussion with a glimpse of what informs decisions in four examples (Boxes, 12.1–12.4).

Key decisions in selecting a programme of study

Core values and beliefs

From the case studies it becomes apparent that what are important in the development or selection of a programme of study or scheme of work in science are the values and beliefs of the teachers and the needs and interests of the children. Thus, at Fosketts (case study 2) science is seen very much as involving the environment and the world outside. Teachers value the exploration of the local flora and fauna. One class, with funding from a farmer, made a CD of the sounds of the meadow, which, with its accompanying notes, was extremely popular in the school and in the village. The teachers believe that children learn best by doing; thus when it came to looking at endangered species, they looked at stag beetles and not just rhinoceroses. At the same time, to feel free to follow exciting trends the staff felt they needed a scheme of work to use as a baseline to check coverage. Selecting the right scheme takes time and care, as well as lots of consultation with colleagues. A number of websites provide reviews. For example, BAYS (British Association for Young Scientists, see website) reviews a wide range, from materials focused on one element of science to whole schemes. Very brief comments are made which can provide a good starting point. However, for reviews by practitioners that attempt to unpick the underlying values of a scheme the reports in *Primary Science Review* are extremely useful. These are now gathered together in the members' section of the Association for Science Education website (see websites).

Meeting the needs of the children

It is also clear from the case studies that the children have different needs that teachers want to be able to meet. In Greston Primary School (case study 3) the priority was for children to focus on activities relevant to their everyday lives, to develop simple skills and to develop their social skills. The 'three bears' topic provided an opportunity to cook and taste, and to talk and share knowledge about cooking and food. Shopping provided an ideal vehicle for a visit to a local supermarket. Opportunities for trips further afield are limited due to the cost of transport, so the locality is an important resource. In St Johns Parish School (case study 4) the issue was not one of material deprivation but rather a need to encourage parents and carers to see learning and play as interrelated and to communicate a sense of fun in learning to parents.

In three of the case study schools investigation was given an additional boost when this element was introduced into the national tests. Making good use of new technologies to enhance rather than replace investigations proved successful, and so resulted in changes to the schools' schemes of work. By seeing what works and does not work, the scheme of work is constantly changing. For example, the impact of parent and children's evaluations of the role-play boxes, as described in St Johns, was such that the school scheme was modified.

Making use of the environment and surrounding area

Each of the case study schools is in a different environment. Yet the staff in both Fosketts (case study 2) in a rural village and Bryn Fellin (case study 1) in an industrial town are extremely keen to make use of the local environment. In Fosketts school this means making use of the countryside; in Bryn Fellin the key was to link with local businesses, such as garden centres. In Greston the local environment could be seen to be rather arid, but a trip to a supermarket (or the dockside), properly planned, provided interest and relevance. Children were encouraged to ask questions about a facility they knew well. Through questioning and observation the children learned about bread making and food preservation and discussed the origins of some of the fruit and vegetables on display. The quality of learning from this was, according to the teachers, remarkable.

Of course, as in all school activities, safety is of utmost importance. An essential guide for schools is the Association for Science Education's booklet *Be safe!* (ASE, 2001). Prior visits to sites to assess the risk are key (obvious when visiting building sites and wasteland but just as important when working in the school garden). Indeed risk assessment is as important to the success of the activity as careful forethought being given to exactly what learning outcomes are anticipated and therefore what activities should be planned and what questions asked during the visit. (See chapter 9 for more discussion of out-of-school visits.)

Other curriculum subjects

In each of the case study schools the value of capitalising on cross-curricular links is apparent, although how far the curriculum is planned on the basis of topics or themes varies greatly. In Fosketts, projects such as growing a wartime garden brought together history, drama, art and science, while at other times subjects are taught separately. The selection of a commercial scheme in sympathy with this approach helped to support teachers without constraining them.

Greston, with its concern for the basics, used a literacy-led approach to cross-curricular planning. This could have the effect of skewing the curriculum diet experienced by the children if not carefully monitored. The solution at Greston was for teachers to stick closely to the QCA scheme of work to give them the confidence that they were covering what was required. What teachers in this school noticed was that they were covering the curriculum easily, meeting more objectives in a topic than were suggested in the scheme. However, once they realised this they were happy to continue as they felt that the scheme provides a rigour that would otherwise be lacking. This is something that schools were accused of prior to the introduction of a National Curriculum in 1989, but how far this constrains the teachers' creativity in curriculum planning is a thorny question. (See Chapter 7 for further discussion of links to other subjects.)

A published scheme or not?

Although the approach and the level of prescription was different in different countries within the UK, the introduction of externally devised curriculum guidelines in the 1980s and 1990s led to many teachers spending hours taking the curriculum to pieces or interrogating guidelines and building school schemes of work. It was at that time that curriculum planning moved from the level of the individual teacher to the school level, with year group or key stage teams planning together. It could be argued that teachers were replicating effort across the country. Although the purchase of published schemes of work increased at that time the focus was on teachers planning together. The advantage of this approach is that teachers get to know the curriculum very well and are able to imbue it with their own values and to make it relevant to their children. The disadvantage is that it involves a lot of precious time; where published schemes have done the work, this may not be the best use of such a valuable commodity.

Finding the right balance is not easy. In Greston teachers were afraid to go too far down the route of cross-curricular topics without having the security of the QCA scheme of work. This is understandable given their poor showing on national tests. But the desire to meet the needs of the children better led to a compromise, which gave them confidence. In St Johns, teachers felt confident to work without using a prescribed scheme, but with a wide variety of resources, including published schemes and materials downloaded from the many websites that offer support, such as Planet Science resources (see websites).

Supporting planning

The purpose of a school scheme of work is to establish a shared view of what it is important to teach. It shows how, in terms of the overall philosophy of the school and subject, the curriculum might be delivered and then, linked to this, how that should be structured (cross-curricular, separate subjects). The order in which aspects of the curriculum are to be taught is important (see Chapter 13). The scheme of work provides an analysis of the curriculum in terms of progression: what should be covered and roughly when it should be covered. Decisions about, for example, how often to revisit a science topic are made at this stage. This is important to help teachers as they plan for the medium term. For example, one London school included in its scheme of work the importance of environmental education. In developing medium-term plans it was decided that every class should visit the Greenwich Environmental Centre at least once over the following two years. The scheme then informed decisions about when classes might go and what they should be focusing on (Barr, 2003).

The issue of ensuring good progression without overloading the curriculum, which in turn tends to stifle creativity, was key for a group of science subject leaders in the London Borough of Newham. They worked together to plan a scheme of work in which science could be taught rigorously through the expressive arts. They decided that there were far too many learning outcomes in the QCA scheme and so identified the key learning outcomes for their project. They then decided on the appropriate progression routes and built this into their scheme, making direct links with the prescribed National Curriculum and to ideas for creative outcomes. This provided a rich, and well-structured basis for medium- and short-term planning in the schools in the cooperative (Iiyambo, 2005).

Once a scheme of work has been developed it provides the basis for selecting appropriate resources so that teachers can be confident, when they make their medium- and short-term plans, that the resources are available (see Chapter 15).

Conclusions

The scheme of work provides the structure within which teachers can make their medium- and short-term plans. The best schemes of work are in sympathy with a school's beliefs and aspirations and meet the needs of the children. Schools can either develop their own tailor-made scheme or use a published scheme and adapt it. Both approaches have their advantages. A bespoke scheme can be time-consuming to produce and requires a lot of knowledge and resources on the part of teachers; however, it can result in a scheme that is well understood and flexible. A published scheme can save time initially and can provide a structure and content coverage that gives staff confidence in delivering the required curriculum. However, it is important that the scheme is modified to suit the needs of the school and the children. Indeed, a good scheme is ever-changing as we learn from our teaching, as new ideas and resources become available, and as teachers grow in confidence.

References

ASE (2001) *Be safe! Health and safety in primary school science and technology*. Hatfield: Association for Science Education.

Barr, K. (2003) Managing science and technology: one school's approach. *Primary Science Review*, **79**, 4–7.

Goldsworthy, A. (2000) *Raising attainment in primary science*. Oxford: GHPD.

Iiyambo, R. (2005) Planning a creative science curriculum. *Primary Science Review*, **88**, 16–19.

Naylor, S. and Keogh, B. (2003) *Concept cartoons in science education* (CD-ROM). Sandbach, Chesire: Millgate House.

QCA (1998) *A scheme of work for key stages 1 and 2*. London: Qualifications and Curriculum Authority.

Websites

ASE (Association for Science Education) *Primary Science Review*: http://www.ase.org.uk/htm/members_area/journals/psr/

BAYS (British Association for Young Scientists): http://www.york.ac.uk/org/ciec/
    GRG/General_primary%20reviews.htm
CREST awards: http://www.the-ba.net/the-ba/ResourcesforLearning/BACRESTAwards/
DfES (2003) National Primary Strategy: http://www.standards.dfes.gov.uk/primary/
    publications/literacy/63553/pns_excell_enjoy037703v2.doc
Planet Science resources: http//www.scienceyear,com/under11s/
SEED (2004) *A curriculum for excellence*. Ministerial Response:
    http://www.scotland.gov.uk/library5/education/cermr-00.asp
Science Clips: http://www.bbc.co.uk/schools/scienceclips/index_flash.shtml
Science Web: http://www.scienceweb.org.uk/

Chapter 13 Progression and continuity in the school programme

On what basis do we decide to involve children in certain activities? Addressing this question

Bob Kibble

involves consideration of whether there is, or is not, a sequence dictated by the logic of the subject or the cognitive development of the children. Although there are national and local frameworks for curriculum planning that schools can follow if they wish, it is still important to understand what is involved in making decisions that provide for progression and continuity in children's experience. This chapter considers these complex matters and their implications for individual schools' long-term planning. It deals with sequence in conceptual understanding and in the development of enquiry skills and attitudes, and comments on how curriculum organisation can influence children's opportunities for learning in science.

Sequences within and between science domains

Learning in science is often presented as a sequential journey, with new understanding being built upon more fundamental ideas. Such a sequential structure ought to help teachers make decisions about the order in which topics might reasonably be taught. However, the science-learning landscape is not without grey areas. For example, should children learn about the parts of a plant before learning about the properties of materials? In this case there are too few connections between the areas to allow a case to be made for teaching one before the other. Plants and materials reside in two distinctly different domains of science.

Box 13.1 offers four curriculum topics from a typical primary school science programme. What reasons are there for any one topic being taught before another?

Box 13.1

- The idea of a complete electric circuit – be able to make a simple circuit.
- The idea of a material undergoing change – irreversible and reversible change.
- The planets in the solar system – motion and order.
- Frictional forces and their effect on motion.

The topics in Box 13.1 seem to occupy sufficiently different domains that they do not relate to each other in any obvious sequence. They might reasonably be taught in any order. In contrast, consider the five topics from a primary school science programme listed in Box 13.2. If there is a sequence evident in these statements it is evident because the statements are located in the same science domain, that is, *forces*, with ideas from two sub-domains, friction and gravity.

Box 13.2

- A force as a push or a pull, a twist or a stretch.
- Friction as the name of the force that helps to prevent sliding.
- Forces being measured using a force-meter. The newton as the unit of force.
- The size of a frictional force depending on the weight of the sliding object.
- The effect of gravity giving everything a weight, which is a downward force.

In order that children experience a learning journey that allows for conceptual progression, the curriculum-planning process, out of which a school science programme emerges, needs to make a clear distinction between unrelated domains (those not requiring sequencing but perhaps needing to offer a balance of topics) and related domains within which there is more likely to be an inherent sequential science storyline.

Sequences and spirals

It is unlikely that the curriculum will allow the complete *forces* domain to be tackled at one sitting. It is more likely that learners will revisit a domain such as this on more than one occasion. Such a spiral approach to the curriculum allows children the opportunity to experience a rich variety of science-learning contexts, each revisited at a suitable later stage, when particular language, number and science process skills have been developed.

However, just because learners are a year or two older, there is no guarantee that a revisited topic will offer a sound foundation for further learning. Teachers need to be sensitive to the experiences and learning outcomes that characterised the learners' previous achievement within a topic, and ensure that the second exposure offers real progression, with tasks that build upon and extend previous learning.

Considering the sequencing of activities helps develop the forward-planning skills that enable a whole-school, spiral-structured science programme to be charted. For example, Box 13.3 lists a set of statements from a domain within science. Considering how they might be placed in a meaningful sequence for learners is a useful stimulus to reflection on how they might be located within a spiral structure.

Box 13.3

How might these be arranged in sequence?

Electricity needs a complete circuit before it flows.	You can measure electric current using an ammeter.	A switch will make or break a complete circuit.
Most electrical conductors are made of metal.	Materials which don't conduct electricity are called insulators.	Materials which conduct electricity are called conductors.
The more bulbs in a series circuit the harder it is for the electricity to pass through.	A battery provides a push for the electrons. It gives them energy.	In an insulator there are electrons but they are not free to move around.
Electrons don't come from the battery. They are already part of the metal in the wires.	When a circuit is complete an electric current flows around the circuit.	The electric current is the movement of tiny particles called electrons

It is easy to see that some particular statements in Box 13.3 must come before others. Other statements are harder to place in any sequence. Teachers need the confidence to identify the key conceptual connections between different parts of the sequence. It is through a progression of such connected concepts that learners will start to be able to tell their own science stories.

Cognitive sequences

As with any good storyline certain features need to precede others. The lighthouse keeper's lunch will not appear until after breakfast. Understanding pollination will require that the parts of a flower and their functions are appreciated. However, unlike the lighthouse keeper's lunch, which finds its place in the story simply by virtue of a temporal sequence, understanding the structure of a flower is an essential prerequisite to understanding the process of pollination. Such sequential ordering is critical to support understanding and is an example of a cognitive sequence. Children trying to understand pollination face a very steep learning curve if they have yet to appreciate that a flower has a structure and that each part of the flower has a function in reproduction. Understanding how volcanoes work will come after an appreciation of the internal structure of the Earth. Understanding of series and parallel circuits will follow after learning the concept of a complete circuit. These are all examples of cognitive sequences, each part of a science storyline and each located within a particular science domain.

Some storylines, even within a science domain, do not lead naturally to conceptual progression. Consider the following three statements:

- Describe the pattern of movement of the Sun in the sky.

- Make use of a globe and torch to explain night and day.
- Know that planets orbit the Sun. This is called the solar system.

These three statements from the 'space' domain have been chosen because they incorporate one of the great cognitive challenges in school science. A teacher will be able to create a set of learning activities that allows most children to achieve each individual statement. For example, the first statement might be interpreted through children drawing around shadows in the playground and linking observed changes in shadows during the day with the movement of the Sun. The second might involve torches in a dark room and stick-on people having an imaginary telephone conversation from 'night' and 'day' locations. The third might have children wearing planet hats and enjoying circular orbits in the playground as they model the solar system. However, does one statement lead naturally on to the next?

The transition from the first to the second mirrors one of the greatest challenges in the history of science. Does the Sun orbit the Earth or the Earth orbit the Sun? This episode in the history of science, in which Nicolaus Copernicus offered a Sun-at-centre model of the universe, is known as the Copernican revolution and here it is in the primary curriculum for 7-year-olds. So here is the challenge for both learner and teacher in the primary classroom. No sooner has the learner established that the Sun doesn't just appear in the daytime but that it moves across the sky from east to west, he or she then has to accept that this is simply an optical illusion. The Sun doesn't really move around the Earth at all. It is the Earth that spins and orbits the Sun. Here, then, is an example of curriculum statements that are apparently sequential but are, in fact, anti-sequential. Does the first idea mitigate against an understanding of the second?

With the story of night and day and a spinning Earth established, it is a small hop to accept that there are other bodies, much akin to the Earth, also experiencing night and day and all members of the same happy family in relation to the Sun. An understanding of the solar system therefore does indeed build on the notion of the Earth–Sun system, but is an appreciation of the solar system a more challenging cognitive concept than the night and day story?

The sequential nature of learning

Any parent/carer or primary teacher will be able to describe the differences in cognitive behaviour between children at the start and the end of primary school. These differences will be evident through the children's use of language, their attitude to learning and to listening, their ability to see life as others see it, and their ability to handle more complex ideas, perhaps with more than two variables. The work of Jean Piaget attempted to offer a scientist's approach to describing such cognitive changes. He used a language of stages, from pre-operational to formal thinking, to describe a pattern of progression in conceptual development that all children were thought to exhibit. Of course, as with all science models, there is an element of assumption and simplification built into Piaget's conclusions. However, his model of learning provided a starting point for a significant research study, the fruits of which are evident in many schools today.

In the 1980s a team of researchers led by Michael Shayer looked at the match between the cognitive expectations of the science curriculum and the cognitive levels of learners, using a Piagetian model (Shayer and Adey, 1981). Their analysis revealed a considerable mismatch, with the curriculum demands generally exceeding the cognitive abilities of learners struggling to cope with a particular element of the curriculum. This work eventually led to attempts to accelerate cognitive development through focusing on how children think about problems, how they group and classify, and use and interpret evidence. Projects such as CASE (Cognitive Acceleration through Science Education) (Adey, Shayer and Yates, 1995), *Let's think!* and *Let's think through science!* have their origins in Shayer's early work. (See also Chapters 1 and 24.)

As well as specially designed 'thinking' activities such as these, all planning of science programmes needs to take account of the development of enquiry or process skills. In exactly the same way as discussed earlier in relation to concepts, progression in the skills of scientific enquiry has to be considered,

---

Box 13.4

Characteristics of children's ways of thinking relevant to development of enquiry skills and attitudes

Children in the early years:

- need to carry out actions to see their result, rather than being able to 'think through' actions;
- look at things from their own point of view and may not realise that a different point of view makes things look different;
- focus on one aspect of an object or situation and so may not see that a combination of factors causes a particular outcome;
- identify only parts of a sequence of related events.

Children in the middle primary years:

- begin to see a simple process as a whole and put all parts in sequence;
- can think through a simple process and mentally reverse it;
- can identify that a result may be the result of two or more factors in combination;
- are able to relate cause and effect in simple, familiar and concrete phenomena.

Children in the later primary years:

- can use a wider range of logical relationships and so mentally manipulate more things;
- show less tendency to jump to conclusions and a greater appreciation that ideas should be checked against evidence;
- can use measurement and recording as part of a more systematic and accurate approach to problems;
- can think through possible steps in an investigation and produce a plan of necessary actions. (Based on Harlen, 2006)

taking account of the characteristics of children's thinking at various stages as summarised in Box 13.4.

Long-term planning in practice

Head teachers carry the statutory responsibility for ensuring that all aspects of the curriculum are covered within their school. In planning for science, a science subject leader or local authority adviser might assist or take a lead in this process. In England, the Qualifications and Curriculum Authority (QCA) offers a scheme of work which could serve as the basis of a school plan for science. In Scotland, the 5–14 Curriculum Guidelines for science have been interpreted by some local authorities, which have produced their own model schemes of work often shared with other local authorities.

A critical element in the success of any whole-school scheme is the shared awareness across the whole staff of just where the key conceptual progression journeys occur. Not only is such a shared awareness needed to avoid unnecessary overlap, it is critical in presenting learners with challenges and experiences appropriate to a particular stage in their learning journeys.

Whichever template is chosen, there will always be room for local innovation and variation. A school located near a paper mill might choose to include an extended curriculum project based on materials or sustainability. Another school might make use of a nearby farmers' market to run an extended curriculum project designed to focus on the variety of living things, the cycle of life or even food and digestion. An urban school might make good use of local roads to carry out traffic surveys, with spin-off projects relating to speed, measurement and forces. The opportunity to tailor specific curriculum experiences to local opportunities is there to be seized by enterprising curriculum planners. Not only do such opportunities locate science learning in a local and more tangible context, they help to forge stronger links between school work, parents/carers, employers and the community, each of whom might play a part in the enterprise. Such enriching contexts for learning ought not to be bolt-on activities, planned at the last minute. Planned in advance, they can form an integral feature of the learners' journey, supplemented by pre- and post-activity tasks. Teachers also stand to gain from such projects, through professional development which is informal and secured in real time.

In striving to maintain curriculum balance when planning, it is important not to lose sight of those aspects of a science education that fall outside the realm of content. The development of science process skills and of attitudes towards science needs to be built in to any curriculum map. The characteristics of children's thinking listed in Box 13.4 have clear implications for the way in which content is addressed at various stages. For example, children in the early years need plenty of opportunity to look, handle, collect and sort, group and classify, take things apart, make and model. The types of investigation most appropriate for them are classifying and exploring. In the middle primary years, children can undertake tasks that require close observation of details and the effects of change, and problems that require fair comparisons; they should be expected to try to give explanations for what they find. In the upper primary years, there should be opportunity for a wide range of activities and investigations extending beyond the 'fair-testing' type to include pattern-finding and the exploration of relationships or models. At all stages children need opportunities to talk, listen, explain, reflect and respond to others.

It is a poor curriculum indeed that leaves such process skills as 'added extras' to be covered should time permit. It is an impoverished curriculum that delivers such learning only through end-of-topic 'investigations'. Far better is the situation where the school has looked at just how children experience such enquiry skills, year by year, as they progress through the primary science curriculum. Such a school is likely to be able to chart the opportunities afforded to learners as they experience topics in science.

In helping teachers to reflect on the extent to which they have engaged in such a whole-school debate, Box 13.5 suggests a few questions, chosen to illustrate this area of curriculum planning.

Box 13.5

Planning opportunities to develop process skills and attitudes

When in our programme do children have the opportunity to:

- create a chart from some results?
- analyse a pattern from a set of results?
- plan their own investigations?
- appreciate the tentative nature of their own discoveries?
- share experimental results with others, thereby appreciating the importance of community in science research?
- speak up and present their own work to others?
- make observations of a changing process in real time?
- appreciate that scientists use models to help to explain difficult ideas?
- critically evaluate the work of another group of children?
- record measurements over an extended period of time?
- use ICT to help record data?
- use ICT to help process data?
- make their own predictions?

Extended periods of learning

A glance at the timetable for any school will reveal immediately the fragmented structure that dominates everything that happens in schools. The week is subdivided, not only into five working days but into perhaps 25 learning periods. As a result, children are presented with opportunities to learn that can be severely truncated. Need the school pattern of learning be structured like this? What might an alternative model offer? If schools were to devote an extended period of time to a particular area of learning, perhaps a half day doing an extended piece of science, what might be gained? Such an extended time period would allow for more open-ended tasks, in particular investigative tasks.

Observations of children engaged in investigations show that they often try out various approaches quickly before appearing to start again and work more systematically. Short periods of science often prevent them from moving beyond the stage of superficial trial and error. They need a longer time to engage with problems at a level where real learning can take place.

Extended time-frames also allow time for learners to offer presentations about their work while that work is fresh in their minds. By being immersed in activities and discussion on a particular topic, individuals can explore learning at a pace and in a style that suits them. Any teacher who has managed learning over an extended period will know just how surprising the outcomes can be, particularly for learners who perhaps do not manage to find their feet in a shorter time-frame.

References

Adey, P. S., Shayer, M. and Yates, C. (1995) *Thinking science: the curriculum materials of the CASE project*. London: Thomas Nelson.

Harlen, W. (2006) *Teaching, learning and assessing science 5–12*. 4th edn. London: Sage.

Shayer, M. and Adey, P. S. (1981) *Towards a science of science teaching*. London: Heinemann.

Chapter 14

Using ICT in teaching and learning science

The use of information and communication technology (ICT) has changed many aspects of

Roger Mitchell

our lives and has the potential to alter aspects of the way teachers teach and children learn. The aim of this chapter is to help teachers keep up with the range and potential use of technology-based tools for learning and teaching. After listing the main types of ICT it considers how some of these are applied in different parts of scientific enquiry: gathering evidence, organising and interpreting evidence, accessing information sources, communicating and discussing results. A list of useful websites for obtaining further information is included at the end.

Types of ICT

Broadly speaking, the ICT capability available can be placed under the headings in Box 14.1. With the possible exception of the last item in the list, all the types of ICT listed are used by both teachers and children at various times. Morris and Wardle (2006) provide a helpful table summarising use in different activities for different purposes.

Most of the elements in Box 14.1 will be useful to enhance different aspects of learning science at different times during activities. So the various pieces of hardware and software are considered here in relation to the purpose they serve in learning science. Due to the variety of products currently available, and the pace of change, it is probably more helpful to consider types of hardware and software rather than specific products, although some examples will be provided.

Box 14.1

Types of ICT

- Generic software packages that can be used in relation to science, e.g. word processors, spreadsheets, databases, graphics packages.

- Multimedia simulations, animations and secondary information sources, e.g. CD-ROMs and materials available online.

- Observational tools, e.g. data-loggers, digital microscopes, digital cameras and other imaging tools.

- Interactive teaching technologies, e.g. interactive whiteboards and graphics tablets, digital presenters (visualisers), hand-held voting systems, wireless devices such as laptop computers and PDAs (personal digital assistants).

- Communication technologies, e.g. Internet and Web-based resources, email, webcams.

- Content management and personalised learning, e.g. VLEs (virtual learning environments) for the organisation of digitally based curriculum content, task management and assessment.

Gathering evidence during practical activities

ICT has a useful role both in enabling detailed observations and in recording them. In relation to recording observations or events, photographs taken with a digital camera can be an invaluable resource in recording what equipment was used and key aspects of how an investigation was undertaken. These can be used in children's recording of their science work by importing them into a word-processed report, or they can be printed and displayed.

Digital microscopes

Digital microscopes can provide a photographic record of close observations that would have been hand-drawn in the past. Most schools in the UK now have at least one digital microscope, with the Intel QX3 and the Motic DS300 being the most common. (An Intel QX3 digital microscope was given to every maintained school in England during Science Year, 2000.) Some points about the use of digital microscopes are given in Box 14.2.

Data-loggers

The use of ICT can be very effective in moving children on from descriptive qualitative to quantitative data collection. This is where sensors and data-loggers come into their own. An example of an investigation with potential for this quantitative element would be the investigation of the brightness of bulbs in a series circuit as more bulbs are added. Rather than depending on children's descriptions of the brightness, which does not easily allow identification of patterns in results, the introduction of a light sensor connected to a data-logger provides quantitative results that can be more readily compared. Box 14.3 gives some advice on introducing data-loggers.

Box 14.2

Using digital microscopes

Probably the main concern is the concept of magnification. Digital microscopes have the facility to magnify at different levels (usually between x10 and x200). Children frequently do not have a good understanding of what is meant by magnification and younger children often find it hard to relate the magnified image to the actual object. In these circumstances, x10 magnification is often perfectly adequate. However, the whole magnification issue is made harder by the fact that the magnification seen depends on the screen size as well as on the microscope. The same image will be of different size displayed on a 15 inch monitor as compared with a 17 inch monitor, or – an extreme case – projected on to a large screen.

Similarly, the colour of digital images will vary depending on the colour-balance settings of the screen on which they are displayed and on the type of light source illuminating the object. Tungsten-filament lights tend to make images pinker and fluorescent lights to make them bluer, as compared with natural sunlight. This is the cause of the pinker images captured using the Intel QX3 microscope, which can also be under-lit at higher magnifications. However, this is less of a problem with the Motic DS300 which uses a white LED for its light source, or if flash photography is used with digital cameras.

The possibility with digital microscopes of undertaking time-lapse photography is extremely useful. This is particularly easy to set up with the Intel QX3, and advantageous when undertaking extended investigations such as those involving germination or the formation of crystals.

Box 14.3

Introducing data-loggers

When first introducing young children to data-loggers it is important to establish the relationship between the action that is being recorded and what they see as a visual representation of it. Most software packages that accompany data-loggers provide the option to view sensed inputs in real time and in a clear visual way. So it is possible to make the connection between a quality being measured (say brightness) and its representation as a simple bar on a chart in the display and then to show how the bar decreases in height when the sensor is covered. Such real-time representations of cause and effect are vital if young children are to get a firm understanding of what can be a quite abstract representation of the world around them.

As well as allowing quantifiable measurements to be made, data-loggers with hand-held recording devices allow data to be recorded and stored remotely for later use. This means that children can take readings anywhere without the need to be close to a computer. Data-loggers can be set up to take readings at different time intervals, allowing data to be collected over a longer period of time and in the absence of the children. For example, readings can be taken for light, sound and temperature over the course of 24 hours in a school. The stored data can then be uploaded to a computer when they return the data-logger to the classroom. The data can normally be presented in a tabular and graphical form, and these can then be used to identify key points in the school day, such as break times (increased noise level). The facility to represent collected data in various graphical or tabular forms is particularly useful when the focus is on the interpretation of the results as opposed to the construction of the table and the graph.

The range of sensors available for use with data-loggers is wide and varied. However, in the primary school setting, most needs can be covered with light sensors, sound sensors, temperature probes and heart monitors. Other sensors available are more relevant to secondary school science.

Although no data-logging equipment is cheap, the level and quality of the display is currently the biggest determining factor in the price of such devices. Built-in displays range from simple black-and-white LCD readouts to colour screens of the quality found in hand-held computers. It is important that the school considers which features are absolutely necessary when thinking about investing in this type of equipment.

Organising and interpreting evidence

The essence of scientific activity is to make sense of observations of the world. This means it is very important that children's science activities don't stop when observations have been made and recorded, but that they are interpreted in ways that help to develop understanding. Databases and spreadsheets are effective tools for organising data and searching for patterns that help this process.

Databases

Databases provide a means of recording information in what is essentially an electronic card-file system. The power of the database is that it can be searched according to single or multiple categories. Databases can be created by children from their own data, but there are also many ready-made ones available. These include databases of characteristics of plants and animals. For example, searches could be undertaken to call up records about all six-legged animals that have wings and are shorter than 1 centimetre.

A slightly different format is the branching database. Here, children are able to analyse and create their own keys in order to group and classify different things. Again, the most obvious use in primary science is in the context of living things. However, databases can be put to equally good use in other areas, such as the properties of materials.

Spreadsheets

Spreadsheet software provides a powerful tool for analysing the data collected from investigations. Many schools use Microsoft *Excel* as a spreadsheet package with older primary pupils. However, various other spreadsheet packages are available that are more accessible for younger children. There are two main advantages in using a spreadsheet package to record data from science activities. The first is the ability to sort data automatically according to different criteria, for example numerically, in ascending/descending order, or alphabetically. The second use is the facility to convert tables of data into graphical form. Most spreadsheet packages will also intuitively offer the most appropriate type of graphical representation. In other words, where the variables are discrete, the software will prompt children to create a bar chart. Where the variables are continuous, the software will provide a line graph.

The use of spreadsheet software makes it far easier to analyse and manipulate data, identify patterns and present findings in an understandable graphical format. Such software also makes it easier to identify any collected data that do not fit into the pattern of the rest. This can lead to evaluative discussions on the reliability of the data and the experimental methods that were employed.

Accessing information sources

Science education involves children building their understanding not only through direct investigation but also through using sources of secondary information. Once, textbooks would have been the source of this information. Now there is a wealth of multimedia material available to schools, notably with the explosion of resources in CD-ROM format. Increasingly, the Internet is being used as a source of readily available information.

The problem for teachers is that, with so many resources available, it can be difficult to choose what to use. In selecting appropriate materials there are some points to bear in mind. There are many instances of 'wrong' information on the Internet. For this reason, it is very important to establish scientifically secure sources of information. Linked to this is the fact that some of the information available may be pitched inappropriately for the children, either wholly or in part. The complexity of the formats of some webpages also means that children need to be helped to access the information in them (see Chapter 15).

Simulation and modelling

In addition to providing information, such resources can be used for simulating and modelling phenomena that cannot readily be demonstrated through direct experience. For example, although it is possible to observe directly the phases of the Moon, a good simulation shows how changes in the relative positions of the Earth, Moon and Sun cause the part of the Moon that is lit, and so its apparent shape, to change over time.

A recent development of ICT resourcing for science is that of the interactive CD-ROM or web resource in which virtual investigation can be carried out. Such resources allow the user to select and change variables in a variety of different investigations and see the effects. These materials have their place in terms of introducing an activity or reinforcing concepts and process skills. However, it must be stressed that they are no substitute for real, practical science activities.

Multimedia CD-ROMs can be an excellent resource but can also be expensive. With the growing number of online resources available, decisions will need to be made as to whether a school should invest in materials on CD-ROM, or alternatively subscribe to an online service. Although there are advantages to both options, the message is the same. It is important to establish what such resources will do to enhance what is already happening in the classroom. The starting point will be the school's scheme of work. This will identify the learning objectives for the particular area of interest. Only once these are clear should the resources that will best support these objectives be sought. In this way we will be promoting a learning-oriented rather than an activity-led curriculum.

Communicating

Word processing

While spreadsheets provide a method of communicating the results of science activities, there is also a need in recording science activities to provide information on how the activities have been carried out. This is where word-processing software comes in. One valuable feature of word processing is that the teacher can create templates to support and model good-quality science writing.

Writing frames (Lewis and Wray, 1997) combined with word-processing capability enable teachers to provide this structure at different levels. Templates can be written, providing varying degrees of scaffolding for children, which can be stored and easily accessed as necessary. However, the greatest power of the word processor is the convenience it offers to writers for editing and revising their writing. This means that children are able to respond to discussions with their teacher and their peers, and act on any changes in their thinking without having to revise a report from scratch.

Word-processing software is also highly versatile. Objects such as digital images, tables and graphs can be imported and laid out with the text. Combined with the editing facilities, this means that children can create a complete and polished-looking piece of work.

Using the Internet for communication

The other element of communicating with ICT is the use of the Internet to receive and send information. Any work that is produced electronically can be posted on the school's website so that it can be viewed by the wider community. As well as providing a showcase for the work of the school, this also facilitates writing for a wider audience. When children are required to write for an unknown reader who may be far away, the writing needs to be more precise, complete and coherent. There is great value in setting up a joint science project in which children exchange their investigative findings, by email or using webcams, with children from another school, be it in the same town or on a different continent.

Promoting whole-class discussion

There will be many opportunities for discussion at different levels in any science lesson. Much of it will take place on a one-to-one basis. Some of it will be in small groups. Recent developments in interactive-teaching technologies have meant that ICT can now be utilised to facilitate interactive whole-class teaching. This is an exciting new area for ICT as it takes its role in promoting dialogue to a higher level.

Interactive whiteboards

Introduction of interactive whiteboards into many classrooms has enhanced the ability of the teacher to involve children more actively in whole-class teaching elements of lessons. In addition, the presence of a large projected image with which children can interact provides a multimedia focal point that is very effective in catching attention. That said, there is much to consider in the use of these new technologies. Most importantly, it must be remembered that this new equipment places an even greater onus on the teacher to be well prepared and for the lesson to be of high quality. Things can go wrong with all technology and it is good practice to be prepared to teach the lesson without the whiteboard should anything untoward occur.

The children will need some basic tuition in using an interactive whiteboard. For example, they need to get used to standing to one side of the area with which they are interacting and not looking into the light beam from the data-projector as they turn back towards the class. Some of these problems are avoided by the use of a graphics tablet, or 'slate', which can be passed around the class to allow interaction with the screen. Essentially, this is a sophisticated wireless mouse, whereby a 'pen' is used on the hand-held 'slate' to manipulate the images on the screen. Children are able to interact without leaving their seats, which can assist in maintaining the pace of the lesson. Use of a graphics tablet also allows the children to interact with the entire screen area as nothing is out of reach when they have the graphics tablet in front of them.

There is an increasingly wide range of software for use with interactive teaching technologies. Two of the most popular are Research Machines *Easiteach Science* and the online subscription service *Learn Premium*. However, interactive whiteboard lessons will only be as good as the teacher preparation that has gone into them. A good example of the use of an interactive whiteboard for developing enquiry skills is given by Earle (2004).

A recent development in this area of educational ICT is the digital presenter or visualiser. This is essentially a digital camera that captures images and projects them on to a large screen or imports them into a computer. The images are real time and in colour. The camera can zoom in to allow even very small items to be seen easily by the whole class. For example, a child can demonstrate how he or she has connected a simple circuit and others are able to see what is being described and explained. When everyone is able to see what is going on, everyone is able to offer an opinion or take part in an informed discussion.

Organising and accessing ICT-based resources

Virtual learning environments (VLEs) are more common in secondary schools than in primary schools. However, the increasing occurrence of server-based networks in primary schools means that VLEs are worth a brief mention here. At a basic level, a VLE is essentially a way of cataloguing digital resources that are stored on a central server so that they can be easily identified and utilised in the creation of learning and teaching programmes. For example, an animation of the water cycle might be catalogued as being relevant to science for evaporation and condensation. However, it could also be catalogued in relation to the geography curriculum. This means that the same resource can be identified for both purposes without being duplicated on the server.

VLEs can pull together such resources, along with *PowerPoint* presentations, word-processed materials and the like, to create an electronic scheme of work that can be accessed from anywhere on the school network. It can also be used to allocate to specific children, or groups of children, tasks that can be accessed remotely, such as online homework. This facility could be utilised to address elements of the personalised learning agenda. Electronic mark books and assessments can also be included. However, as with many other elements of ICT, the VLE will only be as good as the information that is fed into it.

References

Earle, S. (2004) Using an interactive whiteboard to improve science-specific skills. *Primary Science Review*, **85**, 18–20.

Lewis, M. and Wray, D. (1997) *Extending literacy: developing approaches to non-fiction*. London: Routledge.

Morris, P. and Wardle, J. (2006) Teaching science with ICT. In *ASE guide to secondary science education*, ed. Wood Robinson, V. Hatfield: Association for Science Education.

Websites

Becta Educational Software Database (BESD): http://besd.becta.org.uk/

Branching databases: http://ngfl.northumberland.gov.uk/science/databases/default.htm

Digital imaging (including digital microscopes), data-logging, using ICT, integrating planning: http://www.sycd.co.uk/primary/ict/using-technology.htm

Digital presenters (visualisers) in education: http://www.bardaglea.org.uk/testbed/uploads/Samsung%20Case%20Study%20A4.pdf

Education Guardian article: http://education.guardian.co.uk/evaluate/story/0,14726,1298340,00.html

General advice on ICT in education: http://www.becta.org.uk/schools/index.cfm

Interactive teaching technologies: http://www.jisc.ac.uk/uploaded_documents/interactivewhiteboards211102.doc

VLEs: http://www.becta.org.uk/page_documents/research/VLE_report.pdf

Writing frames in science: http://www.chester.ac.uk/~mwillard/sci_ed/writing/writing.htm

Chapter 15   Resources

Active learning is widely agreed to be necessary for learning with understanding in any area of the curriculum. **Mick Dunne** and **Liz Lakin**

curriculum. Both mental and physical activity are involved and for learning science the activity requires resources to support enquiry either at first hand or through interactive media. These resources are the subject of this chapter. Aspects discussed are: selection, with cost and provision for progression in learning in mind; maintenance; storage; health and safety; and the use of living things. The types of resources discussed fall into three main groups: written; computer-based; and other equipment for first-hand enquiries. The main concern in this chapter is the last of these. The first two are the subjects of other chapters and so are only briefly mentioned.

Written resources

As with all resources, a starting point in selection is to have a clear idea of:

- Who is going to use them?
- For what purpose?
- How will they be used?

Resource choice and effectiveness is strongly influenced by the identity and purpose of the user. The resource may be for the class teacher, for the classroom assistant to use for reference purposes to top up their own subject knowledge, or it may be for children to use directly as part of quality activity work or for reference. All three situations demand that careful thought be given to selection to ensure that the most appropriate provision is identified and that fitness for purpose is maximised.

Children need access to reference books for information beyond that which a teacher can supply, to satisfy their curiosity and, sometimes, their appetite for collecting names and facts. Information books for young children are difficult to write. It requires an expert in the subject matter to find a way to present information in simple understandable terms; the best such books are written by scientists or doctors (for example, the award-winning books by Balkwill and Rolph, 1990a and 1990b). Introducing fantasy as a vehicle for telling 'the story of a meal' or 'the life of a drop of water' does not necessarily aid understanding.

In choosing reference books for children the criteria are not very different from those for good reference books for adults: large, clear, coloured photographs, with straightforward text and an easily used index or other way of locating information. However, modern reference books, as in the case of webpages, now use more complex formats than straightforward blocks of text with linked illustrations. There are more often diagrams where the layout is part of the message, with arrows, icons and most of the text spread out in boxes or labels. Children need to learn how to take the messages from these more varied ways of presenting information. Peacock (2004) gives the following advice:

Children tend to look first at blocks of text, but it is usually more helpful to encourage them to look first at titles, captions, icons, questions or pictures. When a child has identified the page they need to use, you can help by 'teaching the page'. This means asking questions as the child tries to 'navigate' around the page, such as: What is this? [points to heading, picture, icon, caption, diagram, etc.] Why did the author put it there? What does it tell you? What else tells you about ...? (Peacock, 2004, p. 7)

There is also a wealth of possibly unexplored scientific resources within other parts of the curriculum, but specifically within English. Books introduced during literacy often have potential outside this curriculum area. *The bad-tempered ladybird* (Carle, 1982) is a case in point (see Box 15.1).

Box 15.1

The bad-tempered ladybird (Carle, 1982)

This is a wonderful resource for exploring feelings and emotions, but there is also a wealth of science and mathematics loitering just below the surface. Telling the time and exploring size are the obvious contenders, but what about sorting and classifying organisms? How does the hyena differ from the praying mantis and can these differences be used to sort some of the other animals mentioned in the story? There are engaging examples of adaptation and variation to explore, the elephant's tusks and the rhinoceros's horn, the wasp's sting and the stag beetle's jaws, not to mention the fireflies' glow! Then there is the environmental message sounded loud and clear by using ladybirds to control the aphid population.

Computer-based resources

These include software to show real events (such as volcanoes and time-lapse sequences of plant growth or flowers opening) or to simulate real events. Many such resources are available on-line. While globes, torches, the overhead projector and balls of different sizes are important, as well as the children role-playing the relative movement of the Earth, Moon and Sun, some web-based resources provide another level of engagement with learning. An excellent example is the Virtual Solar System (see website). These resources enable practical learning activities that would otherwise be too difficult, time-consuming or impossible to achieve, but which enrich the learning. An example is the Bradford Robotic Telescope (see website) that is free to all primary school users.

Data-loggers and software to display results in various ways enable children to engage with the questions they are investigating rather than practicalities of measurement. For example, in order to use a standard spirit thermometer reasonably well children need to recognise and know negative and positive numbers, read a scale and be able to match the level of the spirit against the scale (they actually need to do much more but the point has been made). Given that thermometers are used in many practical tasks, then the choice of the one that best matches the learner's knowledge, understanding and skills is very important. Data-loggers provide a direct reading, as can any standard digital thermometer, and might be preferable to a glass thermometer. Clearly there must be a match between the type of resource and its purpose. If the purpose really is to learn how to read a thermometer scale or to explore how a thermometer works, then the instrument clearly has to be used. A data-logger is preferable if the purpose is to investigate a phenomenon where measuring temperature is a means to a conceptual end. For example, the simple investigation of the cooling of warm water in different containers involves using a thermometer (and so knowing how to read it), taking down readings at particular times (and remembering to do this, or risk dubious results) and then drawing a graph or displaying the results so that comparisons can be made. This takes much time and energy and if the purpose is to understand something about cooling, there is too much activity intervening between asking the question and obtaining the answer. The use of sensor probes and data-logging using a computer removes these intervening steps and enables children to focus on their results. Portable and hand-held (pocket-book) computers enable this kind of work to be carried on outside as well as inside the classroom.

There is much more about using ICT in Chapter 14.

Other equipment for first-hand enquiries

Most curriculum materials and schemes of work provide lists of resources needed for the activities they suggest. Box 15.2 lists, under three headings,

Box 15.2

Everyday objects and materials	Consumables	Specialist equipment
Boxes, plastic bottles, other containers, string, scissors, rulers, paper clips, sticky tape, drawing pins, elastic bands, glues, card, plasticine, plant pots, spoons, straws, marbles, toy cars, rocks, pieces of fabric, ...	Flour, bicarbonate of soda, soap powder, plaster of Paris, mirror card, wood for hammering, batteries, wire for shaping, aluminium foil, fruits or flowers for cutting, seeds for planting, ...	Pooters for collecting insects, torches, mirrors, glass blocks, triangular prisms, hand lenses, measuring cylinders, spirit thermometers, tuning forks, stopclocks and watches, springs, bathroom scales, pulleys, filter paper, gardening and other tools, magnets, bulbs, wire etc. ...

(Fom Harlen and Qualter, 2004, p. 211)

some examples of the sorts of things that will be needed.

Any discussion about resources quickly turns to economic considerations; while it is recognised that there are many advantages to using cost-effective freely available bits and pieces, such as 35 mm film canisters, there is also a clear requirement for more specialised equipment. This raises the question of the criteria to be used in selecting equipment: when is it appropriate to use everyday materials and when specialist equipment? What difference do the ages and stages of the children make? How is progression catered for?

Everyday or specialist equipment?

In many cases there is no choice: investigating magnets requires magnets. But in other cases there is the potential for home-made devices: a windsock made from a stocking, a home-made rain gauge and an anemometer constructed with yoghurt pots, rather than more sophisticated instruments. These will be designed by the children to do the job that they have defined; they will not be starting with an instrument whose function they have to learn. Using more sophisticated equipment later will make more sense with this foundation. The more children help in designing the ways they interact with their surroundings the more they will realise that they can investigate and learn about the world around through their own activity. When involved in using complex equipment children's attention is absorbed by the minutiae of how to use it rather than the phenomenon they should be studying, occupied by procedures instead of trying to understand.

Selection for progression

Planning for progression has implications for equipment choice as much as for selection of activities and written resources. Planning that reflects the progressive development of enquiry or process skills should take account of the points just made about familiarity of equipment as well as the age and ability of the children.

Take, for example the devices used to magnify objects. Those simple magnifiers that do not require the observer to hold them but are placed directly over the specimen are much easier to use than the traditional magnifying glass that has to be held correctly and moved together with the head until the best image is obtained. It would appear logical then to find more of the former in the lower primary years and vice versa. It is very easy to overlook the cognitive and skill demands made by even the most simple science resource.

Strategic deployment of equipment in different age ranges should reflect teaching and learning needs. As a general rule, non-standard measurement resources that do not require the ability to recognise and use number are more usefully provided in the nursery, reception or lower primary classes. Those requiring some ability to use standard measurement (such as measuring cylinders, thermometers, balances, force-meters) would mainly be found in upper primary classrooms. As children become more skilful and knowledgeable they need more sophisticated and accurate equipment. In order for children to make genuine decisions about equipment as they progress, a wider choice of resources also needs to be provided.

Building progression into teaching and learning resources in science can ensure that the sparkle and enthusiasm are maintained. Attention to the overall use of different materials in primary science can ensure that the children's experiences are not unnecessarily limited or repetitive. For instance, the main plants used in studying living processes are cress, broad beans and the sunflower. Generally the selection does not vary much at secondary level, save for the introduction of the geranium. The potential boredom can be avoided by carrying out an audit of resources used throughout the foundation, infant and junior phases, and ensuring that this information is available to all teaching staff. A rolling programme of alternatives interspersed with the age-old favourites can be compiled and implemented.

Possible alternatives to the well-tried ones include:

- nasturtiums – fast-growing, brightly coloured, edible flowers;
- capsicums (sold as peppers) – easy to grow in warm places from seed;
- mung beans – excellent alternative to cress, cheap, quick growing, less fiddly than cress, possibly more relevant to some children;
- wheat – another excellent alternative, probably more contextually relevant than cress.

Similar points apply to other materials. Invariably milk chocolate is used for illustrating change in materials, with the danger that it has been 'done to death' by the time the children reach the middle primary years. Box 15.3 shows how one school ensures variety in the choice of material being studied.

Box 15.3

Key stage 1 record of materials studied by each class group

Plastic	Paper	Bread	Glass	Cake mixture	Ice
Wood	Metal	Rocks & stones	Soil	Wool	Water
Clay	Play dough	Sand	Magnets	Chocolate	Brick

Teachers mark the class group when the material has been studied in the appropriate square. A ring is placed around any material that has been exhaustively studied. Spare squares can be added for materials not listed. The materials above are not considered obligatory, but they are the commonest used.

Auditing resources

Auditing the school's science resources is part of the role of the science subject leader. All teachers need access to the inventory and to working and reliable equipment as and when it is required. The audit should also include the 'everyday' items in Box 15.2. As noted earlier, it is often possible to investigate scientific phenomena at the required level using very basic materials, perhaps born out of necessity rather than by design. String telephones and rubber-band guitars are used to explore sound. Pastry cases and film canisters work admirably to demonstrate the effects of air resistance. Junk modelling is used time and again to illustrate the parts of a flower and the principles of wheel and axle arrangement in vehicles.

To ensure continuity and progression in terms of resources it is useful for teachers to be aware of the resources used both before and beyond the particular stage children are entering. Awareness of resources used outside the immediate age range can be a valuable asset for special educational needs at both ends of the spectrum. Gifted and talented children may benefit from accessing resources a year or so ahead of their chronological age. Likewise, the less able will benefit from a less complex approach to the same concept area. It is also valuable to know how to use certain equipment flexibly to suit different ages, for example the digital microscope (see Box 15.4).

Box 15.4

Versatile use of the digital microscope

Every primary school in England and Wales has a digital microscope and in too many schools they remain in their original wrapping gathering dust. This stimulating, sturdy piece of kit needs to be connected to a computer. Its use extends across the age range and not just for science education. It is relatively cheap, robust, versatile (especially when it is taken out of its stand) and straightforward to use. With a minimum of guidance 5-year-olds can use it, not only to observe an object but even to take photographs of magnified specimens. In the majority of schools foundation stage children rarely have the opportunity to use one. This is a missed opportunity: connect the digital microscope to a computer, LCD projector or interactive whiteboard and it will be hard to stop children of any age experiencing the 'WOW' factor!

Sharing resources

Some primary schools operate within school cluster groups. Greater cost-effectiveness is gained through coordinating the purchase of specialised resources or through sharing equipment, although there can be planning, financial and storage implications. These resources are not required all the time and a careful loan system, signed up to by all concerned, can work well if managed properly. Some clusters include the local secondary school that often willingly provides access to a wealth of specialist equipment and the expertise that goes with it. This of course can work both ways and the benefits become mutual.

The use of living things in primary science

Imagine teaching football to children without any footballs. A similar point can be made about teaching some of the biological elements of primary science without using living specimens, resources that are on the decline in primary classrooms. The English National Curriculum identifies the need for *'pupils to observe, explore and ask questions about living things'* and to be taught *'that animals, including humans, move, feed, grow, use their senses and reproduce'* (DfEE/QCA, 1999, pp. 16–17). It is quite possible for a school to keep living representatives of many of the major groups of animals and plants and observe them directly. Yet before animals are brought into the classroom a number of important questions need to be asked:

- Who will care for them both in term time including weekends and over the holiday periods?
- Do they present any health and safety hazards? Is there space?
- Are they easily maintained?
- Do I (we) have the specialist knowledge and skills needed?

These are very real questions and while it is impossible to resolve all of them the choice of animal helps to reduce many concerns. Giant land snails are superb as they are easy and cheap to maintain and present little in the way of health risk if obtained from a reputable source. CLEAPSS (2005) provides good-quality information about the care of this animal and others such as the different species of stick insects and cockroaches. The safety matters associated with the choice and care of living things are also covered in the ASE publication *Be safe!* (ASE, 2001). Children have an inherent fascination with living things and they can be used to good effect in promoting quality investigative and observational work and challenging attitudes and values.

Storing equipment

The obvious way to store the specialist items of equipment is in a central store, so that only one or two class sets of things such as hand lenses, mirrors and bulb-holders need be purchased. There are disadvantages, of course, especially when equipment is not returned or is present but 'lost' through poor organisation. Careful labelling and indexing (using a computer database that can be accessed by all) are important, and records have to be kept of replacements needed. It is also desirable to have some means of easily transporting equipment around the school (trolleys are invaluable except where stairs need to be negotiated). It is the responsibility of the science subject leader to set up a system that all teachers find workable and to ensure its operation. Feasey (1998) gives some useful advice on managing resources.

It is as well to anticipate expansion of resources. They never seem to diminish. Items brought to school to add to a display or to the range of materials being investigated are generally donated. In this way, useful items such as an old camera, clock, clockwork or battery-driven toys, metal and wood off-cuts, are added to the store and room has to be available for them. The store should also house a range of containers and other general equipment that is extra to that required in each classroom for activities other than science (Harlen, 2006).

Sources and resources outside the school

We should not forget the resources not discussed directly in this chapter but described elsewhere in this book. The classroom, school building and school grounds can be valuable resources (see Chapter 9). Local supermarkets and other businesses are often very keen to provide useful items such as cardboard tubes, sheets of plastic, packaging materials or information sheets. Local secondary schools, FE colleges and universities can be very generous in providing long-term 'loans' of items such as simple optical microscopes and even 'experts' for a day. Purchasing new resources can be problematic and so resource reviews and seeking advice from the many institutions and individuals eager to give it become important. Finally, the teacher and the children are perhaps the best resource of all.

References

ASE (2001) *Be safe! Health and safety in primary school science and technology*. 3rd edn. Hatfield: Association for Science Education.

Balkwill, R. and Rolph, M. (1990a) *Cell wars*. London: Collins.

Balkwill, R. and Rolph, M. (1990b) *Cells are us*. London: Collins.

Carle, E. (1982) *The bad-tempered ladybird*. London: Penguin.

CLEAPSS (2005) *Science publications CD-ROM*. Brunel University, Uxbridge.

DfEE/QCA (1999) *Science: the National Curriculum for England*. London: Qualifications and Curriculum Authority.

Feasey, R. (1998) *Primary science equipment*. Hatfield: Association for Science Education.

Harlen, W. (2006) *Teaching, learning and assessing science 5–12*. 4th edn. London: Sage.

Harlen, W. and Qualter, A. (2004) *The teaching of science in primary schools*. 4th edn. London: David Fulton.

Peacock, A. (2004) We need good navigators: choosing and using science books for children. *Primary Science Review*, **84**, 6–7.

Websites

Bradford Robotic Telescope: http://www.telescope.org

The Virtual Solar System: http://www.solarsystem.org.uk/

Chapter 16 | Science in the early years

Advances in children's understanding in each stage of education are built on the | **Max de Bóo**

preceding one, so science in the early years (ages 3–5 years) is as important as science at later stages. As at other stages, provision has to match the learning needs and characteristics of the children. This chapter therefore begins by describing the characteristics of young children's thinking. It then considers the learning objectives – the attitudes, enquiry skills, knowledge and understanding relating to science education. Subsequent sections look at the provision for achieving these objectives, the teacher's role and the importance of developing children's language. The final section briefly considers ways of keeping track of children's progress.

How young children learn: the value of play

The experiences to which young children are exposed in their early years form the foundations for their subsequent learning in science. Nowadays, most children from the age of 3 receive some of their education in settings such as playgroups and nurseries, as well as at home. However, whether at home or in a larger social group, the development of young children differs from that of 6–8 year-olds. The 3–5 year-old children are learning largely through the medium of exploratory play or 'playful activities' (Moyles, 1989; Anning, 1994). They are exploring or 'playing with' the objects and materials in their immediate environment, exploring their own capabilities and exploring language. Play is vitally important to the development of intelligence, developing abstract (symbolic) and divergent thinking skills which then foster problem-solving skills. In their daily playful activities, we can see *the germ of children thinking about problems and solutions* (Moyles, 1996, p. 56). The more opportunities that young children have to explore their environment, the greater their scientific development is likely to be (Johnston, 1996).

It is inappropriate to use formal approaches too soon (QCA/DfEE, 2000). Young children need an active, non-sedentary, social environment, with opportunities and encouragement to explore a wide range of objects, materials and events:

> First-hand experiences are essential elements in this if children are to make sense of their wonderful, but sometimes confusing world. Books, pictures and posters can enhance their learning but these cannot inspire the awe and wonder that accompanies exposure to reality. (French and Randall, 2000, p. 68).

Some characteristics of young children's thinking

Young children construct their knowledge from isolated, practical experiences, such as floating objects in the bath, pushing and pulling wheeled toys, 'helping' with cooking, measuring their own growth on their birthdays, from informal, often overheard, pieces of information and from stories. Such experiences result in these characteristics:

- Their overall knowledge is fragmentary, giving rise to misconceptions or alternative conceptions. Young children require experience of concepts in a variety of contexts before the knowledge can be 'decontextualised' and lead to conceptual understanding.
- Their enquiry skills, such as observation, classification and early explanations, reflect this intermingling of personal, anthropomorphic and objective criteria.
- Their attitudes *towards* science enquiries are almost always positive. Young children find practical explorations exciting and stimulating because they do not depend on ability to read or compute. Their attitudes *within* a science enquiry are more problematic. They may have had less experience of cooperating with other children; they may feel uncomfortable with 'uncertainty' or 'not knowing'; their curiosity and enthusiasm may be great but lacking in the kind of restraint needed in a more scientific enquiry.
- Their language can be rich and inventive but will often mix more scientific terms ('push', 'pull') with terms that are less scientific ('disappeared' for evaporated, 'melted' for dissolved).

Learning objectives for children in the early years

There is a general consensus throughout the United Kingdom about the kind of experiences to which our young children are entitled. Some of these are outlined in the QCA/DfEE (2000) document, *Curriculum guidance in the foundation stage*, within the chapter entitled '*Knowledge and understanding of the world*'. Children should be given opportunities for:

> exploration, observation, problem-solving, prediction, critical thinking, decision-making and discussion (p. 82)

and encouraged to:

> Investigate objects and materials by using all their senses as appropriate.
> Find out about, and identify some features of living things, objects and events they observe.
> Look closely at similarities, differences, patterns and change.
> Ask questions about why things happen and how things work. (p. 86)

These science experiences are described as the 'stepping-stones' towards learning objectives defined in National Curriculum documents and guidelines for older children. Here we spell out in a little more detail the goals of learning, under the headings of attitudes, enquiry skills and knowledge and understanding.

Attitudes

It is arguable that, for young children, the development of positive attitudes is the first stepping-stone to their scientific development. Personal and social attitudes are important in the way young children approach science, attitudes such as:

- independence;
- perseverance;
- cooperation;
- respect for evidence;
- creativity and inventiveness;
- open-mindedness;
- sensitivity to living things.

We also need to encourage children to think positively about science itself and to think of themselves as 'aspiring scientists' (Siraj-Blatchford, 2000). For example, 4-year-old Ann thinks that she is a good scientist because she *measures things carefully and likes looking through the microscope*'. Johnston (1996, p. 94) claims that:

> children who think of themselves as good thinkers / good scientists and problem-solvers perform better than children with less confidence in their abilities.

Enquiry skills

As emphasised in *Curriculum guidance in the foundation stage*, 'observing' is probably the most important enquiry skill for very young children to learn. It is not only a component of exploratory play but also a characteristic of good scientific enquiries. Observations can lead to 'investigating' and 'asking questions', but we need to encourage a wider range of thinking skills. If young children are not invited to articulate their ideas we do not gain access to how they are using and developing their thinking skills.

Sorting and classifying

Sorting and classifying is often overlooked as part of a young child's development in science and dealt with using mathematical criteria only. However, scientific classification is crucial to developing knowledge and understanding (e.g. living/not alive; floats/sinks/dissolves). Young children frequently offer a range of personal as well as objective criteria, but scaffolding their thinking by using the strategy of '*My turn*' often results in the children revealing their ability to think in terms of abstract criteria (see Box 16.1). Classifying by a variety of criteria is the first step towards seeing patterns, making generalisations and truly making sense of a confusing world.

Reasoning

This includes predicting, interpreting results, explaining patterns and drawing conclusions. Simple reasoning develops children's language skills (cause and

Box 16.1

Sorting and classifying

Two reception-class children are sorting cards illustrating objects, some of which use electricity.

Teacher: *Which things do you think go together?*

Nathan: *It's the same – it's got the same sort of job.* [vacuum cleaner + iron]

Teacher: *Anything else?*

Carita: *I think these – because they're both black.* [bicycle + frying pan]

Teacher: *Anything else?*

Nathan: And these – 'cos that's a motor and that's a motor. *[car + lawnmower]*

Carita: *You can put these together so they stay nice and neat.* [lines up two cards edge to edge]

Teacher: *My turn. Can you guess why I've put these ones together?* [lawnmower, computer, vacuum cleaner and iron]

Carita: *'Cos you like them.*

Nathan: *'Cos they are all electric. 'Cos you switch them on – only my mum says I mustn't.*

effect) as well as thought processes: *'Fast cars will go furthest'* (Box 16.2). Making predictions on a regular basis helps children become comfortable with the concept and begin actively to listen and look for information on which to base their predictions and reflect on the test results. Children's predictions can give the practitioner an insight into the children's ideas (Box 16.3).

Box 16.2

Predicting

Teacher: *Which car do you think will go the furthest?*

Prakash: *The white one.*

Ben: *No. The blue one. That went fastest last time.*

Box 16.3

Interpreting and explaining

Teacher: *Which car went the furthest?*

Children: *The white one!*

Teacher: *Why do you think that it did?*

Prakash: *'Cos it's a police car.*

Albert: *'Cos it's got the biggest wheels.*

Teacher: *The biggest wheels?*

Albert: *Yeah – 'cos my dad's car's got big wheels and it goes really fast.*

Susie: *No! 'Cos Richard pushed it.*

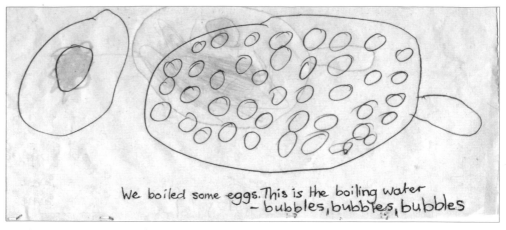

We boiled some eggs. This is the boiling water – bubbles, bubbles, bubbles

Figure 16.1 **Given encouragement and time, young children are keen to offer their ideas (Lisa, 4 years, 10 months).**

Creative and intuitive thinking

Creative thinking involves making a leap of the imagination to offer explanations or simple hypotheses (see Figure 16.1). Young children may show surprise or remain silent when asked for their explanations if they are unaccustomed to giving their ideas. When given plentiful opportunities and encouragement, they become very enthusiastic about offering their ideas.

We should not be deterred by the possibility that young children's early hypotheses are unscientific. In responding a teacher has to find a balance between challenging these ideas and damaging the children's self-esteem. For example, the teacher might offer another object or opportunity to challenge their ideas or agree with the child that, 'It certainly looks like that, doesn't it'. This values the child's response without confirming a misconception. Encouraging children's hypothetical thinking stimulates self-esteem, develops children's language skills and encourages positive attitudes towards science.

Problem-finding and problem-solving

Challenging children or encouraging them to pose their own problems develops social and personal skills as well as enquiry skills, such as curiosity, innovative lateral thinking skills, open-minded debate and a practical approach to solving the events and conflicts of everyday life.

Reflective and critical thinking

As with hypothetical thinking, young children need encouragement to think reflectively about the processes of enquiry, difficulties experienced and successful outcomes. Awareness of ideas *as* ideas stimulates the beginnings of critical thinking and ultimately leads to metacognitive thinking. Comments such as 'What a good idea!', 'What made you think of that?' and 'Good thinking!' give positive approval and make children aware of themselves as thinkers.

Knowledge and understanding

Prescribing 'Knowledge and understanding of the world' in the foundation stage ensures that young children are offered learning opportunities to which they are entitled, knowledge such as:

- *knowing that* most apples float and most pears sink; sunflowers grow tall with flowers and water flows.

- *knowing how to* help seeds grow by regular and careful watering; behave fairly by releasing cars down a ramp without pushing them; look through a hand-lens. In the early years this knowledge is still developing. Unlike older children and adults, younger children are less aware of what they need to know in order to carry out a task. This applies particularly to young children's inability to think about and control the variables in a science enquiry.

- *knowing why* the apples floated and the pears sank. This requires an ability to reason and explain and is closest to 'understanding'. Not all young children can achieve this. Setting a goal of 'understanding' in the early years may be somewhat over-optimistic and difficult for adult practitioners to find the evidence for when assessing young children (de Bóo, 1999).

- *knowing that we know*, meaning that children are not only aware of their own ideas but know that *they* thought of them. This is less evident in young children's interactions. But, *knowing that we don't know* can lead to *knowing how to find out* which is a major goal of education at all levels.

Knowledge acquired in the early years gives children the 'feel-good factor', empowers them, helps them solve problems and communicate, gives them pleasure and self-confidence in their own and others' eyes and, ultimately, becomes part of their identity. Of course, such knowledge is not free of the influence of values or culture. Young children acquire the kind of knowledge that their parents or carers and their society deem relevant and appropriate; this may not always match the kind of knowledge that is accepted by the scientific community.

Working to achieve the learning objectives

In a good early-years setting, learning is a combination of child-initiated and teacher-directed activities.

Child-initiated activities

A setting where there is a mixture of familiar and unfamiliar objects and events, such as unexpected objects in the water tray, displays of unusual fruits and vegetables, a 'garden centre' in the role-play area, will prompt children into posing and solving their own problems. Children who identify and 'own' the problem perform with greater creativity, offer more varied responses and have a greater sense of achievement.

Teacher-directed activities

Learning by exploration is effective but not always efficient:

> *Free play can be imaginative and exploratory, but it can also be limited, repetitious and 'boring'.* (Johnston, 1996, p. 54)

Teachers can set the scene for children to discover or address problems, for instance by adding lengths of drainpipe and a plastic spider to the water tray (Feasey, 2004), which meet learning objectives yet leave enough flexibility for children's self-initiated enquiries. Children may sometimes identify a problem but are not always able to test out their own solutions without adult help. Sometimes adults need to define the problem for children and provide appropriate resources to solve it.

The teacher's role

Adult practitioners are role models. So they need to let children see their own curiosity and enthusiasm, uncertainty and areas of ignorance. Practitioners need to respond positively to children's own suggested enquiries, allowing children sufficient freedom to follow up their ideas, whilst providing resources and support to ensure some successful outcomes. It is important to show how much children's responses and ideas are valued, even when these run counter to received scientific thinking. Children who know that *all* their ideas are welcomed will develop skills in language as well as thinking skills. Asking person-centred and open questions (see Chapter 21) gives children the opportunity to make decisions, such as deciding how and where to plant the sunflower seeds to be fair to everyone, who will have a turn next, or whether we will measure the distance travelled by the toy cars from the top or the bottom of the ramp. Children whose decisions are valued and acted upon whenever possible, develop greater self-confidence.

Children need challenging enquiries both indoors and in the outdoor environment. The science experiences should be set in contexts that are relevant and appropriate to young children, such as observing changing materials when making jellies and cooking cakes, and simplified so that children can learn from them. Enough time needs to be allowed for the different aspects of the enquiry – something we often underestimate when young children are acquiring new skills and knowledge.

Children need good-quality hand lenses and access to binocular microscopes (monocular microscopes are not easy for young children to use), strong magnets (weak magnets do not show the wonder of repelling forces), simple and digital balances, digital cameras to record transitory events and achievements (e.g. plant growth or constructions that have to be dismantled). Adults need to introduce tools and train children to use them safely and appropriately – allowing time to explore these as objects too. And they need to capitalise on the potential for science enquiries in all aspects of the early-years classroom, such as:

- wet and dry sand and water play: the nature of materials, liquids and solids, floating and sinking;
- construction kits – balancing forces and strength, materials;
- role-play, in the baker's shop, garden centre, toy shop – cooking, growing, moving toys;
- small world play, e.g. farm, zoo, houses for the 'three little pigs' – living things, forces;
- a science corner – displaying a range of different shells with hand lenses for close observation, ferrous and non-ferrous objects with magnets to explore them, sealed yoghurt pots with beans, seeds, rice or sand inside.

Developing children's language

With 3–5 year old children, oracy comes before literacy. We want the children to be confident and articulate in speaking and listening. Speech or 'thinking aloud' *'aids the expression of thinking, and ... the very use of talk initiates and refines the child's thinking'* (Tough, 1973, p. 88). It is important, then, to welcome all ideas and encourage children to:

- use scientific vocabulary appropriately;
- enjoy using scientific language;
- communicate their ideas and experiences in science.

The teacher's role in developing scientific language is to help children make connections between the object or event and the word. The appropriate time for introducing new scientific vocabulary is when children have had experience of objects or phenomena and show that they have the relevant knowledge for the word to label something that has meaning for them. This helps children whose first language is English and those for whom English is an additional language. For example:

Robert: *Car won't move. It's stuck.*

Teacher: *Yes, it's sticking, isn't it? There must be a lot of friction stopping it moving.*

It is important to recognise that children who are silent are also participants in the discussion. Young children may lack confidence or may have not previously tried to express scientific thinking. Silence does not necessarily mean a lack of understanding and children will often communicate with gestures.

Encouraging children to talk about their scientific enquiries has the added benefit of being an effective strategy for assessing their knowledge and understanding (e.g. Figure 6.2).

Recognising and recording children's achievements

Remembering or recalling later what children have said or done is not impossible but can be unreliable. A strategy is needed for recognising and recording children's achievement on a regular, preferably daily basis. In a setting where there are two or more adults, it is possible to schedule short periods of time for one person to observe children involved in an activity (e.g. 5–10 minutes). The use of an audiotape recorder can serve the same purpose, for the same periods of time. Children become used to the presence of the recorder, stop 'reacting' to it and enjoy listening to their own responses (used selectively and positively).

Structured assessment of children's achievements usually occurs during an activity when practitioners are simultaneously challenging the children's thinking and developing their knowledge and understanding of the world. The assessment is most often based on what the children do and what they say, rather than what they draw and write. However, children's work (paintings, drawings, written work) gives a tangible record and enables them to discuss their observations (see Figure 16.2), compare data with others, and contribute to a display. Adults have material evidence of achievement and opportunities to discuss and question the children's ideas:

- *Why did you think that?*
- *Would you do it any differently next time?*
- *Why's that?*

We need to share our assessments of children's achievements with the children themselves. Through this they develop awareness of their own learning and

Figure 16.2 **Children's drawing can offer opportunity to discuss and question their ideas. Here the labels have been added to Alex's drawing after discussion with an adult (Alex, 4 years 11 months).**

take greater pride in and responsibility for it.

Planning for and putting science into practice in the early years can be hard work – but it is often a magical experience for young children – and for us too!

References

Anning, A. (1994) Play and the legislated curriculum. Back to basics: an alternative view. In *The excellence of play*, ed. Moyles, J. R. Buckingham: Open University Press.

de Bóo, M. (1999) *Enquiring children: challenging teaching*. Buckingham: Open University Press.

Feasey, R. (2004) In *The early years handbook*, ed. de Bóo, M. Sheffield: Curriculum Partnership.

French, M. and Randall, A. (2000) Managing science in the early years. In *Science 3–6: Laying the foundations in early years*, ed. de Bóo, M. Hatfield: Association for Science Education.

Johnston, J. (1996) *Early explorations in science*. Buckingham: Open University Press.

Moyles, J. R. (1996) *Just playing? The role and status of play in early childhood education*. Buckingham: Open University Press.

QCA/DfEE (2000) *Curriculum guidance for the foundation stage*. London: HMSO.

Siraj-Blatchford, J. (2000) Promoting equality and citizenship. In *Science 3–6: Laying the foundations in the early years*, ed. de Bóo, M. Hatfield: Association for Science Education.

Tough, J. (1973) *Focus on meaning*. London: Allen and Unwin.

Section 4 Classroom level: Lesson planning

Chapter 17

Planning with goals in mind

What ends up as learning activities for children begins in the plans that teachers make and the goals they intend children to

John Dabell, Brenda Keogh and Stuart Naylor

achieve. This chapter is about the process of moving from overall goals to plans for specific classroom experiences. It begins by identifying the role of goals of learning at three levels of planning. Two subtly different ways of planning the same lesson illustrate how goals can be shared with children and how they guide child-centred approaches to teaching. Finally, some key aspects of good planning are suggested.

What do we mean by goals?

The goals we are concerned with here relate to children's learning. They can be small scale and short term or described in broader terms over longer periods of time. In science they include not only conceptual but procedural, attitudinal, experiential and social goals. The most obvious learning goals are conceptual, but on their own these will not provide the broad coverage of science to which children are entitled; nor will they engage and inspire children.

In many curriculum documents, goals are expressed in very formal language, meant for teachers. But it is possible to expressing learning goals in more child-friendly language, often as questions, and share them with children. This makes it more likely that the goals will provide a challenge that directs the learner's attention, enhances motivation and promotes learning (see the example in lesson B in Box 17.1).

How do goals influence planning?

Planning is about more than 'coverage'. Its purpose is to translate goals into practice and to make the teaching and learning experience as effective, and enjoyable, as possible. There are different levels of planning, which can be illustrated by thinking about planning for a holiday. Goals for a holiday are determined by what someone sees as the purpose of going on holiday: whether spending time in cafes and restaurants, in museums and art galleries, by the beach and pool or in bars and discos. These general goals will determine the plan of where to go, who with, for how long, and so on. Then the time of year, transport, accommodation, budget, and so forth need to be planned. Finally, on arrival, the day-to-day planning is strongly influenced by local circumstances, such as what the weather is like, the local transport system and whether places of interest are closed on certain days.

These three levels of planning are evident in planning for teaching and learning:

- **Planning with goals in mind requires a whole-school perspective.** It provides a broad sense of direction and paints a big picture in which goals are clearly evident. It assumes that teachers will work together to avoid unnecessary repetition and identifies in general terms where new ideas and experiences can best be introduced. It emphasises what goals will be achieved rather than what will be taught.

- **Planning at the class level** provides an overview of goals across a year or a block of work and how these goals will be achieved. It draws on whole-school planning and identifies a sensible and manageable sequence of work. It refers to skills and understandings from other curriculum areas that need to be introduced in order to enable children to make sense of the science.

- **Short-term planning** still takes overall goals into account but is responsive to the particular needs or interests of the class. It draws on the teacher's knowledge of the children, the progress they are making, the potential of the particular topic being studied, and the teacher's subject knowledge and understanding of approaches to teaching and learning science.

At each level of planning it is important that teachers have a clear picture of the goals for children's learning and experiences. Planning is a creative interaction between goals, objectives, activities and practicalities in the quest for an effective learning experience. It is not simply a matter of making a 'to do' list; it is about deciding when, where, why, and how a certain lesson is taught.

How are classroom goals for science established?

A good number of starting points exist for planning at the school level: the National Curriculum (DfEE/QCA, 1999), the Scheme of Work published by the Qualifications and Curriculum Authority (QCA, 1998), and other published material. The authors of these have worked hard to indicate a reasonable sense of progression across different areas of science. However, it would be unwise to view these as sacrosanct, since defining any precise conceptual progression in science learning is difficult and can vary from child to child (see Chapter 25).

For planning at the class level, teachers need to draw on their experience and their knowledge of their own class to adjust their planning. They will also adjust and amend plans in the light of the children's responses as they put these plans into practice. The children's likely misconceptions need to be taken into account. These help to define both the content of and the approach to teaching so that misconceptions are challenged and children are likely to move on in their thinking. The whole area of misconceptions (or alternative conceptions) has been extensively researched in recent years so there is plenty of published material available to help teachers anticipate what these misconceptions may be. Probably the most valuable source is the series of Nuffield Primary Science Teachers' Guides (1995). Equally, there are many valuable approaches that can be used to anticipate and explore children's possible misconceptions at the same time as beginning the learning process, such as predict–observe–explain (White and Gunstone, 1992) or concept cartoons (Naylor and Keogh, 2000).

Cross-curricular goals for the school will influence the goals for science teaching and learning. This is a two-way process. Goals for science may depend on progress that children have made in other areas of the curriculum, such as independent writing, using bar charts or observational drawing. Equally, learning in science can make a valuable contribution to broad cross-curricular goals, such as raising questions, using evidence to justify ideas, or independent enquiry.

There is also a complex set of other factors that interact to influence and modify goals for science. These include information from other teachers, children's views about their own goals for learning, how they respond in science lessons, information from formal and informal assessment, and so on.

Sharing learning goals with children

It is now common practice for teachers to share learning goals or objectives with children at the start of the lesson. There is a sound research base for the value of doing this. Part of the purpose of sharing learning goals in this way is about tuning children in to the context of the lesson and helping them to recognise when they are making progress.

In science teaching especially it is important to think about how and when to do this so that sharing learning goals is meaningful and appropriate. It is possible to share learning goals in such a way as to take away any surprise or challenge for children, which can be demotivating and counter-productive. For example, if a teacher writes on the board that the learning goal is to show that metals are good conductors of electricity, then a lesson to explore which materials are good conductors becomes rather pointless. Children may also recognise that this statement is what the teacher wants to hear them say by the end of the lesson. Whether they understand it or not, they know that the correct answer is that metals conduct electricity. Reproducing the learning goal in the form in which the teacher wrote it on the board can give the appearance of learning whilst possibly masking a lack of understanding.

A more effective way to share learning goals could be to present children with a problem that provides a reason for wanting to find something out. For example, why we get an electric shock from an uncovered wire but not from a covered one. A suitable learning goal would then be for children to identify which materials do or don't conduct electricity. This learning goal gets children more engaged at the outset. It presents science as a series of problems to be solved rather than instructions to be carried out. It gives children a stake in the process rather than seeing learning goals as something received from the teacher (see also Chapter 23).

This more child-centred approach also helps to make differentiated learning goals more manageable. It isn't realistic for a teacher to set individual learning goals for children. It *is* realistic for teachers to help children to personalise

137

learning goals through engaging in problem-solving activities, building on their ideas and giving some degree of choice in the activity.

What does planning with goals in mind look like?

There is more to planning than identifying learning goals. Successful learning depends on the way that learning goals have been implemented. This is

Box 17.1

	Lesson A	Lesson B
Learning goal	Children will be able to describe that light cannot pass through some materials and that this is how shadows are formed.	Children will be able to explain that light cannot pass through some materials and that this is how shadows are formed. Children will have an opportunity to experience the excitement of exploring shadows
Introduction	Write learning objective on the board and share it with children. Use recall questions about what they know already: *What did we do in last week's lesson about light shining though materials? Who knows what transparent/opaque means?* Identify children's ideas: *What is a shadow? Who can tell me what a shadow looks like?*	Quick reminder of previous lesson – brief questioning about evidence for what they learnt: *How did you know which objects were translucent or opaque in last week's lesson? Why did some of you have problems deciding which objects were transparent or opaque?* (buddy discussion and feedback). Introduce learning goals using child-friendly language: *We are going to observe shadows on the playground and then see if we can explain what shadows look like and how they are made.* Go outside to explore shadows – chasing shadows, running away from shadows, hiding shadows. etc. Back in class: true/false statements for paired discussion: <ul><li>*Shadows are the same size as the person.*</li><li>*Shadows are the same colour as the person.*</li><li>*Shadows are attached to the person.*</li><li>*You get shadows when it's dark.*</li></ul> These will start to identify children's ideas and help them set their own more precise learning goals.

Setting up whole-class work	Explain what children will do during the next part of the lesson. First fill in the sections of your planning sheet: *'What we want to find out'*, *'What we are going to do'*, and *'Predict what will happen'*. Work in your usual groups. Then we will go out into the playground in groups to observe shadows.	Briefly share ideas. Identify areas of disagreement across the class. List these on the board. Discuss with children what they need to do next to find out which ideas are true and which are false.
Class activity	Children complete worksheet. Children look at shadows in the playground. Return to class to complete worksheet.	Children go out into the playground in their usual groups for more focused observation of shadows, including looking for shadows in dark places. Reminder to focus on areas of disagreement. In class: collaborative annotated drawings to show what they have observed.
Plenary	Select and share some examples of children's work that show good understanding. Can they tell me what they have learnt?	Return to true/false statements. Class vote on true or false. Ask them to justify views. Focus discussion on any remaining disagreement or where they are confidently wrong. Identify questions that remain unanswered; save these on class question board.
Resources	Planning sheet. Classroom assistant for outside work.	True/false statements. Classroom assistant for outside work.

illustrated in the two lessons in Box 17.1, both of which are based firmly on the National Curriculum.

In lesson A, the teacher's questioning is unlikely to involve all children and some of them may opt out of thinking. The work in the playground has little obvious sense of purpose for children. Slow writers may spend far longer on completing the worksheet than finding things out. The plenary offers limited scope for all children to be involved or challenged.

By contrast, lesson B actively involves all children throughout the lesson. They are involved in setting their own learning agenda and they challenge each other's ideas. There is a greater emphasis on thinking and investigating than on recall and writing, and the lesson also begins to set an agenda for future learning.

When we think of planning with goals in mind we are really thinking of children and strategies for maximising their learning. Planning with goals in mind is planning with children in mind. Planning is about promoting learning, not just teaching, and inspired, enthusiastic children are better learners than bored, demotivated ones. A well-planned lesson will engage and challenge children, make science an enjoyable experience and enhance learning:

> Science stimulates and excites pupils' curiosity about phenomena and events in the world around them. (DfEE/QCA, 1999, p. 15)

By contrast, an emphasis on narrow learning objectives makes it all too easy to plan a lesson that offers children no stake in the process of creating learning goals and that misses out on engagement and challenge. Schemes of work (such as QCA, 1998) can be very valuable for defining learning objectives and suggesting suitable activities for children. However, they may fail to provide any sense of context or purpose for activities, making it more likely that children will not be engaged or motivated.

Some prerequisites for effective planning

Building in time for talk

One important aspect of planning that can sometimes be neglected because of the pressure to cover curriculum ground is interaction among children. Planning opportunities for actively engaging children in situations that involve collaboration is essential. Unlike watching a play, learning is not a spectator sport. Children are expected to take an active part. A silent classroom is not normally a good learning environment. Children need to discuss ideas, build on each other's expertise, use each other as sounding boards and work creatively in a community of learners (see Chapter 20). They need to interact with others to plan, explore, discuss and direct their activities; in doing so they try out and modify their ideas. Children engaged in active learning are making their own meaning and constructing their own knowledge in the process.

Forming groups

Grouping children for collaborative science activities presents a challenge. The usual groups used for literacy and numeracy are not necessarily helpful for science, where attainment and interest may be very different. It is not uncommon for low-attaining children in literacy and numeracy to be more thoughtful and creative in science. The groupings used may change according to the purpose of the activity, with a wide range of groupings being used over a period of time. These might include friendship pairs ('learning partners'), mixed ability/interest groups, mother-tongue groups, and so on. There is some logic in getting children used to working in a variety of groupings so that they can switch from one grouping to another with minimal fuss, instead of expecting always to work with their friends. There is also research evidence to support children working with others of different abilities and with different ideas; those in heterogeneous groups make more progress than those in homogeneous groups (Howe, 1990).

Being informed and creative

Inevitably, good subject knowledge is helpful. Although subject knowledge varies widely between teachers, a commitment to further study is part of good professional practice. Being confident in a subject area can help teachers to go beyond 'knowing about' a subject to 'playing with' a subject, providing the energy and mental space to be creative and bring a topic alive. A small creative episode can make a big difference to a lesson (see Chapter 26). Even teachers who do not feel creative themselves can research and use the creative ideas of others in their lessons.

Reflection

Including time for reflection in the plan is also important. Children need time to reflect on an experience and what they have learned from it. Encouraging them to pause and reflect on the insights they have gained and the things that don't seem to make sense will help them to take control of their learning in a new way. They will develop new understandings, learn how to manage misconceptions and respect themselves as learners.

Collaboration

Where it is possible to organise it, planning in teams is always helpful. It shares subject expertise, maximises the range of ideas that can be used and promotes creative thinking through interaction between colleagues. It also makes it more likely that a commitment to engaging, inspiring planning with goals in mind becomes a whole-school perspective rather than one restricted to a single teacher.

References

DfEE/QCA (1999) *Science: the National Curriculum for England*. London: Qualifications and Curriculum Authority.

Howe, C. (1990) Grouping children for effective learning in science. *Primary Science Review*, **13**, 26–27.

Naylor, S. and Keogh, B. (2000) *Concept cartoons in science education*. Sandbach, Cheshire: Millgate House Publishers.

Nuffield Primary Science Teachers' Guides (1995) Various titles. London: Collins.

QCA (1998) *A scheme of work for key stages 1 and 2*. London: Qualifications and Curriculum Authority.

White, R. and Gunstone, R. (1992) *Probing understanding*. London: Falmer Press.

Chapter 18

Scientific investigations in the context of enquiry

Scientific enquiry enables children to develop understanding through a range of activities

Rosemary Feasey

including investigation of materials and phenomena, consulting books and other sources of information including experts, and through discussion. This chapter deals with the first of these, a key aspect at the primary level. There are various types of investigation, as pointed out in the first section, but research shows that the 'fair-testing' type dominates current practice. However, even this common form of investigation often lacks attention to important features, such as the use of language, planning, data handling and the use of mathematics. Ways of improving these aspects of practice are discussed, with examples, in subsequent sections of the chapter.

Types of scientific investigation

Scientific enquiry both requires and enables children to develop the ability to take the lead in thinking and working scientifically. It has become embedded in primary science curricula throughout the United Kingdom and many other countries across the world. Where scientific enquiry (especially fair-test type investigations) is successful there are common elements which underpin that accomplishment. Ian Richardson, HMI Specialist Adviser for Science, indicates that:

> In a survey of schools which have the highest standards or have made the most significant improvements in science, we find scientific enquiry (Sc1) at the heart of pupils' work ... belief in the significance of Sc1 to learning is underpinned by clear inclusion of Sc1 in schemes of work such that a progression in Sc1 is set out, through planning of science activities, effective

sharing of good practice and systematic monitoring of teaching and learning. (Richardson, 2005)

For teachers, scientific enquiry has made many demands on their approaches to teaching and learning in science. It must be remembered though, that it is less than 30 years ago that a curriculum for science was set out in the UK, so it is a relative newcomer to the curriculum. There is still much to learn about how children learn in primary science and what kind of approaches to learning have the potential to support teachers and children.

During that period research into scientific enquiry has been limited to a few large-scale projects. The most recent is the AKSIS (Association for Science Education/King's College Science Investigations in Schools) project which looked into how investigations are carried out in schools. The project identified a number of issues and provided some suggestions for future development and strategies for supporting teachers and children in science. One of the outcomes of the research was to suggest that while schools carried out fair-test investigations, a greater range of types of investigation could be included, for example:

- **Fair testing.** Fair-test investigations where factors (variables) are changed and measured.
- **Classifying and identifying.** Organising objects and events into sets.
- **Pattern seeking.** Observing and recording natural phenomena or carrying out surveys.
- **Exploring.** Observing objects or events.
- **Investigating models.** Deciding what evidence needs to be collected to test a model.
- **Making things or developing systems.** Usually technological where children design an artefact or system to meet a human need.

  (see AKSIS website)

The impact on schools across the UK of these alternative types of investigation has been limited and until there is major curriculum change it is unlikely that the suggested alternatives will be adopted by schools in a way that will impact on primary science. The AKSIS research did, though, provide some insights into how teachers and children approach fair-test type investigations. The research findings suggested that:

- teachers and children were confused in the language used to describe and discuss investigations;
- most teachers placed emphasis on children planning and carrying out the investigation and less emphasis on analysing results and evaluating the process of investigations;
- most teachers gave prompt sheets to children, but many children used these without understanding the purpose behind them and the use of prompt sheets tended to reduce the openness of investigations.

Given that this is the case in most schools, the question must be *'What strategies can schools adopt that have the potential to support both teachers and children?'* The following sections suggest some approaches that are targeted to addressing some of the areas of weakness indicated by the AKSIS research.

Language of scientific enquiry

Primary science aims to develop children's ability to think and work scientifically. This requires children to learn and apply a new and different vocabulary, not just the vocabulary of scientific concepts such as electricity, magnetism or changes of state, but also of scientific ways of working and thinking, such as carrying out investigations, considering data and drawing conclusions. It is helpful to classify the different kinds of vocabulary that teachers need to teach children, in order that teachers can target vocabulary that will support children in becoming articulate and confident communicators in science. Some examples are given in Box 18.1

Box 18.1 Examples of types of vocabulary

Vocabulary of description. Children should develop language related to describing objects and phenomena in science, which includes describing emotions, awe and wonder.

Examples: *huge beautiful strange level speckled awesome*

Vocabulary of measurement. This is crucial to scientific enquiry. Numerical evidence is the way in which scientists recognise patterns, trends, are able to compare and offer proof of what happened. Children must develop mathematical competence in understanding, using and applying a range of measurement, but most importantly they must be able to transfer these skills across to science.

Examples: *centimetres milligrams scale accurate reliable newton metre*

Vocabulary of comparison. Science requires children to compare objects, phenomena and data. Comparative language includes words such as similar, different and positional language.

Examples: *higher smaller similar different heavier above inside lower more less declining*

Vocabulary of explanation. Children must be able to explain ideas, things that happen, data and even instructions. For example, when children draw conclusions they need to explain what they have found out and give reasons, and use a range of words to make statements and justify these using evidence and conceptual understanding.

Examples: *think pattern predict because evidence reasons*

The teacher can support the development of specific language relating to scientific enquiry by:

- ensuring that the language of scientific enquiry is displayed around the classroom, including individual words, phrases and sentences;
- teaching children sentence openers and phrases that they can use when thinking and talking about science, particularly scientific investigations;
- ensuring that they model language when talking about science, not just words related to concepts such as electricity and friction but in relation to planning, predicting, hypothesising, handling data, drawing conclusions;

- challenging children to use the correct language, for example, axis, centimetre, volume;
- providing children with speaking frames to scaffold their thinking into talking about science (see Box 18.2).

Planning a fair-test investigation

As primary science has developed there have been numerous approaches to supporting children in planning for scientific investigations. Such frameworks can be useful and provide a starter for children but, as the AKSIS project suggested, they can be formulaic and take away the necessity for children to make sense of the processes of investigations.

Such frameworks are least effective when the same framework is used throughout the whole school, without differentiation. Where teachers differentiate frameworks they often do so in terms of those children with special needs in language development, and rarely in relation to capability in science.

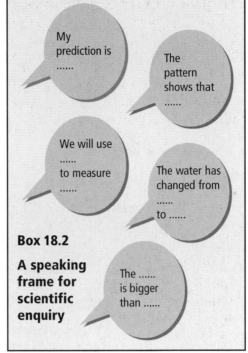

Box 18.2

A speaking frame for scientific enquiry

My prediction is ......

The pattern shows that ......

We will use ...... to measure ......

The water has changed from ...... to ......

The ...... is bigger than ......

Planning frameworks should not be rigid; they should certainly differ in format from year to year. The 'Post-it' method (Goldsworthy and Feasey, 1997), illustrated in Figure 18.1, is flexible and encourages teachers to use whichever part of the framework the children need. It has the advantage that the teacher can take children through the planning process step by step and it shows how the different parts of the investigation link together, in particular how data in the table relate to the graph and the final conclusions.

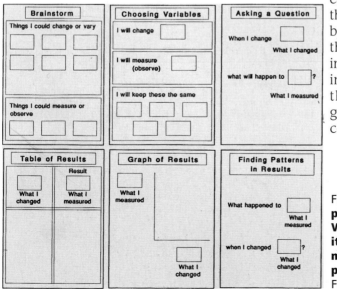

Figure 18.1 **A 'Post-it' planning framework. Variables written on 'Post-its' or cards can easily be moved from poster to poster** (Goldsworthy and Feasey, 1997, p. 12).

Figure 18.2 **Some more examples of planning frameworks** (Feasey, 2005, p. 62).

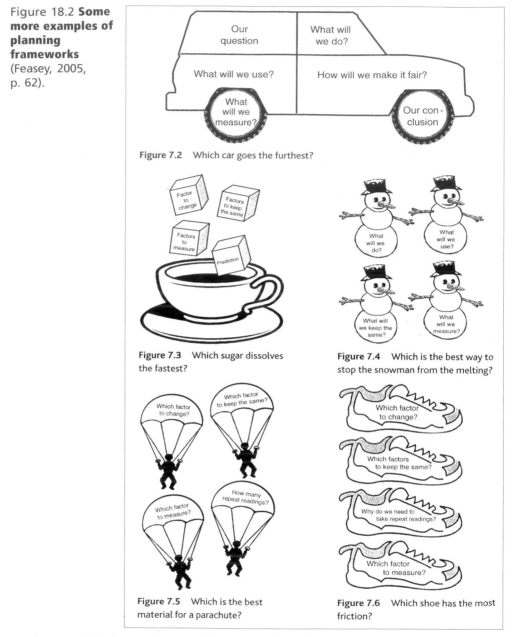

Figure 7.2 Which car goes the furthest?

Figure 7.3 Which sugar dissolves the fastest?

Figure 7.4 Which is the best way to stop the snowman from the melting?

Figure 7.5 Which is the best material for a parachute?

Figure 7.6 Which shoe has the most friction?

Figure 18.2 shows some other examples of visual planning frameworks. Using frameworks such as these, particularly as large wall displays, can serve a number of purposes:

- provide a visual stimulus for planning;
- help to raise the profile of scientific investigations in the classroom;
- provide a focus for discussion at all points of the activity;
- be changed according to different questions and focuses;
- contain words and phrases to support discussion and writing.

Building from these examples, teachers have created their own visual planning frameworks according to the needs of the children. Science subject leaders have found these useful for auditing progression across the school. By looking at the visual planning framework displayed in each classroom, subject leaders can ascertain what kind of investigations the children are engaged in, the type of language used and the level of the investigation. For example, the car planning framework in Figure 18.2 is used with younger children, whilst the parachute framework relates to an investigation for upper primary. Note the differences: for example the use of the word 'factors' in the parachute framework and the focus on repeat readings. Differentiation in terms of questions is important and should relate to the changing demands of investigations as children move through the primary school, for example, moving children:

- from using non-standard measures to standard ones;
- from 'things to change, things to measure and things to keep the same' to using the word 'factors';
- from taking single readings to taking repeat readings where appropriate;
- from merely reporting results to using data to draw conclusions.

Data handling

The AKSIS project indicated that teachers and children have become adept at predicting and carrying out a fair test, but data handling is less developed and AKSIS stated that:

> As part of our research we analysed pupils' uses of graphs in investigations. We found that over 75% of their graphs were incorrectly constructed and most pupils regarded graphs as an end in themselves. Only a few pupils referred to their graphs when considering their evidence. We found that many teachers we interviewed recognised the difficulties that pupils had with graphs, but few had made a point of teaching pupils about the construction and use of graphs. (Goldsworthy, Watson and Wood-Robinson, 1999, p. 2)

Some of the more specific difficulties include:

- transferring information from tables to graphs;
- knowing whether to use a bar or a line graph;
- understanding scale;
- remembering the basic rule for creating graphs;
- describing relationships in data;
- explaining results;
- understanding why some measurements need to be repeated.

What became obvious from the AKSIS project was that teachers needed specific teaching strategies to support children in data handling in science generally and investigations in particular. There are many different ways of supporting children in managing data; the following section offers a few suggestions.

Developing children's understanding of graphs in science

One of the areas children find difficult is deciding which type of graph, if any, they need to produce. Sometimes all that children (and teachers) need is a simple rule of thumb, as suggested by Goldsworthy and Feasey (1997) in Table 18.1.

Table 18.1

Factor I changed	Factor I measured	Type of graph
words	words	no graph
words	numbers	bar chart
numbers	words	no graph
whole numbers only	numbers	bar chart
numbers	numbers	line graph

(After, Goldsworthy and Feasey, 1997, p. 38)

The AKSIS project offered teachers a range of strategies for supporting children, including the inspiring 'human bar chart' in Figure 18.3. This enables children to develop a 'feel' for graphs by becoming part of a human graph, offering a very practical approach to a challenging concept.

Another useful strategy is the 'scale selector' (Golds-

Figure 18.3
Making a human bar chart
(Goldsworthy, Watson and Wood-Robinson, 1999, p. 9).

Figure 18.4 **A checklist such as this will help children ensure that their graphs are complete.**

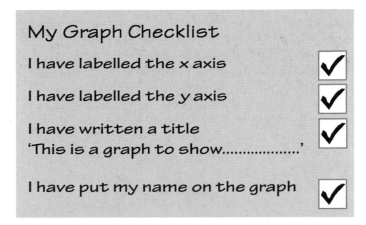

My Graph Checklist

I have labelled the x axis ✓

I have labelled the y axis ✓

I have written a title ✓
'This is a graph to show................'

I have put my name on the graph ✓

worthy, Watson and Wood-Robinson, 1999, p. 48), designed to support children in selecting the correct scales for horizontal and vertical axes. This comprises a paper 'ruler' with different scales on it to help children develop an appreciation of why different scales are used and how to choose the most appropriate scale.

Teachers often report that children do not complete their graphs, forgetting, for example, to label axes and put a title on the graph. A very simple solution is to create an A4 laminated checklist such as the one in Figure 18.4. Before the children finish their work they take the laminated checklist and, using a whiteboard pen, tick those parts that they have completed and finish those that they have forgotten. This 'prop' can be taken away once it has become second nature to children to make sure that their graph is 'finished'. This checklist can be produced for a bar chart or a line graph and can be adapted to meet the needs of children with differing skills in constructing graphs.

Using individual whiteboards to support investigations

Many children find it difficult to 'talk about data' and write simple sentences relating to aspects of investigations and data handling in particular, such as patterns, anomalies, conclusions and evaluations. An important element of developing the ability to handle data is to make sure that children have as many opportunities as possible to talk through their ideas and phrase what they want to say. The use of 'talk partners' is important in science and particularly when engaging children in data handling. Children need 'thinking time' and 'talk time' (see Chapter 17) so that they can share their ideas with their partner, and draft and redraft statements on their individual whiteboards before exposing them to the teacher or the rest of the class. For the teacher, using individual whiteboards also has the advantage of providing immediate access to ideas from the whole class and not just a few individuals. Talk partners working on individual whiteboards is a strategy that can be used to access children's thinking on:

- predictions;
- hypotheses;
- suggesting patterns from data;
- sketching outlines of graphs;
- offering conclusions;

- suggesting the next number in a set of data;
- identifying which factors to change, measure and keep the same.

Mathematics in investigations

An important element of science, especially investigations, is the level of mathematics that the activity requires children to use. Frequently children have difficulties with an investigation because they are unable to carry out appropriate mathematical procedures. Not only does this impinge on the quality of children's work but also on the level they can achieve, since the assessment level of investigation is often determined by the mathematics required, for example:

- using standard measurements;
- creating a bar or line graph;
- taking repeat readings and working out an average.

It is therefore important that teachers consider the mathematics required in science investigations. This needs to be identified in lesson planning and the maths extracted during the lesson and re-taught, so that when children need to use it they can do so with confidence.

Conclusion

Many aspects of conducting investigations still need to be developed in order to give primary children a wider experience of learning through enquiry.

There is no limit to the kinds of investigative work that can be carried out with children; the only limits will be those set by the teacher. A great deal depends on how science is managed and supported in the school and on the confidence and competence of the science subject leader (see Chapter 11). To date, opportunities for professional development for science subject leaders have been too limited, but the developments in professional development provision, outlined in Chapter 5, should make available the necessary training to ensure that scientific enquiry is given the time and energy it deserves by both teachers and children.

References

Feasey, R. (2005) *Creative science – achieving the WOW factor with 5–11 year-olds*. London: David Fulton.

Goldsworthy, A. and Feasey, R. (1997) *Making sense of primary science investigations*. Hatfield: Association for Science Education.

Goldsworthy, A., Watson, R. and Wood-Robinson, V. (1999) *AKSIS investigations: Getting to grips with graphs*. Hatfield: Association for Science Education.

Richardson, I. (2005) Summer Newsletter. Science Learning Centres.

Websites

AKSIS: www.kcl.ac.uk/depsta/education/research/AKSIS.html

Chapter 19

Access and engagement for all

Any classroom contains children of widely differing interests, experience, ability and motivation for learning, presenting a considerable challenge to their teachers who have to maximise opportunities for each one to learn. This chapter sets out the principles for meeting this challenge in a primary science classroom. It begins with the description of a lesson where these learning opportunities are indeed present and then discusses six aspects of teaching that are significant in providing engagement for all in learning.

Brenda Keogh and **Stuart Naylor**

Engaging all children

In Box 19.1 there is a glimpse of a classroom in which the teacher has created learning opportunities for all the children despite their individual differences in development and experience. How has the teacher managed to maximise access and engagement in this way? What factors have been taken into account in planning and teaching the lesson? Some of these factors relate to the nature of the activities provided for the children, but how they are presented makes a big difference to access and engagement. For example, in the activity using true/false statements the teacher was able to:

- create an engaging stimulus that captured the children's attention;
- get children thinking and talking;
- provide problems to be solved;
- help children to set their own learning agenda;
- ensure there was a clear sense of purpose to follow-up activities.

The range of activities that followed also helped to provide:

- further opportunities for discussion and argument;

Box 19.1 A glimpse into a productive classroom

Imagine the situation. You walk into a science lesson. There is an intangible but noticeable buzz as children work. As you look around all the children seem to be productively occupied. They are engaged in activities that maintain their concentration. They are talking animatedly. You can tell from the expressions on their faces that there is a lot of thinking going on.

You find yourself wondering how the teacher achieved this. You talk to some of the children and find out that the teacher began the lesson with a set of true/false statements, which they discussed in small groups. After a few minutes the teacher gathered their ideas together and identified areas where they couldn't agree or were uncertain. This was followed by thinking and discussion about how to resolve these areas of uncertainty. Children used a range of resources to explore their ideas, including models, books, CD-ROMs, Internet access and structured worksheets. Towards the end of the lesson they reported back on what they had found out, with a range of types of evidence gained from the different sources. The teacher asked questions and contributed ideas to clarify, challenge and support their understanding. Finally they summarised their learning in pairs.

- questions to promote thinking and reasoning;
- opportunities for active involvement of children – minds on, not just hands on;
- a range of ways of accessing ideas and information.

Underpinning the lesson was the teacher's awareness of more complex aspects of teaching and learning that influence children's access and engagement. Some of the most important aspects include:

- recognising the importance of children's feelings;
- taking children's ideas into account;
- using a range of teaching and learning styles;
- using a range of differentiation strategies;
- using language to promote access and engagement;
- making good use of assessment.

In the following sections each of these aspects is considered further.

Recognising the importance of children's feelings

This may seem like an odd place to begin to describe factors that influence access and engagement. But learning isn't just an academic, cognitive process. Learners also have emotional and social needs (Hodson, 1998), and if these needs are not met then engagement and learning will suffer.

Children's feelings count. How children feel about themselves, the activity they are engaged in, their teachers and their schools, makes a difference to how they engage in learning (Keogh and Naylor, 2004). As adults we realise how close the connection is between how people respond to our ideas and how we feel about ourselves. Children are no different. If we want them to engage fully with learning activities and to put real effort into their thinking, then we need to provide the kind of learning environment in which they feel comfortable doing that.

That means doing all that we can to provide a supportive classroom climate. We need to respect children as individuals, to respect their ideas, to suspend judgement when they offer their ideas and to maximise opportunities to succeed. Children who are willing partners in learning are more effective learners. Motivated children are more willing to share the responsibility for their learning with the teacher, showing commitment to their learning, working at overcoming problems, asking for advice when necessary and keeping the teacher informed about their progress where possible. This sharing of responsibility helps to ensure that the demands of an activity are reasonably well matched to their capabilities and that activities are appropriate and accessible.

Taking children's ideas into account

This can be easier to say than to carry out in practice. Teachers often suggest several reasons why it can be difficult, such as the need to plan lessons in advance, the time it takes to find out children's ideas and the practical difficulties of responding to individuals at the same time as teaching the rest of the class. However, recognising and valuing their ideas is an important part of engaging children. Starting lessons by getting children to share their ideas in a structured way, with the teacher and with each other, helps them to clarify what they think. This provides a focus for discussion and argument and makes follow-up activities more purposeful and engaging.

Of course, taking children's ideas into account can't mean planning a different investigation or activity for every child. In most circumstances this isn't possible. However, it is generally possible to start lessons with children clarifying what they understand and where they are uncertain through some structured activity, so that the purpose of an enquiry or investigation is related to testing out their ideas. In this way, children can be working on the same topic, carrying out similar investigations, but with different purposes in mind. Learning becomes personalised as children build on their individual starting points, and this helps to ensure access at the most suitable level. This is precisely what the teacher did through the use of true/false statements in the lesson described in Box 19.1.

There are many other strategies, such as card sorts and predict–observe–explain, that are ideal for helping children to explore their ideas in this way. When used as the focus for discussion they can make eliciting the children's ideas a natural part of the learning process. More examples can be found in White and Gunstone (1992) and in Naylor, Keogh and Goldsworthy (2004). These kinds of strategies can all be used to present alternative viewpoints, to give children challenges and to link the sharing of ideas with productive learning opportunities. Teachers who use these kinds of approaches are quick to identify how effectively they get children motivated and engaged in the learning process, so that sharing ideas creates a purpose for follow-up activities that help to develop their ideas further.

Using a range of teaching and learning styles

It is now commonly accepted that people can have different preferred learning styles. Some of us may learn most effectively through text, others through discussion, others through hands-on activity, and so on. Clearly this is relevant to access and engagement, since some children will respond better to certain styles of teaching than others.

However, we need to be very cautious in how we interpret this information. Children do not use or learn through just one particular learning style. Each will have a range of learning styles that they use more or less effectively in different settings, and the understanding that teachers have about individuals' preferred learning styles is limited. Making simplistic judgements about a child's learning style will not enhance either access or engagement. The issue of whether to *reinforce* children's preferred learning styles or *extend* their possible learning styles is crucial. When should the teacher attempt to use the children's preferred learning styles? When should the teacher attempt to extend children's capabilities by using other learning styles? There are no easy answers to these questions.

Edward de Bono provided a different perspective in his book, *Six thinking hats* (de Bono, 1985). In this he recognises six different styles of thinking, each of them valuable at different times and for different reasons. Similarly, a good way forward in the classroom is to recognise and use a broad range of learning styles. Since it is difficult to plan to meet individual preferences, offering experiences that encompass a broad range of learning styles will be helpful to all children (as in the lesson in Box 19.1). This will provide valuable variety in teaching and learning, and help to ensure that no children are continually disadvantaged by always using teaching approaches that do not suit them. This can apply to how activities are presented, how they are recorded and how much independence children have during the activity. Offering children some choice of learning styles where possible increases the opportunity for personal preferences to be taken into account.

Using a range of differentiation strategies

There was a time when differentiation in science teaching and learning seemed to mean that teachers should provide different activities for children of different 'abilities'. Teaching often became organised around a series of graded worksheets for children to follow. As well as presenting severe practical difficulties, this approach did not necessarily lead to better engagement by children. Learning sometimes became fragmented as children did everything on their own, and 'death by a thousand worksheets' became a common expression. Another consequence was that children with less well-developed linguistic skills were often given tasks that were scientifically undemanding.

There are now many useful outlines of a wider range of strategies that can be used to promote better differentiation in science education. These include, for example:

- varying the level of scientific procedural skill required, while the scientific conceptual demand remains the same;
- varying the level of linguistic or mathematical demand in an activity and providing different levels of support in these respects;
- using a wide variety of resources to support learning, including information technology;
- using the same set of activities but varying the pace or sequence of learning;

- offering different types and amounts of support for learning, including small-group tutoring, peer support, careful monitoring, additional guidance and additional challenges;
- expecting different outcomes from children and responding in different ways to these outcomes, including careful use of productive questions;
- providing a degree of choice for children where possible, to enable them to develop their differing interests and aptitudes.

Further details of these and other strategies can be found in Keogh and Naylor (2002) and McNamara and Moreton (1997).

As with learning style, offering variety in the approaches used for differentiation is realistic for teachers and engaging for children. Actively involving children in the learning process is a key principle for maximising engagement. This can include building on their ideas and giving some choice in how an activity is carried out, how it is recorded or presented and what resources are used. If children have a useful part to play in ensuring differentiation then they will find lessons more accessible and engaging than if they view it as a process done to them by teachers.

Using language to promote access and engagement

There are plenty of well-documented challenges concerning the language of science, such as the specialist vocabulary and the formal structure of scientific reports (see Chapter 18). However, good use of language can really open doors for access and engagement.

Variety in the language used in the classroom can make lessons more interesting and therefore more engaging. Using a multisensory approach connects with different children's preferred learning styles and makes science more accessible. Wellington and Osborne (2001) provide very useful guidance about all aspects of language use in science lessons.

Talk

Providing opportunities for talk is crucial, especially talk involving some kind of scientific argument. Talk should not be just between teachers and children, important as this is, but also amongst children themselves. The lesson described in Box 19.1 contains plenty of opportunities for talk amongst children. Child–child talk not only clarifies thinking, promotes understanding and helps them to learn to reason; it also makes a massive difference to their engagement. There are few stimuli more effective at the beginning of a lesson than getting children engaged in an argument about that topic. Unfortunately it is all too easy for teachers to dominate classroom talk. Giving children information, asking lots of recall questions, being judgemental about children's answers, being anxious about talking getting out of control: all of these tend to lead to teachers filling the spaces and leaving little opportunity for children's talk. While confident children are likely to create their own spaces for talk, less confident children can easily be excluded from classroom conversation.

Questions

Talk also involves questions. Questions from the teacher may be closed, low-

155

level and unproductive, or more open, more exploratory and more productive. Which type of question do you find more engaging as an adult? Which type of question do you think children will find more engaging? Questions from children can be a superb stimulus for learning. This is especially evident with young children, who soon begin to recognise the value of asking questions. It is possible to create a climate of enquiry in the classroom in which children's questions are encouraged and valued (see Chapter 21). It is also possible to discourage their questions ('*they ask too many questions, they ask trivial questions, I may not know the answers, it takes too long, ...*'), and it is noticeable how quickly they can get out of the habit of asking questions as they go through school.

Writing

Writing in science lessons can be low-level, routine and time-consuming, so it isn't really surprising that so many children don't like doing it. Low-attaining children are often slow writers and they can easily become bogged down in writing, leaving little time for anything else. Writing can be made more active and engaging by using a wider variety of writing styles, such as news reports, diary entries, information leaflets or sets of instructions. These provide an obvious purpose for writing, but it is important to avoid writing dominating the lesson.

Making good use of assessment

There is no conflict between teaching that is engaging and high levels of achievement by children. Quite the opposite, since engagement and motivation are necessary for effective learning and high levels of achievement. Even dull and uninspiring formal testing doesn't require dull and uninspiring teaching as preparation for the tests.

Assessment also influences how we feel about ourselves, by giving us feedback about how well we are doing, and this can make a big difference to engagement and learning. Harlen (2003) summarises a wealth of evidence that highlights the impact of assessment on self-esteem, motivation and learning. Of course this can be a positive or a negative difference, and one of the challenges for teachers is to try to use assessment in ways that enhance rather than damage self-esteem.

The term 'active assessment' (Naylor, Keogh and Goldsworthy, 2004) refers to activities that begin the learning process at the same time as providing valuable assessment information. Generally these will be used as collaborative activities that promote discussion and argument. The true/false statements in the lesson described in Box 19.1 are a good example of active assessment. Children do not usually view these strategies as assessment, with all the negative connotations that assessment can have for them, but they do provide valuable assessment information. In this way, through a combination of self-, peer- and teacher-assessment, the learning needs of children can become more apparent but without the damage to self-esteem sometimes caused by more formal assessment procedures.

More extensive detail about the links between assessment and learning is provided in Chapters 22 and 23.

Conclusion

Two themes that run through this chapter are collaboration and personalisation. Collaborative activities give children confidence and security; they promote thinking and reasoning; they encourage talk and argument; they enable self- and peer-assessment to occur. Paradoxically, they can also help to personalise learning. As children become more involved in the activity they begin to make judgements about their own ideas in relation to some of the alternative possibilities. As they recognise the boundaries of their own understanding they begin to create their own learning agenda and see the purpose of follow-up activities. For most children most of the time, collaborative learning is accessible and engaging; equally, personalised learning is accessible and engaging.

Other important themes in this chapter are variety, creativity and pupil choice. They are evident in the teacher's choice of elicitation strategies, teaching and learning styles, the approaches used for differentiation, the language register used, and so on. These themes overlap and interact, enabling teachers to develop a coherent teaching style designed to engage and motivate children. Of course there is never any guarantee that children will be engaged, but there is every point in trying to achieve this. As Woolnough puts it:

> If students are motivated, and if they are given the freedom and opportunity, they will find ways of learning. If they are not, they will not bother.
> (Woolnough, 1994, p. 111)

References

de Bono, E. (1985) *Six thinking hats*. London: Penguin.

Harlen, W. (2003) How high stakes testing impacts on motivation for learning. *Science Teacher Education*, **37**, 2–5.

Hodson, D. (1998) *Teaching and learning science*. Buckingham: Open University Press.

Keogh, B. and Naylor, S. (2002) Dealing with differentiation. In *Aspects of teaching secondary science*, ed. Amos, S. and Boohan, R. pp. 269–278. London: Open University Press.

Keogh, B. and Naylor, S. (2004) Children's ideas, children's feelings. *Primary Science Review*, **82**, 18–20.

McNamara, S. and Moreton, G. (1997) *Understanding differentiation*. London: David Fulton.

Naylor, S., Keogh, B. and Goldsworthy, A. (2004) *Active assessment: thinking, learning and assessment in science*. Sandbach, Cheshire: Millgate House Publishers.

Wellington, J. and Osborne, J. (2001) *Language and literacy in science education*. Buckingham: Open University Press.

White, R. and Gunstone, R. (1992) *Probing understanding*. London: Falmer Press.

Woolnough, B. (1994) *Effective science teaching*. Buckingham: Open University Press.

Chapter 20

Talk in science classrooms

Language provides the fundamental means for communicating ideas, but it is

Hilary Asoko and **Phil Scott**

also through talk, either with others or 'in our heads', that we can develop personal understanding. This chapter expands on the reasons for the importance of talk in the classroom and its particular value in science education. It first describes the characteristics of different kinds of verbal communication between teacher and pupils in terms of two dimensions: interactive and non-interactive; and authoritative and dialogic. The nature and impact on learning of exploratory pupil–pupil talk is then discussed.

Why is talk important?

Robin Alexander made the statement in Box 20.1 based on his extensive study of primary education in five countries. In this section we explore some of the reasons for the importance of talk in science learning, the kinds of talk that might be used and how these can be matched to different teaching purposes.

Box 20.1 Talk in science

... in English primary classrooms, although much may be made of the importance of talk in learning, and a great deal of talking goes on, its function is seen as primarily social rather than cognitive, and as 'helpful' to learning rather than as fundamental to it.

(Alexander, 2000, p. 566)

In any classroom, talk is clearly important to the teacher as a way of communicating expectations, giving instructions, explaining ideas, monitoring understanding and controlling activity. However, talk is also central to the process of *learning*. It is a common experience that if we want to make sense of difficult ideas, talking them through with others usually helps. Talk in the classroom provides children with a way to express and to work on ideas, to explore their implications and to share, compare and consolidate understanding.

Science lessons provide plenty of opportunities for talk. There are phenomena to discuss, ideas to explore, practical activities to carry out, results to report and evidence to interpret. Through these activities children can learn how to talk and think about natural phenomena in a scientific, as opposed to an everyday (or common-sense), way. This means using the ideas, explanations and approaches of the scientific community and it is important to recognise that these ideas and explanations are not there to be 'discovered' from hands-on activities. They arise from thinking and trying out ideas and are *'talked into existence'* (Ogborn *et al.*, 1996) with, and by, the children. Language is thus crucial to science learning.

However, everyday ways of thinking and talking may cause confusion. For example, common words such as force, power or weight may have specific or different meanings in science. The ways in which language is used in science may make particular demands, for example when reporting results, structuring an argument or reaching conclusions based on evidence. In some science topic areas there may be big differences between everyday and scientific accounts of phenomena and this can lead to big teaching and learning challenges (Leach and Scott, 2002). For example, there is a considerable difference in the thinking behind an everyday account of a ball falling as a result of a personal action, *'because you let go of it'*, and the scientific view, based on forces acting at a distance, *'because of the pull of the Earth'*.

Effective teacher–pupil and pupil–pupil interactions are the key to supporting children in making personal sense of the science we wish them to learn and in developing their ability to reason scientifically. With this in mind we might begin to think about activities in terms of their potential to stimulate and support different kinds of talk. This is rather different from thinking simply in terms of 'what children will do'.

The word 'interactive' can be used in many senses in relation to teaching. In the next sections we use it in relation only to verbal activity in the classroom and to those aspects of classroom talk that are concerned with learning, rather than with management.

Teacher–pupil talk in the classroom

We can think about classroom talk along two dimensions (Mortimer and Scott, 2003) which address, firstly, who is speaking and, secondly, whose points of view are being discussed.

Who is speaking – the interactive and non-interactive dimension

The interactive/non-interactive dimension describes the extent to which the teacher involves the children in the dialogue. *Interactive* talk allows for the participation of both teacher and children, for example when a teacher engages children in a series of questions and answers. *Non-interactive* talk, on the other hand, involves only the teacher and largely excludes the verbal participation of the children.

Whose ideas are being discussed – the dialogic and authoritative dimension

The authoritative/dialogic dimension describes the extent to which the teacher takes account of different points of view and ensures that these are represented through talk. *Dialogic* talk involves exploring answers or comments further by asking for more detail (*'That's interesting, why do you think that might be?'*), asking other children whether they agree with it or not (*'Do you go along with what Anita has just said?'*), making links to what someone else has said or done (*'That sounds like what David said earlier about ...'*) or writing it down for further consideration (*'Let's just put that down on the board, so we don't forget it.'*). In this way, the teacher makes room in the classroom talk for a whole range of ideas and makes it possible to consider the children's points of view as well as the school science view.

Of course, classroom talk is not always dialogic in form. There are occasions when the teacher does not explore and take account of children's ideas as they arise in the development of the lesson but keeps the focus on the science point of view. If ideas or questions are raised that do not contribute to the development of the school science story they are likely to be reshaped or ignored by the teacher. This is *authoritative* talk.

Classes of communicative approach

Any episode of classroom talk can be identified as being largely *interactive* or *non-interactive* on the one hand, and *dialogic* or *authoritative* on the other. These can be combined (Figure 20.1) to form four broad classes of *communicative approach* (Mortimer and Scott, 2003).

	Interactive	Non-interactive
Authoritative	*interactive/authoritative*	*non-interactive/dialogic*
Dialogic	*interactive/dialogic*	*non-interactive/authoritative*

Figure 20.1 **Four classes of communicative approach.**

What might each of these classes of communicative approach look like in the classroom? We start with the two *interactive* approaches. Both involve a great many teacher questions. However, the purpose of these questions and the ways in which children's responses are used, distinguish the two approaches.

Interactive/authoritative communicative approach

This example is from a year 4 class (8/9-year-olds). The teacher is talking about a shadow of a face on a screen. The shape making the shadow has holes for the eyes and mouth.

Teacher: *So what are the mouth and eyes?*
Amy: *Holes*
Teacher: *Yes, and what goes through the holes?*
Amy: *Light*
Teacher: *The light. So what makes the shape of the face?*
Perdip: *The paper's blocking the light.*
Teacher: *The paper's blocking the light isn't it, to make the face. So it's a shadow. So what does that tell us about the light? How does the light travel?*
Fiona: *At light speed.*
Teacher: *Yes, I know it travels at light speed but does it travel in wavy lines?*

Perdip: *No, straight.*
Teacher: *Straight. If it travelled in wavy lines it'd be all scattered over there but because it travels in straight lines we get quite a sharp image.*

Here the teacher wants to use the formation of a shadow to support ideas introduced in a previous lesson, that light travels in straight lines and that shadows are formed when light is blocked. Relevant responses from the children, about light being blocked by the paper but travelling through the holes, are reinforced by agreement or repetition. Fiona's response about *'light speed'* is not directly relevant and, though acknowledged, is ignored; the teacher introduces the possibility of light travelling in *'wavy lines'* to bring the discussion back on track. The teacher is using an *interactive/authoritative* communicative approach. The talk is interactive in the sense of there being lots of questions and answers and is authoritative as the teacher wants to focus on answers that support the scientific view. There is a repeating *pattern of discourse*, with teacher questions directing and structuring the conversation, as in Box 20.2.

Box 20.2 Pattern of the interactive/authoritative approach		
Teacher asks a question:	INITIATION (I)	*So what are the mouth and eyes?*
Child responds:	RESPONSE (R)	*Holes.*
Teacher evaluates:	EVALUATION (E)	*Yes ...*
Teacher asks a question:	INITIATION (I)	*... and what goes through the holes?*
Pattern: I–R–E; I–R–E; I–R–E;		

Interactive/dialogic communicative approach

Of course, there is an alternative to the authoritative form of interactive talk set out above. This is where the teacher sets up interactions that are dialogic in approach. Here the intention is to open up the dialogue to include many points of view or to explore a particular way of thinking. In an earlier lesson the year 4 class had discussed shadows in the classroom which were produced by different light sources:

Teacher: *So what's a shadow?*
Simon: *Darkness.*
Sally: *A kind of reflection.*
Teacher: *A kind of reflection. And you think the same [in response to several children agreeing]? Let's follow this reflection business. In what way is it like a reflection?*
Sally: *It's kind of like a reflection of yourself.*
Teacher: *It's like a reflection of yourself ...*
John: *When you're in the mirror.*
Sally: *But it's not coloured.*
Teacher: *It's like a reflection of yourself except it's not coloured. Why is it not coloured?*
Harpreet: *The shadow's grey and dark.*
Teacher: *The shadow's grey and dark but why is it dark? Yes?*

Harpreet: *Because it's standing in the way of the light so light, when it reflects on to the light it makes it darker.*

Teacher: *Hang on, Sally says it's like a reflection and that puzzles me because a reflection has usually got my own features if it's a reflection of me. I see it wave back to me and it's got eyes and a nose and if I look at my shadow it definitely hasn't and Sally says it's a reflection which is not coloured. Go on Sally.*

Sally: *Well like when light shines on to something and then it makes darkness and then your shadow goes into the light and it makes you look dark.*

Teacher: *So what causes the shadow?*

Michael/Sally [together]: The sun.

John: *It's the opposite ... because of the sun, if the sun was in front, your shadow would be behind you.*

This discussion continued for some time, exploring and clarifying ideas. The teacher, well aware that children often use the word reflection when talking about shadows, used the opportunity to explore the essential differences between the two phenomena and, subsequently, the ideas that children introduced about light being 'blocked' to form a shadow.

The distinctive *pattern of discourse* in this case involves chains of interaction rather than the repeating I–R–E pattern of the authoritative talk (Box 20.3). The teacher started by asking a question, but followed up the response with a series of *prompts* to encourage further contributions from children in relation to the response.

Box 20.3 Pattern of the interactive/dialogic approach		
Teacher asks a question: INITIATION (I)		*So what's a shadow?*
Child responds:	RESPONSE (R)	*A kind of reflection.*
Teacher prompts:	PROMPT (P)	*In what way is it like a reflection?*
Child responds:	RESPONSE (R)	*It's kind of like a reflection of yourself.*
Teacher prompts:	PROMPT (P)	*It's like a reflection of yourself ...*
Child responds:	RESPONSE (R)	*... but it's not coloured.*
Pattern: I–R–P–R–P–R–P ...		

A chain of interaction, I–R–P–R–P–R–P–, is set up and the skill of the teacher lies in sustaining the development of the interaction, encouraging responses from a range of children. When a number of children answer the same question from the teacher, the response from a child might not necessarily address the initial question posed by the teacher; it might be a comment on a previous child's response.

Although question-and-answer sequences have often been criticised as requiring children to 'guess what is in the teacher's head' we can see that, used effectively, they can provide opportunities for teachers to structure dialogue in ways that support children in constructing a scientific explanation (*authoritative*) and allow them to explore and explain their developing understanding (*dialogic*).

Non-interactive approaches

At first glance, the very notion of a *non-interactive/dialogic* communicative approach might seem like a contradiction in terms. How can the teacher be presenting (*non-interactive*) and yet attending to both the science and the children's points of view (*dialogic*)? It is possible if the teacher draws upon a range of ideas, usually in the context of a review or summary.

Consider this example, from the same year 4 class as the previous examples:

Teacher: *I think we're talking about two different things. I think on the one hand we're talking about a patch of light and what we're really trying to talk about is a patch of darkness aren't we? The shadow and not the light. I think we're getting the two things confused ... I hadn't thought about it really until you brought it up just then, that the more powerful light seems to make the darker shadow, but there's also something to do with distance ... but I think the important point that you've made is that the shadow has to do with one light doesn't it? The shadow of the table on the floor has to do with the light from the sun, nothing to do with this [a lamp on the table] ... and the shadow may be dark or light and a lot seems to depend on the strength of the light.*

Right. We'll leave that for the time being. To sum up what we've said so far. To have a shadow you have to have two things. Thomas said you need something to block the light and somebody else, I think it was Sophina, said you need to have a light as well. You have to have two things, light and something to block the light, and the shadow is where the light is blocked and it's dark. Is that right?

Here the teacher is initially using a *non-interactive/dialogic* approach to summarise ideas that have been offered during an extensive discussion of shadows observed in the classroom, how they are made and why some appear darker than others. The question of how the brightness of the source or its distance from the object affects the darkness of the shadow remains open for further investigation. At the point where the teacher says '*Right*' the approach shifts to *non-interactive/authoritative* and the standard science view is clearly presented.

Matching communicative approach to teaching purposes

In the previous sections we have set out and exemplified four distinct communicative approaches that might be used in the classroom. Is one communicative approach intrinsically better than another? For example, is teaching which uses interactive/dialogic talk better than that using interactive/authoritative talk? Is non-interactive teaching bad, simply because it's the teacher who is doing all the talking? These are important and absolutely fundamental questions. The answer to them is that:

Effective teaching involves all of these approaches. It depends on what you are trying to do!

For example, if the aim is to discuss ideas, explore understanding and raise questions then an interactive/dialogic approach which develops chains of discourse is needed (see Box 20.4).

Box 20.4 Pattern for exploring understanding

Teaching purpose: To explore children's understandings.

Communicative approach: Interactive/dialogic.

Pattern of interaction: Open chains of communication I–R–P–R–P–R–P...

If, on the other hand, the teaching purpose is to introduce a key scientific concept, then this approach is unlikely to be helpful. Instead the combinations in Box 20.5 need to be used.

Box 20.5 Pattern for introducing concepts

Teaching purpose: To introduce a scientific concept or develop a clear line of argument.

Communicative approach: Non-interactive/authoritative and/or interactive/authoritative.

Pattern of interaction: Presentational and/or I–R–E.

A non-interactive/dialogic approach allows the teacher to review 'where we are up to in our thinking' by considering and summarising a range of ideas (Box 20.6).

Box 20.6 Pattern for summing up

Teaching purpose: To consider a range of points of view.

Communicative approach: Non-interactive/dialogic.

Pattern of interaction: Presentational.

The 'rhythm' of the classroom talk

What is suggested here is that in any teaching sequence it makes sense to adopt a range of approaches matched to teaching purposes in the ways outlined above. Expert teachers demonstrate a 'rhythm' in their teaching, whereby now they open up matters for discussion (*interactive/dialogic*), now they work on helping children to understand and use the science point of view (*interactive/authoritative*), now they summarise the science view (*non-interactive/authoritative*) and link it to children's thinking and experience (*non-interactive/dialogic*). There is no special order in which they go about these transitions but there is a strong sense of rhythm as ideas are opened up for discussion and then closed down.

Pupil–pupil talk

In a whole-class setting, the opportunities for individuals to talk are inevitably limited. Working in groups or pairs provides opportunities for more children to participate and to explore and develop their understanding but, without the support of the teacher, children may lack the skills to talk productively. Teachers, therefore, have a responsibility to model, in their interactions with children, the kinds of interactive/dialogic talk that they are aiming for in group work:

offering ideas, listening to others, asking for clarification, making links to others' ideas and so on. In addition, the skills needed for such talk can be taught (Dawes, 2004), to allow children to develop their ability to think things through both together and alone.

Although teachers may encourage children to talk in groups, Mercer *et al.* point out that they are rarely given any guidance on doing this effectively:

> *Children cannot be expected to bring to a task a well-developed capacity for reasoned dialogue. This is especially true for the kinds of discursive skills which are important for learning and practising science: describing observations clearly, reasoning about cause and effects, posing precise questions, formulating hypotheses, critically examining competing explanations, summarizing results, and so on.*

(Mercer *et al.*, 2004, p. 362)

Without guidance, talk among children may be 'disputational' (unproductive disagreements) or 'cumulative' (often repetitious and uncritical) but rarely 'exploratory' – the term used when talk has the characteristics listed in Box 20.7.

Box 20.7 Characteristics of exploratory talk

In exploratory talk:
- all relevant information is shared;
- all members of the group are invited to contribute to the discussion;
- opinions and ideas are respected and considered;
- everyone is asked to make their reasons clear;
- challenges and alternatives are made explicit and are negotiated;
- the group seeks to reach agreement before taking a decision or acting.

(Mercer *et al.*, 2004, p. 362)

Mercer *et al.* (2004) investigated the effect of helping children to use exploratory talk on the children's understanding of science. In this study the researchers developed a 'Thinking Together' intervention programme for teachers to use. This comprised a series of lessons in which the children were first introduced to 'ground rules' designed to encourage exploratory talk and then given opportunities to practise these skills in their group work. Various analyses of their talk in groups were conducted; these showed that the programme resulted in increased use of words indicating exploratory talk, with children explaining and justifying their views in longer utterances. Assessment of their science knowledge and understanding showed that the children who had experienced the programme increased their science scores significantly more than control groups of children. Tests of reasoning also showed a significant difference between the gains made by groups with and without the programme.

Concluding comment

Talk, whether initiated by teachers or taking place among children, provides important learning opportunities. How such talk is stimulated, its content and its nature are key to its impact. The framework set out in this chapter enables us to think about the kinds of talk used in teacher–pupil exchanges. Teachers also need to consider how they encourage pupil–pupil discussion so that the talk is exploratory and advances children's thinking. In combination such classroom experiences will support children in developing their scientific understanding. To quote Alexander (2004, p. 5):

Reading, writing and number may be the acknowledged curriculum 'basics', but talk is arguably the true foundation of learning.

References

Alexander, R. (2004) *Towards dialogic teaching: rethinking classroom talk*. York: Dialogos.

Alexander, R. (2000) *Culture and pedagogy: international comparisons in primary education*. Oxford: Blackwell.

Dawes, L. (2004) Talk and learning in classroom science. *International Journal of Science Education*, **26**(6), 677–695.

Leach, J. and Scott, P. (2002) Designing and evaluating science teaching sequences: an approach drawing upon the concept of learning demand and a social constructivist perspective on learning. *Studies in Science Education*, **38**, 115–142.

Mercer, N., Dawes, L., Wegerif, R. and Sams, C. (2004) Reasoning as a scientist: ways of helping children to use language to learn science. *British Educational Research Journal*, **30**(3), 359–377.

Mortimer, E. F. and Scott, P. H. (2003) *Meaning making in secondary science classrooms*. Maidenhead: Open University Press.

Ogborn, J., Kress, G., Martins, I. and McGillicuddy, K. (1996) *Explaining science in the classroom*. Buckingham: Open University Press.

Chapter 21

Teachers' and children's questioning

Questioning is a key feature of scientific activity and of teaching science. Asking questions leads scientists to seek answers through enquiry and so develop understanding of the world around. Children's scientific activity, too, is stimulated by questions, sometimes implicit rather than explicit, sometimes raised by the teachers and sometimes by the children. What is important is the way that a question is accepted by the class and that the child sees it as a question worth answering and is motivated to seek an answer. It is in helping this search for answers through scientific activity that the role of teachers' questions is so important. The chapter begins with teachers' questions and turns later to how to encourage and deal with the questions that children ask.

Wynne Harlen

Questions for different purposes

There are several reasons for giving attention to the questions teachers ask. First, they are by far the most common form of communication between teachers and children. Second, they have the potential to stimulate children's thinking and guide their effort productively. Third, the questions often fail to do this because they are not appropriately worded. For example, research shows that the overwhelming majority of teachers' questions are 'closed' and a large proportion of these ask for facts. Whilst occasional questioning of what the children know is expected, often teachers ask a factual question when what they really want is the children to give their ideas or think things out. Finally, changing questioning is one of the most effective steps to take in improving teaching.

Teachers ask a number of different kinds of questions for different purposes, such as for class control, checking on whether instructions have been understood or routines followed, or asking for information. The questions that

Box 21.1

The wording of teachers' questions

Consider a situation in which a primary teacher has provided lots of home-made and other musical instruments for children to explore as a preliminary to more structured activities aimed at developing the idea that sound is caused by objects vibrating. To find out the ideas the children already have the teacher might ask questions such as:

1 *Explain to me what is happening when you hear the sound?*

2 *Why does the sound change when you shorten the string?*

3 *What causes the guitar to make a sound?*

4 *Explain why you are able to make the bottle make a sound by blowing across the top?* etc.

Or (s)he might ask:

5 *What do you think makes the sound when you pluck the string?*

6 *What are your ideas about how the guitar makes a sound?*

7 *What do you think is the reason for the bottle making a sound when you blow across the top?*

8 *What do you think is going on when the drum makes a sound?*

9 *What are your ideas about why you get different sounds when you shorten the string?* etc.

Or, again, (s)he might ask:

10 *What can you do to make a sound from the bottle?*

11 *What do you see happening when the drum makes a sound?*

12 *What do you think will happen if you make the string even shorter?*

13 *How do you think you can change the note you get when you blow across the top of the bottle?*

14 What could you do to find out if how you pluck the string makes a difference?

The questions in the first set (1–4) are open in form, as opposed to closed questions where a short one-word answer is all that is required. However, these questions ask directly for *the* answer, not the children's ideas about what is happening. By contrast, the questions in the second set (5–9) are expressed so as to ask for the children's ideas, with no suggestion that there is a right answer. They are described as 'person-centred' as opposed to 'subject-centred' questions. All the children should be able to answer the second set, while only those who feel that they can give the right answer will attempt to answer the first set. Thus the open, person-centred questions are preferred for eliciting children's ideas.

The questions in the third set (10–14) are also open and person-centred, but they are more likely to lead to *action* and to the use of enquiry skills rather than to the expression of ideas because they do not ask for explanations. So the content of these questions makes them useful for finding out about children's ability to observe or investigate or use other skills.

Evidently small changes in wording of a question can have a big impact on how children respond.

are our concern here are those asking about children's ideas or encouraging the use and development of enquiry skills. For these questions to be effective their form, content and timing need to be appropriate for their purpose. These three aspects are interconnected and all need to be considered in framing questions. Box 21.1 illustrates how just small changes in wording can make a difference.

The examples in Box 21.1 indicate the difference the form of a question (open/closed; person-centred/subject-centred) can make to how children respond. They also show that the content of the question has to reflect the kind of response intended. If the intention of the question is to encourage children to use enquiry skills then the question needs to indicate the skill that is required. For example, in the case of an activity related to shadows:

- *What would you like to find out about shadows?* (raising questions)
- *What do you think will happen if we move the object this way?* (prediction)
- *What could you do to find out what makes a difference to the size of the shadow?* (investigation)
- *What have you found out about the link between the position of the torch and the size of the shadow?* (interpretation)

Timing is also important. When starting a new topic, children need time to explore and relate new experiences to existing ones before they can be expected to explain what is going on. So, *'How can you make different sounds?'* should come before *'How do you think these sounds are produced?'*

A further important point about teachers' questioning concerns giving children time to answer. Research (Budd Rowe, 1974) showed that, after asking a question, teachers frequently wait no longer than one second before intervening again if no answer is forthcoming. When they were advised to increase the 'wait' time to eight to ten seconds, after asking questions that required explanations, the children's answers were longer and more thoughtful. The 'wait' time is necessary not only to allow the children to think and to formulate their answers, but to convey the message that the teacher is really interested in their ideas or their skills and will listen to their answers carefully. It also slows down the discussion, giving the teacher time to phrase thoughtful questions and the children time to think before answering. The whole exchange is then more productive in terms of giving teachers access to children's real understanding and not just their first superficial thoughts. A teacher's experience of changing this aspect of her questioning, as a result of work described by Black *et al.* (2002), is reproduced in Box 21.2.

Encouraging and responding to children's questions

Another part of the teacher's role in relation to questions is responding to the questions that children ask. There is value to both children and teachers in encouraging children to ask questions. Through their questions, children reveal the limits of their understanding and the nature of their own ideas. But by no means all of their questions will be ones that lead to scientific activity. So teachers need to be prepared to respond to, though not necessarily to provide an answer to, the variety of questions that children ask. Coming to grips with this is particularly important for primary teachers who may be wary of being

Box 21.2

A teacher's experience of changing her 'wait' time

Increasing waiting time after asking questions proved difficult to start with – due to my habitual desire to 'add' something almost immediately after asking the original questions. The pause after asking the questions was sometimes 'painful'. It felt unnatural to have such a seemingly 'dead' period, but I persevered. Given more thinking time students seemed to realise that a more thoughtful answer was required. Now, after many months of changing my style of questioning, I have noticed that most students will give an answer and an explanation (where necessary) without additional prompting.

(Quoted in Black *et al.*, 2002, p. 5)

asked questions that they can't answer and consequently, often unconsciously, discourage questioning. We will come to how to deal with different kinds of questions later; first it is important to get the questions flowing.

Some teachers report that their children don't ask questions, so there is very little chance for them to have the satisfaction of finding answers to their own questions. The likely reason for children not asking questions is repeated past experience of not having any, or any satisfying, answers. The problem may well have its roots at the primary level and it is here where teachers can take action to encourage questions.

Encouraging questions at the primary level

Questions arise from curiosity, so the first point is to have materials, events and sometimes people, to stimulate interest and questions. The materials need not be novel. Often displays of familiar things, such as wood-working tools, different kinds of nails, screws, bolts, and so on, to which children can relate, are more effective in generating questions than the unfamiliar. Provision for children to bring in to school materials and objects to display means that these have built-in interest likely to be shared by other children.

Given a stimulus, questions can be elicited through:

- brainstorming as a whole class – the public acceptance of all questions of whatever kind will encourage those at first reluctant to express their questions;
- snowballing – raising questions in pairs or small groups, and then sharing with merged groups and then the whole class;
- a question box or board where children can post or pin up their questions anonymously;
- deciding the most useful questions to ask a visitor or during a visit out of school;
- discussing different kinds of questions and involving older children in categorising them in the way suggested below for teachers;
- using question stems as prompts to construct questions.

All of these will not only lead to really useful information for the teacher about what children want to know and what their current thinking is, but also make clear to the children that questioning is valued. Holding regular question-raising sessions where children can say what they would like to know about a topic they are working on can provide opportunity for children to find answers to their own questions. Such sessions can serve as a good stimulus when starting on a topic. Displaying the questions, reviewing and adding to them at intervals, enables children as well as teachers to be more aware of their developing understanding.

The easiest way to suppress questioning is to ignore questions, sweep them aside or make children feel foolish for asking. So handling questions in a way that takes them seriously, even if they can't be answered, is essential.

Handling children's questions

A useful first step when deciding how to respond to a child's question is to think about the kind of question it is and why it is being asked. Not all children's questions, as parents and teachers well know, are asked because of real interest in the answers. Some are attention-seeking, some delaying tactics, some probing for hints about what the teacher has in mind. Some questions are really expressions of interest or wonder that are put in the form of questions, but to which no answer is really expected. For example, young children looking at a bird's nest asked 'How do they weave it?' Rather than begin to answer this question by focusing their attention on how it might be done, the teacher judged it to be an expression of wonder in which she joined by saying 'Yes, it is wonderful, isn't it?'; the children's attention quickly moved on to other features of the nest.

Among the genuine questions there are likely to be ones that can be classified as falling into one of these four types:

- **Factual questions:** those asking for simple facts, e.g. 'What's the name of this rock?', 'How long does it take for a bird's egg to hatch?'
- **Investigable questions:** those that could be answered, at least in part, by observation or investigation by the children, e.g. 'What would happen if we plant the seeds/bulbs upside down?', 'Which of these rocks is the hardest?'
- **Complex questions:** those that require complex answers and reference to concepts that are beyond the understanding of the children, e.g. 'How do satellites stay in the sky?', 'Why do you see colours when there is oil in a puddle?'
- **Philosophical questions:** those that may be philosophical, e.g. 'Why do birds only have two legs?', 'Why do we have day and night?', 'Does light travel faster than God?'

Each of these types is best handled in a different way, and knowing some ways of doing this can take the anxiety out of encouraging children to ask questions.

Factual questions

These are questions that cannot be answered by the children's enquiry into the objects themselves because they refer to names, conventions and factual information. They can be answered immediately if the teacher knows the answer, or later when the teacher can look it up or can help the children find it by using reference sources – books, CD-ROMs, the Internet. Suitable questions

171

can be displayed on a board as *'This week's interesting questions'* to encourage other children to seek out answers.

Investigable questions

These are the questions of most value in science education. It is important for the teacher to recognise them and to resist the temptation to give the answer, which may seem obvious but it is of more value to the children if they find it for themselves. There is often need for some discussion of the question before it can be investigated. Turning a vague 'which is best' type of question into an investigation involves deciding what 'best' means in a particular case and whether the comparison is, for example, between types of material or specific objects or pieces of material.

It is quite likely that a question that can be profitably investigated by the children comes up at an inconvenient time. In that case it should be stored, perhaps on a list on the classroom wall of *'Things to investigate'*, or on a 'question tree' in the corner of the classroom, to be taken up at a later time. This is a way of acknowledging that the children's questions are valued – but it is important that they are not forgotten.

Complex questions

These may well seem the most difficult questions to handle, particularly because the teacher may not know the answer and if (s)he does, will realise that the children would not understand it. Giving complex answers may well send the message to children that science is difficult, and if they often find their questions met by answers they can't understand they are likely to stop asking questions. To prevent this, the question has to be discussed and can often be turned into one that children can investigate. For instance, the question about colours seen in an oil film can lead to investigations about where the oil is, that it floats on water, and about whether the thickness of the oil film makes a difference to the colours. This technique of 'turning' was suggested by Jelly (2001) who gave the example in Box 21.3. Jelly admits that the outcome is not a complete answer to the child's question, but it often satisfies the curiosity for the moment and underlines the message that in science answers can be found by enquiry.

Philosophical questions

These questions, also, require some discussion with the children asking them. Only then will it be possible to decide whether *'Why do we have day and night?'* means *'Who decided this?'* or *'What causes day and night?'* Frequently the question will be rephrased to make it clear that it falls in one of the other categories; if not, then it is only possible to agree that it is an interesting question but one to which no one can give a definite answer.

Discussing questions with children

The categories just suggested for teachers to use in deciding how to respond to children's questions can be shared with older children to help them begin to work out how to answer their own questions. The differences can be explained simply for primary children, perhaps by taking a collection of questions and asking them to decide: which can be answered by looking in a book or using another reference source; which can be answered by observation or

Box 21.3

Example of 'turning' a question

Consider, for example, a situation in which children are exploring the properties of fabrics. They have dropped water on different types and become fascinated by the fact that water stays 'like a little ball' on felt. They tilt the felt, rolling the ball around, and someone asks 'Why is it like a ball?' How might the question be turned by applying the 'doing more to understand' approach? We need to analyse the situation quickly and use what I call a 'variables scan'. The explanation must relate to something 'going on' between the water and the felt surface, so causing the ball. That being so, ideas for children's activities will come if we consider ways in which the situation could be varied to better understand the making of the ball. We could explore surfaces, keeping the drop the same, and explore drops, keeping the surface the same. These thoughts can prompt others that bring ideas nearer to what children might do.

(Jelly, 2001, pp. 44–45)

investigation; and which can't be answered by science. The AKSIS project (see website) developed activities, for both primary and secondary level, using model questions to be supplemented by the children's own, to discuss how they can find answers by different kinds of scientific enquiry (see also Chapter 18). Secondary pupils may be able to take this further, to develop understanding of what science is about, the nature of the knowledge it provides and its limitations in terms of the kinds of questions that we can answer through scientific activity. What is important is that questions, and particularly questions generated by children, are at the centre of science learning so that curiosity is stimulated and discussion takes a major role in science education.

References

Black, P., Harrison, C., Lee, C., Marshall, B. and Wiliam, D. (2002) *Working inside the black box*. London: nferNelson.

Budd Rowe, M. (1974) Wait time and rewards as instructional variables, their influence on language, logic and fate control. *Journal of Research in Science Teaching*, 11, 81–84.

Jelly, S. J. (2001) Helping children to raise questions – and answering them. In *Primary science: taking the plunge*, ed. W. Harlen, 2nd edn. Portsmouth, NH: Heinemann.

Website

AKSIS: www.kcl.ac.uk/depsta/education/research/AKSIS.html

Chapter 22

Assessment for learning and assessment of learning

All assessment involves collecting evidence of children's achievements, interpreting the evidence and using it for a defined purpose. This chapter is about carrying out this process for two main purposes: helping learning and reporting on learning. These are described as formative assessment, or assessment *for* learning, and summative assessment, or assessment *of* learning. The first section provides a rationale for the importance of formative assessment and considers what implementing it involves. This is followed by a discussion of how summative assessment differs from formative assessment and the relationship between the two. Other purposes for which children are assessed, not considered here, are for accountability, for monitoring standards over time and for research. In these cases, the purpose of the assessment is not to make decisions about individual children; however, using assessment information for these other purposes can and does affect children through impact on teachers and the curriculum, a point revisited briefly at the end of the chapter.

Wynne Harlen

Why assessment for learning?

Using assessment to help learning is logically necessary for teaching that aims for understanding. It is particularly appropriate in science, but the argument applies to any other learning where the aim is for learners to construct meaning through their own thinking and actions. In science education, the aim is to enable children to build scientific understanding through direct interaction with, and thinking about, materials, events and phenomena in their environment.

The emphasis is on understanding, which, on the basis of modern views of learning, requires action by the learner. It is recognised that learners 'do the learning' by constructing meaning from their experiences and making sense of the world in terms of concepts and mental models. It is now well known from a considerable body of research (for example the research of the CLIS and SPACE projects) that learners construct their own understanding of their experiences, and that these ideas may be in conflict with the widely held ideas about events. The way in which learners come to revise and reconstruct their understanding to bring it more into line with accepted scientific ideas is through interaction with their environment and with the ideas of others. This is elaborated in the socio-cultural view of learning based on the ideas of Vygotsky (1962) and Lave and Wenger (1991) among others (Bransford, Brown and Cocking, 1999) (see also Chapter 20).

When learning is understood in this way, the children are at the centre of the process. It follows that the more they know about what it is intended should be learned – the learning goals – and about where they have reached in relation to these goals, as well as about what further needs to be done to reach the goals, the more they can direct effort usefully for learning. The role of the teacher is to assess where children are in relation to the goals, to decide on appropriate next steps, to help the children take these steps and, importantly, to involve the children in these processes. These actions together comprise formative

---

Box 22.1

Key features of formative assessment

As a result of a thorough review of research on classroom assessment, Black and Wiliam (1998a,b) concluded that the use of assessment for formative purposes can lead to substantial gains in learning when it includes certain key features. These are:

- the provision of effective feedback to children;

- the active involvement of children in their own learning;

- adjusting teaching to take account of the results of assessment;

- a recognition of the profound influence assessment has on the motivation and self-esteem of children, both of which are crucial influences on learning;

- the need for children to be able to assess themselves and understand how to improve.

Perhaps the most significant finding from the research is that the practice of formative assessment benefits all children, but the increase in levels of achievement is particularly marked for lower achieving children. Thus the effect is to decrease the gap between the lower and higher achieving children.

Black and Wiliam acknowledged that such practices require large shifts in teachers' perceptions of their roles in relation to the children, but that considerable gains in achievements are possible as a result.

assessment or assessment for learning:

> *the process of seeking and interpreting evidence for use by learners and their teachers to decide where the learners are in their learning, where they need to go and how best to get there.* (Assessment Reform Group, 2002)

There is, moreover, convincing research evidence that formative assessment has a positive impact on learning. The value of using assessment in this way was the main message from a review of research on classroom assessment conducted by Black and Wiliam (1998a,b). Box 22.1 summarises the main findings.

Implementing formative assessment

How are the essential features, indicated in Box 22.1, put into practice? First it is important to emphasise that formative assessment is not something added to teaching, but is integral to it. Like teaching, it does not happen at infrequent intervals, as in the case of summative assessment. It is a cyclic process; the effect of decisions at a particular time is to alter the learning activity, hopefully towards achievement of the goals, and to lead to a further activity, where again evidence is gathered and interpreted to decide the most useful further steps, and so on. This can be represented as in Figure 22.1.

We can break into the cycle at activity **A**, related to a clear goal of learning. This provides opportunity for teacher and learners to gather evidence about the learners' current understanding or skills in relation to the goal. Evidence can be gathered in a range of ways, such as questioning, discussion, review of what learners write or draw about what they know and can do, and other methods designed to gain access to the learners' existing understanding. The evidence is then interpreted in terms of the goals of the activity, but also taking into account such things as a learner's recent progress and effort put in. This

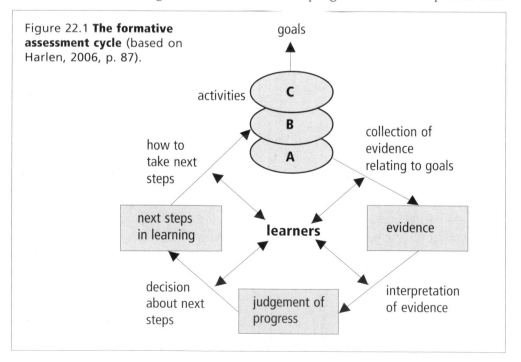

Figure 22.1 **The formative assessment cycle** (based on Harlen, 2006, p. 87).

means the judgement is learner-referenced (ipsative) as well as criterion-referenced.

In the next part of the cycle the judgement of where the learners have reached is used to decide the next steps. This decision requires a clear grasp on the part of the teacher of the goals of the activity and of the course of progress towards them. Once the next steps have been identified the teacher, together with the learners involved, decides how to take them. This can't be planned in detail in advance, since the purpose of assessing within teaching is to guide decisions about how to help learning. However, teachers can, of course, be equipped with a range of strategies – a tool-box, if you like – from which they select according to the nature of the step that needs to be taken (see Chapter 25). The outcome of the process is the next learning activity, **B** in Figure 22.1, which takes learners further towards achievement of the goals. The process then continues in a cycle, leading to activity **C**, and so on. This is, of course, a model and, although described as a series of separate actions, in practice the processes within the cycle often run together.

In all steps there is a role for the learners who, through participating in the decisions, will understand what they need to do and will be committed to making the effort that is required. Chapter 23 and other chapters in this book deal with several of the features of formative assessment identified in Box 22.1. Here we consider feedback.

Feedback and formative assessment

The cycle depicted in Figure 22.1 is one in which evidence is fed back into teaching and learning. This feedback helps to regulate teaching so that the pace of moving towards a learning goal is adjusted to ensure the active participation of the children. As with all regulated processes, feedback into the system is the important mechanism for ensuring effective operation. Just as feedback from the thermostat of a heating or cooling system allows the temperature of a room to be maintained within a particular range, so feedback of information about learning helps to ensure that new experiences are neither too difficult nor too easy for children. In the case of teaching, the feedback is both to the teacher and to the children.

Feedback to the teacher is needed to inform decisions about where children are and what are their appropriate next steps. For these decisions the teacher needs a clear view of progression in the ideas or skills that are the goals of learning. Children obtain feedback directly from self-assessment of their own work, from the teacher and from other children.

Formative feedback

Since much of the communication between teacher and children is through marking written work, the form of the feedback given in this way is of considerable significance if the children are to become involved in taking their next steps. Research shows that, although all feedback through marking is intended to help learning, much of it does not have this effect (Kluger and deNisi, 1996). Some of the most influential studies on feedback by marking have been carried out by Ruth Butler. Box 22.2 summarises one of these studies.

Of course, not just any comment will provide useful feedback. Experience

Box 22.2

Research into feedback that promotes learning

In this study by Ruth Butler (1987) the effects of different types of feedback by marking were compared. Using a controlled experimental design she set up groups that were given feedback in different ways. Pupils in one group were given marks, or grades only; those in another group were given only comments on their work and the third group received both marks and comments on their work. These conditions were studied in relation to tasks some of which required divergent and some convergent thinking.

The result was that, for divergent thinking tasks, the pupils who received *comments only* made the greatest gain in their learning, significantly more than for the other two groups. The results were the same for high and low achieving pupils. For convergent tasks, the lower achieving pupils scored most highly after *comments only*, with the *marks only* group next above the *marks plus comments* group. For all tasks and pupils, *comments only* led to higher achievement.

(Quoted from Harlen, 2006, p. 174)

shows that it is important for it to be non-judgemental and to show where children need to make improvements or direct their future effort. Comments of the type *'Well done!'*, *'A good effort'*, *'Try to draw more carefully'* or *'Always put the date on your work'* do little to advance learning. Black *et al.* (2003, p. 45), working with secondary teachers, quote examples of more useful comments:

> *Richard, clear method, results table and graph, but what does this tell you about the relationship?*

> *Go back to your notes from the 29th September and look up where chlorophyll is and what it does.*

> *Well explained so far but add reasons why the Haber process uses these conditions.*

Harlen (2006) quotes examples of primary teachers' marking in which children respond to teachers' written comments on their work. For instance, one child wrote and drew about making a switch but without making clear how it would be connected into a circuit. The teacher's question about where the wires would be attached was answered by the child before going on to the next activity.

Such comments require time for children to read and respond. A regular time set aside for this is important not only to consolidate or correct the work but to convey the message that responding to the comments is part of their learning. Moreover, children pick up the value of these kinds of comments and use them in giving feedback to each other when they have opportunity for peer-assessment (see Chapter 23).

Box 22.3 summarises some useful advice on feedback drawn from primary and secondary practice (e.g. Evans, 2001; Black *et al.*, 2003).

Box 22.3

Some guidelines for feedback to help learning

- Don't give judgemental comments and particularly not scores or grades since these divert attention from the learning and lead to children comparing themselves with others.

- If regular grades or marks are required by the school policy, keep them in a record book but don't put them on children's work.

- Comment only on certain features, relating to the goals of the work, telling children that this is what you are doing.

- Consider carefully whether to comment on neatness, spelling, etc., unless these were specifically goals of the work.

- Emphasise how to improve by pinpointing aspects that need attention.

- Mark selectively, giving attention to work where children are required to think, rather than just record. Acknowledge that other work has been completed using a signature, stamp or sticker (not a tick, which is judgemental).

- Give time for children to read and discuss comments, reflect on them and respond as necessary.

Summative assessment: assessment of learning

The purpose of summative assessment is to provide a summary of achievement at a particular time. The information needed for this purpose is much less detailed than that needed for formative assessment and for this reason alone it cannot guide teaching and learning in detail. Moreover, it provides information after the event, while formative assessment is an ongoing part of teaching and can affect the learning process. Summative information is used for two main purposes, which we can call 'internal' and 'external':

- **Internal purposes** are for school records and for informing other teachers, parents or carers and the children themselves about what children have achieved at a particular time, generally the end of a term or half-year.

- **External purposes** are for providing those outside the school with information for selection, certification or to give public acknowledgement of achievement.

All teachers are involved in assessment for internal purposes, producing or contributing to records of children's achievement and reporting to parents or carers and others on progress. Those receiving this information will wish to know what has been achieved in relation to levels or standards that apply to all children. Thus the evidence has to be judged against the same criteria in the same way. Levels, as in the English National Curriculum and its equivalents in other countries, are a shorthand for the achievement that they represent.

To ensure consistency in assessment judgements from one occasion to another and one teacher to another (reliability), some form of moderation is necessary. This can take various forms but the most productive involves teachers discussing samples of children's work, comparing judgements and clarifying with each other the operational meaning of the level descriptions or other criteria. Such meetings have the added advantage of enabling teachers to share understandings of certain goals of learning and how to achieve them. Box 22.4 brings together some of these points in comparing the characteristics of summative and formative assessment.

Box 22.4

Comparing characteristics of summative and formative assessment

Formative assessment ...	Summative assessment ...
<ul><li>is an integral part of teaching for understanding. It is not optional; it cannot be taken away without changing the whole nature of the teaching and learning.</li><li>relates to progression in learning but takes individual progress and effort into account; that is, it is both criterion-referenced and child-referenced.</li><li>leads to action that supports further learning.</li><li>can be used in all learning contexts.</li><li>provides information about all learning outcomes.</li><li>involves children in assessing their performance and deciding their next steps.</li></ul>	<ul><li>takes place at certain intervals when achievement is to be reported.</li><li>relates to progression in learning judged against publicly available criteria.</li><li>gives results for different children that are based on the same criteria and so can be compared and combined if required.</li><li>requires methods that are as reliable as possible without endangering validity.</li><li>involves some quality assurance procedures such as moderation.</li></ul>

Using children's achievements for other purposes

Summative assessment for external purposes is often conducted, at least in part, through special tasks, tests or examinations. These can only cover a limited sample of what children can do. When there are 'high stakes' attached to the results, there is a well-recognised consequence that the content of the tests becomes the focus of teaching. The high stakes can be for the children, in terms of grade levels needed for entry to higher education for instance. But they can also apply to teachers and schools when, as in England, children's achievement data are aggregated at the school level and used for creating league tables based on children's performance.

The practice of holding schools responsible for raising levels of achievement as measured by tests, with significant implications if targets are not met, means that the tests dominate the curriculum and teaching. Research (reviewed by

Harlen and Deakin Crick, 2003) shows that even when not teaching directly to the tests, teachers report changing their approach. They adjust their teaching in ways they perceive as necessary because of the tests, spending most time in direct instruction of facts to be tested and less in providing opportunity for children to learn through enquiry and problem-solving (Johnston and McClune, 2000). They also administer frequent practice tests, which take up valuable learning time and are demotivating, especially for lower achieving children. The consequence is that the gap between the higher and lower achieving children widens. When in the grip of summative testing, teachers make little use of assessment formatively and provide fewer opportunities for enquiry-based science.

Concluding comment

This chapter has discussed assessment for different purposes. Formative and summative assessment are not different methods or types of assessment, but are defined by the purpose they serve. A teacher-made classroom test could be used to inform teaching, without any reference to levels, or it could be used to provide a grade or level for end of year or stage reporting. Assessment is only formative if it is actually used to help learning. Once evidence is gathered and used for helping learning it can later be reinterpreted and used to summarise learning. However, there is less opportunity for information gathered for summative assessment to be used formatively.

We have also noted evidence that using children's achievement results from tests for school evaluation leads to inappropriate 'teaching to the test'. The evaluation of schools (see Chapter 10) must be based on far wider evidence than the achievements of children in external tests. Indeed, the criteria for evaluating a school ought to include how well it is using assessment to help learning and that it is providing summaries of achievement as needed and not more frequently, which would inhibit the formative use of assessment.

References

Assessment Reform Group (2002) *Assessment for learning: 10 Principles*. Available from The Institute of Education University of London and from the ARG website: www.assessment-reform-group.org

Black, P. and Wiliam, D. (1998a) Assessment and classroom learning. *Assessment in Education*, **5**(1), 7–74.

Black, P. and Wiliam, D. (1998b) *Inside the black box: raising standards through classroom assessment*. London: nferNelson.

Black, P., Harrison, C., Lee, C., Marshall, B. and Wiliam, D. (2002) *Working inside the black box*. London: nferNelson.

Black, P., Harrison, C., Lee, C., Marshall, B. and Wiliam, D. (2003) *Assessment for learning: putting it into practice*. Maidenhead: Open University Press.

Bransford, J. D., Brown, A. L., and Cocking, R. R. ed. (1999) *How people learn: brain, mind, experience and school*. Washington, DC: National Academy Press.

Butler, R. (1987) Task-involving and ego-involving properties of evaluation: effects of different feedback conditions on motivational perceptions, interest and performance. *Journal of Educational Psychology*, **79**, 474–482.

Evans, N. (2001) Thoughts on assessment and marking. *Primary Science Review*, **68**, 24–26.

Harlen, W. (2006) *Teaching, learning and assessing science 5–12*. 4th edn. London: Sage.

Harlen, W. and Deakin Crick, R. (2003) Testing and motivation for learning. *Assessment in Education*, **10**(2), 169–208.

Johnston, J. and McClune, W. (2000) Selection project sel 5.1: Pupil motivation and attitudes – self-esteem, locus of control, learning disposition and the impact of selection on teaching and learning. In *The effects of the selective system of secondary education in Northern Ireland*. Research Papers Volume II, pp. 1–37. Bangor, Co Down: Department of Education.

Kluger, A.N. and deNisi, A. (1996) The effect of feedback intervention on performance: a historical review, a meta-analysis and a preliminary feedback intervention theory. *Psychological Bulletin*, **119**(2), 254–284.

Lave, J. and Wenger, E. (1991) *Situated learning: legitimate peripheral participation.* Cambridge: Cambridge University Press.

Vygotsky, L. S. (1962) *Thought and language.* Cambridge MA: MIT Press.

Chapter 23

Children's self- and peer- assessment

In the move towards children taking more responsibility for their learning, so that they eventually become lifelong learners, self-assessment has an important part to play. Similarly, peer-assessment promotes understanding that children can help each other towards their learning goals. This chapter concerns the actions that teachers can take to develop in children the necessary skills for self-directed learning through self- and peer-assessment. After some discussion of reasons for making the effort required, the main part of the chapter deals with ways of implementing four key aspects of self- and peer-assessment: understanding learning goals, knowing the quality criteria to apply, looking critically at their work and taking part in deciding next steps. It is emphasised throughout that this requires a classroom atmosphere in which identifying problems is seen as part of progress, and in which collaboration and not competition in learning is encouraged.

Chris Harrison and **Wynne Harlen**

The value of self-assessment

The case for the value of learner's self-assessment is based both on theoretical arguments relating to how people learn and on practical experience. In terms of ideas about learning, a constant theme in the chapters of this book is emphasis on the active involvement of learners if there is to be learning with understanding. Learners 'do' the learning by constructing meaning from their experiences and interactions with others, using existing ideas. It follows that the more learners know about what it is intended should be learned – the learning goals, about where they have reached in relation to these goals, and about what further needs to be done to reach the goals, the more they can direct effort usefully for learning. It is for this reason that the learners are put at the centre of Figure 22.1 in Chapter 22, in the cycle of events in which information about where children are in relation to learning goals is used to decide how to take their next steps in learning.

Involvement of primary-age children in self-assessment has developed only since the late 1990s. Previously, it was argued that children would not be able to understand the goals or reflect on their own progress. These objections have been met by a good deal of development and the publication of examples showing how goals can be expressed in child-friendly ways (see, for instance, Clarke, 1998; Goldsworthy, Watson and Wood-Robinson, 2000) and how children can be helped to decide how to improve their work.

The practical value for learning of learner self-assessment was revealed by the review of research into classroom assessment by Black and Wiliam (1998) noted in Chapter 22. Box 22.1 shows that the key features that lead to gains in levels of achievement include 'the need for children to be able to assess themselves and understand how to improve'. In addition, primary teachers who have implemented self-assessment by children have reported that the advantages listed in Box 23.1 make the initial effort of establishing it as part of practice well worthwhile.

Box 23.1

Some advantages of implementing self-assessment by children

- Children take ownership of their learning.
- Children see assessment as a process in which they are involved and to which they can make a contribution.
- Children have control over their learning and see themselves as partners in the teaching–learning process, raising their self-esteem.
- Teachers gain greater insight into children's understanding by reflecting on the children's assessment of their work.
- Children can use the skills of self-assessment in a variety of learning contexts.
- Self-assessment can clarify ideas for the children, helping them to refine and question their own concepts.
- Children become more self-critical and proactive as learners.
- Children focus upon the next goal in their learning. They feel that the next target is being set by themselves, rather than being externally imposed.

(Quoted from Harlen, 2006, p. 168)

These points refer to the role of self-assessment in formative assessment, which is the focus of discussion here. However, this is only one of four aspects of self-assessment:

- Self-monitoring and checking progress – *Where am I and how far have I come?*
- Diagnosis and recognition of learning needs – *What can I now do and what do I need to take the next step?*

- Promoting good learning practices – *What am I doing that is successful?*
- Linking learning practices – *Can I adopt, adapt or influence my learning techniques in other areas?*

In reality these four aspects interlink. However, the degree to which focus on one aspect can influence and benefit another aspect of self-assessment depends on the emphasis that the teacher gives to it and the classroom climate in which the activities are carried out. If learners are asked to self-assess in the closing minutes of a lesson or open themselves up to ridicule from their peers by the revelation of their inadequacies, or feel that their teacher's expectations may be diminished if they admit to less than full understanding, then there is little chance of self-assessment skills developing.

Self-assessment in practice

Self-assessment is an essential component of formative assessment because it can help children direct their activities towards learning goals. Children need to acquire similar skills to those of their teacher to find out where their leading edge of learning is and where they need to head next. In this way, children can begin to see how the advice from their teacher will help them improve; they also begin to form an idea of what quality looks like within a piece of work. When they can do this, children are able to steer their activity towards the learning goal. Through this process, children become more aware of what they need to do to improve, and as a consequence are often more motivated to learn.

What is needed, then, is for children to:

- understand the goals of a learning activity;
- appreciate the criteria of quality;
- look critically at their work and judge it against the assessment criteria;
- take part in deciding what to do to achieve the goal.

Each of these is now considered in turn.

Helping children to understand goals

Communicating goals to children is not easy and will certainly need different words from those that are used to communicate goals to teachers in official documents. Often there is quite a subtle difference between telling children what they have to do, telling them what they are going to find out and telling them their learning goal. For example, if the teacher's goal is *'for children to understand that the pitch of a sound depends on how quickly the source vibrates'*, the words used to share this with the children might be:

> *Today you are going to try making high and low sounds and see if you can find out what makes the sound high or low*

rather than

> *Today you are going to change the length of the string so that you make high and low sounds* (what to do)

or

> *Today you are going to see that when you make the string shorter it vibrates more quickly and makes a higher sound* (what to find).

185

Sometimes the learning goal is to explain differences or events and develop conceptual understanding. At other times the main purpose of an activity may be to focus on a scientific way of testing something. For example, the more important outcome of the common activity of testing the strength of different kinds of paper is not to find which is strongest but to conduct a fair test. In this case the teacher might not identify the goal as *'finding out which paper is strongest'* but *'testing the papers in a way that is fair so that you can be quite sure that it is the kind of paper that is making the difference'*.

It also helps to reinforce the goals, and check whether they are understood by the children, during the lesson and at the end. Discussing the outcomes of an investigation in terms of the initial goal will not only emphasise the goal but helps to set the pattern of taking note of goals and working towards the intended learning. Of course, sometimes something happens that is not planned and leads to further enquiry. Then it is useful to ask the children *'What did you learn from that?'* Other ways of focusing on goals are:

- writing the goals on the board or on a poster left visible throughout the relevant activities as a reminder;
- when children are discussing what they will do in an investigation, asking them what they think they will be learning;
- checking with groups or individuals to find out whether they know the reason for their activities in terms of what they are learning;
- commenting on the procedures and the outcome of the activities in ways that reflect what they are learning.

Communicating standards of quality

As well as knowing the goals, children also need some idea of the standard or quality of work to aim for. That is, they need to share the teacher's understanding of what is 'good work'. For instance, if they are to make a report of their investigation, it is not just any report that will achieve this goal but one that meets certain criteria, reflecting what can be expected of children at a particular stage. Similarly, what they say they find out about the properties of materials or how to make sounds of different pitch, should meet expectations of conclusions being based on reasoning about evidence.

Some of the ways teachers have devised for helping children to recognise the criteria of quality to be applied, based on Harlen (2006), are outlined in Box 23.2.

Assessing their own work

It is very difficult for someone to look closely at his or her own work and be reasonably objective in applying assessment criteria. It helps to have taken part in deciding the criteria, but it is still useful to practise on someone else's work. Children can use anonymous work, as suggested in the examples in Box 23.2. Since they have no ties or loyalty towards whoever produced the piece of work, they can focus on the characteristics of the work rather than be concerned about the feelings of the person who did it. This allows them to begin to make judgements about quality within a piece of work and to recognise the attributes that illustrate or detract from aspects of quality. Sometimes it is useful to present children with one criterion and ask them to look at whether they can find evidence of it in one piece of work. Care has to be taken that children do not

Box 23.2

Some ways of communicating standards of quality

Using examples

One teacher of 10-year-olds, spent some time at the beginning of the year discussing with her class what made a 'good' report of a science investigation. She gave each group of children two anonymous examples of children's writing about an investigation from children in the same class in earlier years. One was a clear account, well set out so that the reader could understand what had been done, although the writing was uneven and there were some words not spelled correctly. There were labelled diagrams to help the account. The results were in a table, and the writer had said what he or she thought they meant, admitting that the results did not completely answer the initial question. There was a comment about how things could have been improved. The other account was tidy and attractive to look at (the diagrams were coloured in but not labelled), but contained none of the features of the content shown in the other piece.

The teacher asked the children to compare the pieces of work and list the good and poor features of each one. Then they were asked to say what were the most important things that made a 'good' report. She put all the ideas together and added some points of her own, with which the children agreed. She later made copies for all the children to keep in their science folders. But she also went on to explore with the children how to carry out an investigation in order to be able to write a good report. These points too were brought together in the children's words and printed out for them.

Brainstorming

A variation on the above is to brainstorm ideas about, for example, how to conduct a particular investigation so that the children can be sure of the result. The list of what to think about can be turned into questions, e.g. *Did we keep everything the same except for ...? Did we change ...? Did we look for ...? Did we check the results?* etc. Before finishing their investigation they check through their list, which becomes a self-assessment tool for that piece of work.

Discussing 'best work'

This approach can be used with children from about the age of 8 or even earlier. It begins with the children selecting their 'best' work to put into a folder or bag. Part of the time for 'bagging' should be set aside for the teacher to talk to each child about why certain pieces of work have been selected. During this discussion the way in which the children are judging the quality of their work will become clear. To clarify the criteria the children use, the teacher can ask '*Tell me what you particularly liked about this piece of work?*' Gradually it will be possible to suggest criteria without dictating what the children should be selecting. This can be done through comments on the work, e.g. '*That was a very good way of showing your results, I could see at a glance which was best.*' '*I'm glad you think that was your best investigation because although you didn't get the result you expected, you did it very carefully and made sure that the result was fair.*'

approach this with a checklist mentality. The purpose is not simply to find aspects relevant to the criterion but for them gain an understanding of a good example of what it means in the context of that task. Another approach is to take one of the criteria from the list and ask children to discuss how this criterion is played out in a variety of pieces of work; thus they get a feel for the scope and range of ways it can be met before they attempt to exemplify it in their own work.

Taking part in deciding next steps towards the goal

When children have a view of what they should be doing, how well they should be doing it, and how close they are to this goal, they are in position to share in deciding the next steps to reach the goal. Useful questions to encourage children to be reflective about their work and so prompt discussion about improvement are:

What do you think you have done well?

Did you do what were you trying to do in this section?

Why did you do this in this kind of way?

Do you think now that you could do it a better way?

Which bits are you unsure about?

What would you change if you did it again?

What could you add to strengthen this part?

Self-assessment fits well into using KWL (Know, Want to know, Learnt) grids, also mentioned in Chapter 25. The first two, 'know' and 'want to know', are made explicit before an activity and the last as a summary of what has been learned. Any discrepancy leads to discussion of the further steps that might be needed to develop the intended learning. Another strategy is for children to reflect on how confident they feel about what they are learning, during or immediately after an activity. Children might use a traffic-light system (see Box 23.3), a thumb tool or a smiley face to indicate aspects or answers about which they are confident, unconfident or partially confident. This begins the reflective process needed for self-assessment, but at the same time it helps to create the right environment because the judgement is in their hands. The next step is to create discussion about their judgement so that ideas of quality come to the fore. Then the final decision about next steps becomes reciprocal, in that both the child and anyone hearing their judgement are aware of and agreed about what should be done next.

It is also possible to come back to pieces of work several days or weeks later. Teachers can then help children to look through one or more pieces of their work using questions that focus them on what to consider. They might, for example, think about what they found easy/hard in the work, or which bits they are proud of or feel they can now do better. During this process, children will be involved in judgements that help them understand more fully their learning goals and so ensure that their learning progresses both in the individual pieces of work and also more generally. This helps children realise where they need to focus their future efforts and it becomes prospective rather than simply a retrospective exercise.

Box 23.3

Traffic lights

'Traffic lights' is a self-assessment tool that has been developed and used with lower secondary pupils, but has potential at the upper primary level. It involves children using red, yellow and green spots to indicate their confidence in understanding what they have done. It requires gradual introduction and possibly modelling.

The teacher might demonstrate what to do: *'Suppose I've finished or nearly finished the activity, and I read through what I've written and reflect on what I did. If there is something I'm not quite sure about then I put a yellow spot on the top corner. If I really don't understand, then it is a red one. But if I feel it all makes sense, then it is a green spot.'*

The teacher can explain that the spot is not a mark but a way of helping the teacher to know when to go on or to go over things. This approach is particularly applicable to the conceptual understanding in an activity and clearly requires a classroom climate where it is acceptable for children to discuss what they don't understand.

(Based on Harlen *et al.*, 2003, p. 132)

Children's peer-assessment

Peer-assessment, in this context, means children helping each other with their learning, by deciding the next steps to take. It is quite different from children marking each other's work. It has several advantages. For instance, when children are asked to talk about their own and each other's work in pairs:

- they go through their work again and use the criteria of quality that enable them to see where improvements need to be made;
- they express this in words that they understand;
- they are more likely to take seriously criticism from a peer (Sadler, 1989);
- they require less one-to-one attention by the teachers compared with other approaches to self-assessment.

Just as important as the time saved, however, is that the assessment takes place without the pressure that comes from the unequal relationship between the child (novice) and the teacher (expert). It is also consistent with the understanding of learning as the development of ideas through social interaction as well as through interaction with materials. Peer-assessment can help children to respect each other's strengths, especially if pairs are changed on different occasions.

The paired discussion needs to be structured, at least when it is new to the children. For example, the children can be asked to exchange work and then think about two or three questions about the work that reflect the criteria of quality. If the work describes a conclusion from something that has been observed or found from an investigation, the questions might be *'Can you tell what was found?' 'Does the conclusion help to answer the question that was being investigated?' 'What would help to make it clearer (a diagram, or series of* drawings)?' After such a discussion, one child wrote about having her work assessed by another:

> After a pupil marking my investigation, I can now acknowledge my mistakes easier ... Next time I will have to make my explanations clearer, as they said 'It is hard to understand'. (Black et al., 2002, p. 15)

This approach to peer-assessment clearly requires a class atmosphere where cooperation and collaboration, rather than competition, are encouraged. When they have confidence in gaining help from a structured exchange with a peer, children begin spontaneously to ask one another for their opinions. Recognising that they can help themselves and each other enables learning to continue when the teacher is occupied with those who need extra help.

Conclusion

Whether attempting one or all of these approaches, it is essential continually to bear in mind that these tools and processes are designed to engage children in being reflective, both about the task in hand and more broadly about the way they learn. Self- and peer-assessment therefore encourage a deep rather than a surface approach to learning. However, there are no guarantees; by its nature self-assessment is individualistic and so children may not respond in ways expected by the teacher. This puts the onus on the teacher to be even more careful in their approach so that goals are focused on learning and improvement and not simply on tricks and additions that improve performance without affecting underlying understanding.

References

Black, P. and Wiliam, D. (1998) Inside the black box: raising standards through classroom assessment. London: nferNelson.

Black, P., Harrison, C., Lee, C., Marshall, B. and Wiliam, D. (2002) Working inside the black box: assessment for learning in the classroom. London: nferNelson.

Black, P., Harrison, C., Lee, C., Marshall, B. and Wiliam, D. (2003) Assessment for learning: putting it into practice. Maidenhead: Open University Press.

Clarke, S. (1998) Targeting assessment in the primary classroom. London: Hodder and Stoughton.

Goldsworthy, A., Watson, R. and Wood-Robinson, V. (2000) Targeted learning. Hatfield: Association for Science Education.

Harlen, W. (2006) Teaching, learning and assessing science 5–12. 4th edn. London: Sage.

Harlen, W., Macro, C., Reed, K. and Schilling, M. (2003) Making progress in primary science. Study book. London: RoutledgeFalmer.

Sadler, R. (1989) Formative assessment and the design of instructional systems. Instructional Science, 18, 119–144.

Chapter 24

Developing children's thinking in primary science

Natasha Serret

The recognition that primary-school-age children and not just older children can benefit from activities designed to develop their thinking skills is a 21st century development meeting 21st century needs. Previously it was assumed that young children would not be able to 'think about thinking'. This chapter describes the kinds of activities that enable even the youngest primary children to take part in, and enjoy, 'thinking about science'. The key features of thinking programmes, identified as challenge, collaborative group work and metacognition, are discussed in the context of learning science. The challenges to both teachers and children are openly admitted.

A rationale for putting thinking on the learning agenda

An important requirement of formal education is that it equips young people with the skills and attitudes that will enable them to face the demands of the fast-changing and unpredictable world they will inherit. To this end, developing thinking in children appears on the teaching and learning agenda of many schools and teachers. In the Government's strategy for key stage 3 (11–14 year-olds) in England (DfES, 2001, see websites) developing thinking skills is recommended across the curriculum. It has, however, a particular relevance to learning science.

Understanding the scientific aspects of the world requires more than just knowledge and recall of discrete facts. Children get to grips with science through questioning and engaging with the things around them and by having opportunities to use the processes of science to address these questions. Developing thinking is integral to the processes that are needed for developing understanding. It involves making explicit the generic strategies that we can use to solve problems and focusing teaching and questioning on the processes that children go through when developing these strategies, rather than on engineering the learning and responses to produce a fixed outcome regardless of what individual thinking might reveal. Thus, promoting thinking in the classroom also has the potential to give children a greater insight into science processes and how and why they use them. As a result, children may begin to see that they can have greater control over their learning and, indeed, begin to learn how to learn.

When thinking is on the learning agenda, the emphasis is on *'How did you go about?'* and *'Why did you decide to?'* Encouraging children to reflect on how they approached a problem and the strategies they used to overcome the challenges, increases the likelihood that these ways of thinking will be embedded in their minds and not just in relation to one specific context. The principle is to empower children so that they realise that they can think for themselves and have the confidence to approach any unfamiliar problem knowing that they are already equipped with skills to tackle it.

Providing a list of thinking skills might only help to reinforce a view that knowledge and understanding can be neatly packaged into discrete boxes that bear no relationship to one another. What this chapter will do instead is attempt to unpack the pedagogy, roles and expectations that are characteristic of lessons where children are encouraged to think, and illustrate these ideas by putting them into the context of a primary science classroom.

Thinking in the context of the primary science curriculum

What kinds of thinking processes can be developed and how might they relate to science?

At the heart of scientific enquiry is the desire to find ways of gathering and interpreting evidence to try to explain the unexplained. Many key thinking processes apply naturally to learning through scientific enquiry. The two classroom examples in Boxes 24.1 and 24.2 are based on activities found in *Let's think through science!* (Adey *et al.*, 2003) and illustrate how thinking can be developed in a primary science context. Key thinking processes as well as relevant scientific processes and attitudes are highlighted.

What is most important is that children have the opportunity to engage actively in these processes. Then, through reflection on what was going on inside their heads and beginning to identify the complexities involved when thinking in this way, they can later apply a similar set of processes to another context. What is less important is that the whole class end up by putting the materials in the same order of strength, or use the elastic band to describe the proportional relationship between extension and weight.

Characteristic features of thinking programmes

Although the range of thinking programmes currently available may seem varied and overwhelming, there are some key principles that inform many of them. These were identified by McGuiness (1999) in a review of thinking approaches used in the UK. These generic features, if used collectively with some

Box 24.1

Looking at a collection of everyday materials (polystyrene cup, plastic ruler, paper, tin foil, wooden paintbrush) and thinking about putting them in order of strength, groups of children instinctively use all their senses to explore the materials. The challenge is in **reaching an agreement** as a group as to how they define strength. Is it related to the weight? Is it the ability not to snap under pressure? Part of this process will involve **explaining** these ideas, **recognising that there are alternative definitions**, having an **open attitude** to alternatives, being able to **justify** these and eventually reaching a consensus. This may require **willingness to adapt** an idea based on consideration of the evidence and arguments presented. A positive outcome of unresolved thinking about the order is that is motivates the children to **question and investigate** further in order to reach a more conclusive solution. Why couldn't they agree on the order of strength? Can they remember how different children explained what being strong means? If they could agree, what kind of test could they do to help them be sure of the order?

Box 24.2

Groups of children try **to construct together** a method of using a plastic carrier bag, which has its handles tied together with a piece of string with an elastic band attached at its other end, to find out which of their four potatoes is the heaviest. They have to present a **rationale** for what they are doing: how does this tell them which potato is the heaviest? Through discussion and exploration, they notice that the elastic band stretches each time a potato is put in the bag. They try to **look for a relationship** between the stretch of the elastic band and weight. The need to **generate reliable evidence** stimulates some children to ask for a ruler to measure the length of the elastic band. Later they **compare** the weight of their heaviest potato with a 100 g weight by looking at the relative lengths of the elastic band. They try to **predict** what will happen to the length of the elastic band if 200 g is used. There is genuine surprise and **cognitive conflict** when they **observe** that the elastic band is not double the length it was for 100 g. This motivates them to **look further for patterns** in the data to **seek an alternative generalisation**: '*Look, it goes up 2 cm each time we add 100 g.*'

(Based on activities in *Let's think through science!* – see website)

understanding of the theory underpinning them, can potentially stimulate children's thinking when working on tasks in a science context. One of the approaches that featured in this review was 'cognitive acceleration through science education' (CASE) that aims to improve children's thinking in the context of science. Figure 24.1 summarises the key features of a thinking science lesson. The underlying principles of this intervention programme draw from a Piagetian and Vygotskian perspective on cognitive development. This will be explored a little later in this chapter. Some of the ideas and examples from this illustrate

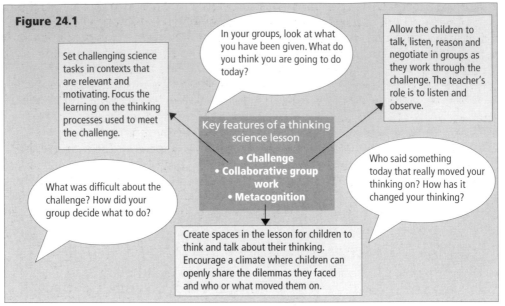

Figure 24.1

Set challenging science tasks in contexts that are relevant and motivating. Focus the learning on the thinking processes used to meet the challenge.

In your groups, look at what you have been given. What do you think you are going to do today?

Allow the children to talk, listen, reason and negotiate in groups as they work through the challenge. The teacher's role is to listen and observe.

Key features of a thinking science lesson

• **Challenge**
• **Collaborative group work**
• **Metacognition**

What was difficult about the challenge? How did your group decide what to do?

Who said something today that really moved your thinking on? How has it changed your thinking?

Create spaces in the lesson for children to think and talk about their thinking. Encourage a climate where children can openly share the dilemmas they faced and who or what moved them on.

how the theory behind these features is transferred into everyday classroom practice.

Setting a challenge where children can use their range of ideas and engage their thinking

The level of challenge and what the teacher expects the children to gain from experiencing the challenge is crucial. The challenge has to be cognitively demanding and set in a context that is, in some way, relevant and motivating to the children. This means that, although it will be important to check that the children will not be disadvantaged linguistically or technically, some kinds of support a teacher might intuitively provide could be unhelpful. For instance, a testing task for the teacher is to resist the temptation to ask leading questions, or to over-resource a challenge so that access is made easier and the children avoid cognitive conflict. During many CASE professional development programmes, teachers have reflected on the extent to which they tend to underestimate children's abilities. Many go on to remark on just how much their children surprised them with their ability to rise to a challenge when they 'stepped back'. A useful approach is to recognise that the learning expectations are more connected with the complex thinking processes the children go through trying to meet the challenge than with a particular outcome. So the teacher's role is about setting up the challenge, allowing the children to experience the challenge for themselves, and listening to and observing them carefully so that the subsequent questioning is tailored to encouraging the children to identify the thinking that they encountered during that challenge.

Collaboration in groups

Vygotsky (1978) drew attention to the notion that, as a society, we instinctively collaborate as teams, think-tanks, parliaments and unions when faced with a challenge. Counselling services offer people the opportunity and support to talk through problems in order to help tackle them. If being able to participate in a group and understanding the dynamics involved is such a vital element of adulthood, then children need to engage in similar situations as part of their learning and thinking development. But, however instinctive it may be to want to share a problem and work together effectively as a group, it still requires skills that only experience and practice can develop and refine. Learning how to negotiate, when to initiate, when to step back and listen, and how to ensure that everyone feels valued and can contribute without external intervention can be a painful process for both the children and the teacher!

Classroom management may seem less complicated when children are working individually. But it is only through working in mixed-ability, mixed-gender groups, that children might begin to recognise all the different academic, social and emotional qualities that individuals can bring to a group and that exploiting this powerful mixture can bring about greater success. For example, when faced with a problem:

- it helps to have someone who will be prepared to take risks and start the process;
- at some points, having someone who questions decisions and demands clarifications moves the process on;
- those with awareness of who is feeling less involved and the skills to encourage inclusion may help to bring in more ideas;
- sometimes the turning point is brought about by someone who has said the least, but has been listening and weighing up all the ideas and is then able to generate a solution from this.

Are these roles fixed? Are some people 'natural born leaders'? How will it help if children are assigned to these roles at the start? To what extent should a teacher intervene to ensure inclusion? Is there a place for allowing children to explore these roles naturally as they work collaboratively and even to encourage recognition of these roles through ongoing reflection? Some of these dilemmas remain unresolved and are debated beyond the confines of thinking, science and education. What is important is that when children have to think collaboratively to meet a challenge, they are more likely to appreciate their peers as a potential learning resource that can be used to help move them into that zone of proximal (or potential) development.

Learning from the process: creating space for metacognition

Metacognition means 'self-awareness that we can use to develop our own thinking process' (Claxton, 1999, p. 131). Providing for it requires more than a plenary discussion or moments when different children share what they have done. It may start by prompting individuals to recall the journey that led to the thinking. Through questioning, this journey is probed further to explore and unpack the thinking that went on and what triggered it (see Box 24.3). Making thinking explicit by encouraging children to articulate what is going on in their heads requires a classroom culture where being open about cognitive conflict and challenging opinions is respected and valued; where skilful questioning, listening and modelling by the teacher give children access to a language for talking about thinking. Establishing this kind of learning environment and

Box 24.3

Questions that help to promote metacognition

- Can you remember what happened when ...?
- What did you do?
- What made this difficult?
- Did you all agree? Why not?
- How did you decide?
- What do you think happened in your brain?
- Who said or did something that changed your thinking today? What was it? Why do you think this happened?

developing this way of talking about thinking is demanding for the teacher and the child. However, this kind of dialogue does increase the chance that the thinking will be embedded and later transferred to other problems in a variety of contexts.

Talking and listening

At the heart of the features indicated in Figure 24.1 is using classroom talk as a vehicle to present, explain and reflect on the thinking processes used. The teacher does not have exclusive ownership over this dialogue and its development can be less predictable than traditional lessons. The agenda is not about guessing what is in the teacher's head; it is about responding to the different views and ideas exchanged between children at that given moment. Children are expected to be active listeners in a discussion and not rely on the teacher to summarise or rephrase opinions expressed by their peers. Children need to recognise that their development of thinking through challenges, group work and metacognition depends upon their participation as speakers and listeners.

Dilemmas

When a thinking programme is set in the context of a curriculum subject such as science, one dilemma for the teacher might be about expectations for the children and the teacher. This is especially true in a climate where learning is compartmentalised neatly into different subjects, further broken down into discrete topics that eventually reach the children in the form of tight objectives. On some professional development programmes for *Let's think through science!*, teachers ask, '*Am I supposed to be teaching thinking or science?*'

It might appear to be an impossible juggling act. On one hand, the teacher's role is to cultivate a less threatening learning environment where opinions are exchanged, valued and questioned and children as well as the teacher share the ownership of new knowledge brought to the discussion. On the other hand, the teacher has a responsibility to help children to seek, recognise and eventually use scientific explanations, particularly when these challenge the alternative concepts that children might hold. In letting go of the reins and giving children more control of classroom discussion, misconceptions are likely to be aired.

Past research has warned us that telling children the right answer doesn't guarantee that this is embedded in their thinking. It is important for teachers to use their professional judgement about when to step in, and to give themselves time to think about the best strategy for addressing unclear understanding in science. One way to avoid promoting misconceptions, whilst ensuring that children feel their ideas have been valued, is to summarise points arising from a discussion in the form of questions. These questions can be pursued later through investigation or research at an individual, group or whole-class level. This also helps to reinforce a model of the nature of science where curiosity and a desire to seek better or different explanations are paramount.

When children are encouraged to think for themselves in science lessons, perceived boundaries between thinking and science become blurred. The level of scientific experience that children bring to a discussion will shape the kinds of arguments and justifications put forward. Similarly, children's ability to think, explain, reason, value and be open to alternative ideas will contribute to expanding that scientific experience further.

References

Adey, P., Nagy, F., Robertson, A., Serret, N. and Wadsworth, P. (2003) *Let's think through science!* London: nferNelson.

Claxton, G. (1999) *Wise up: the challenge of lifelong learning.* London: Bloomsbury (Stafford: Network Educational Press, 2001).

McGuiness, C. (1999) *From thinking skills to thinking classrooms: a review and evaluation of approaches for developing pupils' thinking.* London: Department for Education and Employment.

Vygotsky, L. S. (1978) *Mind in society*. Cambridge, MA: Harvard University Press.

Websites

Department for Education and Skills (DfES) (2001) The Key Stage 3 National Strategy: www.standards.dfes.gov.uk/keystage3

Let's think through science! professional development unit: http://www.azteachscience.co.uk/code/development/case.htm

Chapter 25

Teaching for progression in conceptual understanding

Progression implies progress, and progress suggests a journey. Conceptual progress might be considered to be a journey through a landscape of developing ideas and it is a journey travelled by learners. It is, of course, a lifelong journey. This chapter considers what is known from practice and research about the ways in which children learn about science concepts and how teachers might best support them during their journey. It begins by identifying the main dimensions of conceptual progression. It then discusses the challenges that teachers must meet to promote progression in learning. Two case studies are used to illustrate how teachers can meet these challenges while using individual strategies for helping children's progression.

Bob Kibble

Progression – a journey through reconstruction

For each learner the path taken on their journey in developing understanding will be different if for no other reason than that they will be starting from different places. If we know anything about learning we know that children come to us having already travelled far and along quite different and varied paths. Each child will have had a variety of life experiences and as such will have constructed a host of emerging ideas about the world, mostly from a personal perspective. Some of these home-grown, often egocentric ideas will be fusing into an emerging grand picture of life, the world and everything and this picture will be set against a backdrop of emerging values and aspirations.

What does conceptual progression look like?

Progression isn't about simply learning more and more things. It is more about revisiting ideas in more depth, in extending the range of contexts in which ideas exist and about an increasing complexity both in the nature of concepts and also in the language used to describe them. Perhaps most significantly it is about articulating changes in one's thinking. It also applies to the development of science process skills such as observation, evaluating and designing investigations.

Particular characteristics of conceptual progression in science, articulated by Harlen (2000) and Harrison, Simon and Watson (2000), provide the basis for a summary of how the thinking of young learners might differ from that of older learners. Here are three dimensions of conceptual progression that will be evident in classrooms.

Moving from descriptions to explanations

Young children confidently describe what they see: the obvious colours of the light, the parts of a flower, the brightness of the bulb. The progression journey to be taken will lead these learners to suggest reasons why things are as they are and explain their observations. They will be able to suggest that the glass block does something to the light to create the colours, the flower parts each have a role to play in the life cycle of the flower, the bulb brightness is a result of the number of cells in the circuit.

Moving from small to big ideas

There are perhaps no more than a dozen 'big ideas' in science. The conservation of energy, plate tectonics, the germ theory of disease, natural selection and kinetic theory are candidates for the top ten. Being able to relate a small-scale result to a larger picture which is part of a big idea is evidence of progression. Such linking requires learners to have experienced a number of cases that help to define the common features of the big idea. Therefore, the transition to big ideas takes time, requires a rich set of related experiences and a teacher who can draw out the interlinking messages. The progression that the pioneering psychologist Jean Piaget describes as the transition from concrete to formal operations might be seen as an example of the small-to-big ideas transition.

Moving from the naive personal to the scientific general

Young children see the world from their own standpoint. Learning to see the world as others see it takes time. This part of the journey is supported by the teacher who engineers social interaction, group work and shared discussion. Within this progression we can include the move from a personal language towards a new language, in particular a new shared vocabulary of science which is recognised by and which characterises the science community. Such a vocabulary will include the accepted ideas and models that form the repertoire of a scientist–explainer. In appreciating how others see the world, the learner is exposed to other ways of thinking and seeing. This is an early step in the process of metacognition, whereby learners start to appreciate themselves as learners among other learners, each with an opinion that can be valued but also exchanged or refined.

What can a teacher do to promote conceptual progression?

This section looks at some practical ideas for helping children make conceptual progress. The main messages are concerned with practical professional knowledge, that is, ways of helping to support children. However, the challenge starts with teachers' own personal learning journeys and the absolute requirement to understand the science to their own satisfaction. This is the quest for personal knowledge. The second challenge is to develop pedagogical knowledge – an understanding of the particular cognitive challenges faced by children. The final challenge is to plan activities that promote conceptual progression

Personal knowledge

Some journeys are open ended with a certain pleasure in unknown outcomes. However, the science-learning journey that children take at school is expected to lead to a set of well-defined outcomes. These are stated as learning outcomes or attainment targets in curriculum guideline documents. The first requirement for teachers therefore is to know where they expect children to be heading. It is an expectation that teachers ensure, through their own study and professional development, that they have a correct and sufficiently detailed personal grasp of the key ideas to be covered in the science curriculum. Being confident with personal knowledge, being able to tell oneself the explanatory stories, is an absolute prerequisite. Such knowledge and understanding might be secured through private study, through conversations with colleagues or though engagement with a leader/mentor. Of particular value is training offered by specialists with experience in helping teachers to unravel their own preconceptions. It is not until such training is experienced that teachers discover the frailty of their own understanding. Such a personal journey can be an uplifting experience, as expressed so well by Nobel laureate Richard Feynman, who wrote in a letter to a school teacher:

> *I was born not knowing and have had a little time to change that here and there. It is fun to find things you thought you knew, and then to discover you didn't really understand it after all.* (Feynman, 2005, letter to Armando Garcia, 11 December 1985)

Given that scientific explanations might be offered at a number of levels of complexity, how deep does the teacher's own explanation need to go? In *Beyond 2000* Millar and Osborne (1998) suggest that teachers ought to aspire to be able to tell 'explanatory stories' with confidence. The stories that need to be told, be they about particles during the process of dissolving or about food during digestion, demand a confidence in science equivalent to no greater than GCSE/Standard grade, but they do need to be correct. Such stories are not for direct telling wholesale in classrooms. They are best as an intellectual backdrop from which teachers can select appropriate parts for sharing. Their critical importance in this chapter lies in their ability to help teachers see where children's conceptual progress ought to be heading.

Pedagogical knowledge

To be aware, again through reading and professional courses, of the ideas children have about science concepts, including the most common misunderstandings and how they arise, is a second target for professional development. There is no shortage of examples of those misunderstandings which children are likely to bring into the classroom. Such prior learning, rich in preconceptions, naive interpretations and partial ideas, needs to be prepared for. It is unlikely that, within a class of 30 children, there will be 30 different starting points, 30 different preconceptions. There will be only a few dominant misconceived notions in relation to any key idea and these can be found in the research literature and books that draw on such research. Armed with this prior knowledge the teacher can anticipate where the main cognitive challenges will be. Learning experiences can then be planned either to tackle such preconceptions head-on, getting children to test predictions based on their ideas if possible, or to explore the ideas further through alternative learning tasks, perhaps drawing on a variety of learning styles, role-play, drama, card sort/sequencing tasks, and so on.

To revisit the journey analogy, in order to know how to guide learner travellers teachers need to know where these learners are starting their journey from. Such pedagogical knowledge can be acquired through reading and attending courses that tackle specific conceptual 'hot-spot' areas. SPACE (Science Processes and Concept Exploration) and CLIS (Children's Learning in Science) were two influential projects that helped to chart those common misconceptions held by both children and adults in key areas of science. The fruits of this type of work can be found in many publications, most directly in the Nuffield Primary Science Teachers' Guides (1995).

Practical professional knowledge

How might teachers develop a range of methodologies that support children in articulating and sharing their prior thinking, provide experiences designed to redirect such thinking, and thereby help learners to reformulate, reshape and refine some key curriculum concepts in science? To be steered by seeking answers to this question is to be a teacher guided by constructivist principles. It presents a challenge to be met by teachers drawing on their practical professional knowledge. It is this part of teaching that allows for creative ideas and innovation. It is about how lessons are planned.

Constructivism is a major influence on contemporary science education, although by no means is it the only influence. It does, however, provide teachers with a compelling world view of how children develop understanding and how teachers might engage with such understanding and thereby help reform and develop it. A curriculum founded on constructivist principles will chart the development, the routes for progression and the interlinking of key concepts. Such a curriculum will offer teachers an insight into the continuity of concepts and in particular will articulate the journey towards the development of some important big ideas. In contrast, a knowledge-based curriculum might offer a sequence of unrelated topics, dominated by the need to know things and organised within traditional subject boundaries.

It is likely that most teachers will have experienced a knowledge-based curriculum, delivered by a transmission model of learning and dominated by the spectre of high-stakes summative assessment, placing a considerable emphasis on memory. Becoming a teacher more sensitive to a constructivist approach will demand a rejection of such a transmission model of learning and a reappraisal of what constitutes good teaching and learning. This reshaping of a personal view of what constitutes an appropriate science education is a considerable challenge for new teachers.

Theory into practice: so what does this look like in a classroom?

Armed with a secure personal knowledge and an interest in pedagogical knowledge, what strategies might a teacher use to increase the chance of conceptual progression? A good starting point is to activate prior learning on the topic in question, first by focusing on the topic and then by encouraging learners to explore what is already known about it and even what they would like to know or find out. A KWL grid (what do I Know, what do I Want to know and what have I Learnt?), a concept cartoon (Keogh and Naylor, 2000), a group concept map and a diagnostic, person-centred question (see Chapter 21) are examples of strategies that activate and explore prior knowledge.

Case study 1: Exploring ideas about gravity

Jane is the class teacher of upper primary children aged 9 and 10. She explained:

> Our topic for the month has been 'forces'. I wanted to explore ideas about gravity and in particular the concept that the effect of gravity was to pull everything to the ground and that by weighing things we could measure and record the strength of this gravity effect. I also wanted to extend learning to the idea that, living on a planet, the direction of the force due to gravity was towards the Earth's centre. We have covered ideas about planets and the solar system so this should help.

Jane has a clear personal knowledge about the importance of gravity as an effect that forces objects towards the Earth's centre, and that forces can be measured. Implied in her comments is an awareness that some children in her class will be operating with a framework that there is an absolute down, even in space. This is a common misconception and in recognising it Jane is drawing on her pedagogical knowledge.

Jane's strategy was built around a group task that made use of two sketches. Children were presented with A3 sheets on which one or other of the two sketches, Figures 25.1 and 25.2, was drawn. Each sketch was accompanied by a challenging question and children were invited to talk about the sketch and think about the question. After ten minutes the groups swapped sketches. Each group engaged in leading the ensuing discussion.

The challenge facing Jane and her class is not insignificant. The round Earth versus flat Earth issue is counter-intuitive. The floor seems pretty flat to most observers. Considering what might happen in Australia adds further complications, not the least being that children can't test out their predictions. Some might not have a clue about Australia and its relation to their home. Jane's choice of activity is founded in constructivist methodology. It encourages discussion and the articulation and then sharing of ideas. By including a question, Jane has driven the groups forward towards the goal of seeking a resolution. Conceptual progression in such a lesson will not be achieved through

Figure 25.1

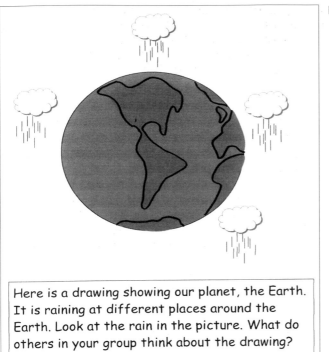

Here is a drawing showing our planet, the Earth. It is raining at different places around the Earth. Look at the rain in the picture. What do others in your group think about the drawing?

Figure 25.2

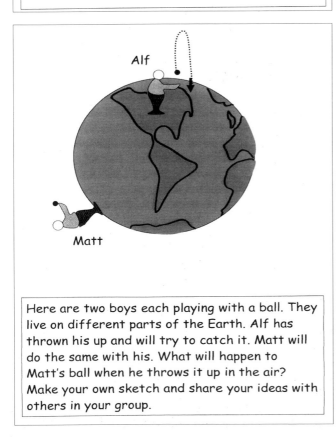

Here are two boys each playing with a ball. They live on different parts of the Earth. Alf has thrown his up and will try to catch it. Matt will do the same with his. What will happen to Matt's ball when he throws it up in the air? Make your own sketch and share your ideas with others in your group.

the sort of cognitive conflict that an obvious experimental test might provide. In Jane's class learners will progress through a series of social exchanges and shared views. Opinions will be reformulated through listening, sharing and reasoning. Australians are good cricketers. When they throw a ball it doesn't get lost in space: it comes back down to Earth.

Case study 2: Exploring ideas about electricity

Geoff teaches a mixed middle primary group with children aged 7, 8 and 9. He has been introducing the topic of electricity and electric circuits. It is the first time that children in his class have been introduced to electricity in a formal sense. He explains:

> I want to get children to appreciate the idea of a complete circuit with the idea of what goes in comes out (conservation of current). With luck we'll extend the work to connecting two bulbs in series and apply the same idea. With a mixed group I'll try using two different concept cartoons to initiate group discussion. One will tackle the complete circuit idea and the other will explore ideas about two bulbs. Both groups of learners will benefit from hearing the ideas from the other group. The older children will benefit from explaining their ideas to the younger group. We have some small bulbs, wires and batteries to test our predictions. I want to leave time for some practical exploration.

Geoff has chosen to access previous learning using concept cartoons. This decision, together with the use of group work and shared dialogue, is again a constructivist approach that explores prior ideas. In this example, the children in Geoff's class can draw on first-hand observations and test their predictions about two bulbs. The concept cartoons chosen have been created to target specific 'hot-spot' areas of misunderstanding (see Figures 25.3 and 25.4). It is evident from Geoff's approach that he is basing his teaching on his pedagogical knowledge about specific difficulties the children are likely to have with circuits. Geoff started his lesson with the concept cartoons pinned up around the room. He didn't take any time to help children focus on electricity and perhaps this was a missed opportunity to set the scene.

Geoff made a point of listening to the discussions among children in each group. He picked up messages about prior learning, in particular that everyone predicted that the two bulbs would be different brightness, justified most frequently by a 'used up' type of argument. Geoff knows that current is conserved and he is confident that he can talk himself through his own storyline about what is happening. He thinks he will introduce the language of energy transfer as a way of exploring a quantity that is 'shared' by the two bulbs. Here Geoff is drawing on his personal knowledge to help select appropriate explanations.

Commentary

The cases of Jane and Geoff illustrate teaching strategies that show an awareness of helping children to move along their own conceptual journeys. There are other strategies but most will involve some form of collaborative, shared learning and all will benefit from teachers who plan from a baseline of secure personal knowledge and an insight into pedagogical issues. These two scenarios not only illustrate the first part of the journey but also hint at how the learning might be developed as the lesson progresses. In Jane's case, dialogue

Figure 25.3

I think the bulb will light. The electricity can get along the wire from the battery.

I think the the electricity will get to the bulb but it will only be half bright. You need another wire to make it fully bright.

I think the electricity needs a complete path. You need another wire to make the bulb light.

battery

Figure 25.4

I think only the first bulb will light up. The electricity gets to it first.

I think both bulbs will light up but the first will be brighter. There is not much electricity left for the second bulb.

I think the electricity passes through both bulbs and goes back around the circuit.

battery

and story telling will play critical parts. She might choose to develop the storyline through a role-play activity involving a telephone conversation with a cricketer in Australia or a weather forecaster in South Africa. In creating an appropriate script for a role-play, children will need to share their ideas about just what should be said. This is social constructivism in its raw state, with children having to share and reformulate ideas in real time, with the support of others and driven by a dramatic context.

For Geoff the way forward lies in experimental testing and verification followed by articulating explanations for the surprising and challenging observations. The children in his class will also do much talking and thinking. They will also be engaged in planning a test, in making observations and making sense of these observations. The language of 'electric current' and 'complete circuit' will be used by Geoff as he models ways of describing a circuit in 'science speak', thereby leading the children from personal/naive ideas to shared/scientific explanations.

In both these scenarios, children have been encouraged to find their own voice and teachers have found a role as listeners rather than presenters. Such experiences are recognised as good practice by those who pioneered the 'Assessment for learning' initiatives. The movement which is *Assessment for Learning* (see Black *et al.*, 2003) and publications such as *Active assessment* (Keogh, Naylor and Goldsworthy, 2004) share a philosophy of teaching and learning that is essentially constructivist in that it places great emphasis on learners being given a voice. It is also a philosophy that encourages teachers to be learners and listeners and so adopt a formative assessment role, being skilled in asking particular types of open question, to appreciate the value of wait time, and to engineer activities that scaffold learners so that they might achieve through making their own challenging but accessible steps.

References

Black, P., Harrison, C., Lee C., Marshall, B. and Wiliam, D. (2003) *Assessment for learning*. Maidenhead: Open University Press.

Feynman, R. (2005) *Perfectly reasonable deviations from the beaten track*. London: Basic Books.

Harlen, W. (2000) *The teaching of science in primary schools*. 3rd edn. London: David Fulton.

Harrison, C., Simon, S. and Watson, R. (2000) Progression and differentiation. In *Good practice in science teaching: what research has to say*, ed. Monk, M. and Osborne, J. pp. 174–189. Buckingham: Open University Press.

Keogh, B., Naylor, S. and Goldsworthy, A., (2004) *Active assessment*. Cheshire: Millgate House.

Keogh, B. and Naylor, S. (2000) *Concept cartoons*. Cheshire: Millgate House.

Millar, R. and Osborne, J. ed. (1998) *Beyond 2000: Science education for the future*. London: King's College London.

Nuffield Primary Science Teachers' Guides (1995) various titles. London: Collins.

Chapter 26

Creativity in teaching and learning science

'Do you consider yourself to be creative in any part of your life?' *'Do you think that you are creative in primary science?'* **Rosemary Feasey**

When asked these questions the majority of a sample of teachers did not consider themselves creative at all, least of all in science, citing a range of constraints that seemed to impinge on their ability to be creative in the classroom. This chapter explores the meaning and value of creativity in primary science and examines what primary teachers feel constrains creativity in teaching and learning. It discusses the conditions and resources for supporting creativity, the role of information and communication technology (ICT) and language in fostering it and how signs of creative thinking can be recognised.

What is creativity?

There are many definitions of creativity. One of the most useful has been developed by the National Advisory Committee on Creativity and Cultural Education in the report *All our futures: creativity and culture in education* (NACCCE, 1999). This seminal report suggests that creativity is:

> *Imaginative activity fashioned so as to produce outcomes that are both original and of value.* (NACCCE, 1999, p. 29)

This definition is expanded in terms of characteristics of creativity as follows:

> *First, they [the characteristics of creativity] always involve thinking or behaving **imaginatively**. Second, overall this imaginative activity is **purposeful**: that is, it is directed to achieving an objective. Third, these processes must generate something **original**. Fourth, the outcome must be of **value** in relation to the objective.* (QCA Creativity in the National Curriculum, see website)

207

This definition provides a useful starting point and it is easy to apply the statements to primary science. Creativity should be a partnership between children and teachers.

Constraints on creativity

One hundred teachers were asked the question, *'What do you think are the constraints for teaching and learning creatively in the classroom?'* The majority of responses focused on:

- increase in paperwork linked to school inspection;
- the high level of planning for subjects across the curriculum;
- feeling exhausted and unable to find the time and energy to be creative;
- the amount of content required in terms of curriculum coverage;
- not enough time to allow children the opportunity to be creative in the class room;
- the concern that, if they taught creatively, it would jeopardise school results in national tests and school positions in performance tables.

All of the above responses are important; they indicate a level of stress that has pervaded much of the teaching profession for a number of years. However, we cannot, as a profession, allow these responses to excuse lack of creativity in teaching and learning. Everyone has the right to be creative: teachers have the right to work creatively, and they also have the responsibility to encourage and develop the creative potential of children. In an ideal world creativity would not be singled out for special treatment. To do so:

> uncovers a basic misconception about the nature of creativity. Creativity is not an add-on to the curriculum but an integral part of thinking and planning for teaching and learning episodes. Creativity requires that teachers are open to different possibilities and also appreciate that developing creativity is not an option to be disregarded but that as professionals we have a duty to be creative and develop creativity in children. (Feasey, 2005, p. 35)

Nevertheless, it is important to debate the nature of creativity and how to develop creative approaches to teaching and learning.

Children's views of creativity

Whilst teachers might understand the nature of creativity what about the children? How can they become partners in developing their creative potential in primary science? One way is to ask children what they think is special about a creative person. Box 26.1 shows just some of the responses from a mixed class of children aged 8–11 who were asked exactly that question.

What do the responses in Box 26.1 tell us? Well, certainly they tell us that children are able to think about the concept of creativity and offer profound and intuitive contributions to the debate. Their ideas include many of those that researchers and writers in the area of creativity mention, and at times with more eloquence and a sense of excitement about creativity. They are important contributions and help to provide some basis for thinking about creativity in science. The idea that creativity in science should encourage free thinking is important since it recognises that children should be engaged in

Box 26.1

Children's ideas on characteristics of a creative person

A creative person:
- *is a free thinker;*
- *is daring;*
- *thinks of lots of ideas not just one;*
- *is always thinking of new things;*
- *reaches new heights;*
- *is encouraging and joyful;*
- *lets the imagination run wild.*

(Feasey, 2005, pp. 9–10)

thinking that is not bound by the existing knowledge and expectations of the teacher. Allowing children to collaborate and discuss their ideas encourages them to share ideas and spark ideas off each other, supporting a free flow of many ideas.

The idea of being daring, a risk taker, is an important one, mentioned by writers such as Sternberg (1999) and the NACCCE report (1999). Risk is often associated with situations that are potentially harmful in science, such as using a Bunsen burner or chemicals. In the context of creativity, risk relates to a person being able to take a risk with ideas, with solutions to problems. These ideas might be different from those of their peers; they might sound ridiculous at first hearing, or be 'off the wall'. In a learning environment that supports and celebrates creativity in science, children will feel able to risk sharing ideas and ways of working with teachers and peers. To develop creativity in primary science children need to be encouraged to move out of their comfort zone and think the unusual. This might also require the teacher to do the same. A good example of this is the use of concept cartoons (Keogh and Naylor, 1997), an important tool for eliciting children's ideas in science. The cartoons are in themselves a creative teaching approach, but used carefully they can encourage children to think and work creatively, particularly where the teacher encourages them to:

- share their thinking;
- consider alternative ideas;
- explore ways of challenging and testing the ideas.

'*Always thinking of new things*' is another important aspect of creativity. In this context '*new things*' are relative to the children and their peers. The fact that the teacher already knows a solution to a problem should not invalidate children thinking of the same idea, since it may be the first time that a child has come up with that idea. It is also important that the teacher allows children to work through ideas, problems and solutions. Too often teachers give children the answer in science, either because of perceived time constraints or because they worry about frustrating children. It is important to remove the barriers to risk taking and failing. When teachers iron out problems and make choices for children (e.g. resources, solutions), this denies children opportunities to:

- tackle problems;
- consider and try out alternatives;

- take risks with their ideas and strategies;
- work as a team;
- persevere when things do not work.

The suggestion that in the process of being creative a person is able to *'reach new heights'* is exactly what we as teachers strive to do, helping a child to shift his or her personal parameters for how they think and work scientifically.

Finally, the enthusiasm and energy of a creative person is acknowledged by children's suggestions that a creative person is *'encouraging and joyful'* and is able to let their *'imagination run wild'*. This underlines how important it is for the teacher to be enthusiastic and be willing to take a risk in his or her approaches to primary science.

What might creative science look like in the classroom?

It should be acknowledged that creativity in science is less likely to flourish where schools have a rigid approach to science based on a scheme of work that lacks the basic tenets of creativity. Of particular concern are the links between school science and everyday contexts that are local and personal to the children and school. Science needs to be freed from the constraints of being taught in a 'curriculum' vacuum, in single lessons where links are not adequately made across different aspects of science and with other areas of the curriculum and children's experience. Ofsted reports that creativity needs:

> *unbroken time to develop. Primary schools which maintain sufficient flexibility in their timetables for lessons to be blocked, or extended to accommodate planned events or just to provide more time for creative activities, found it easier to enable this kind of development.*
> (Ofsted, 2003, p. 12)

Opportunities for children to work and think creatively in science might take place in weekly 10-minutes sessions where children explore and enjoy science outside the 'formal' lesson. Children might be offered science in the form of a weekly '10-minute science extravaganza', where they are shown interesting and awesome artefacts, video-clips or activities. The aim of these sessions is not to teach to a formal curriculum, but to offer children opportunities to be fascinated, awed and inspired by something and be encouraged to explore and engage in a free flow of ideas and suggestions not bound by right or wrong. Creativity in primary science requires carefully structured lessons where the teacher offers children a rich and wide range of experiences that capitalise on their different learning styles, interests and enthusiasm.

Resources for creative teaching and learning

In planning for creativity, teachers should consider the kind of resources needed to support creative teaching and learning in science. The science subject leader needs to makes purchases that support and develop creativity in the school and can be justified by considering the following questions:

- Can it be used across the school from early years to the end of the primary?
- Can it be used for a number of different purposes, such as role-play, as well as offering children opportunities to use it for revision?

- Is it interesting and will children enjoy using it?
- Can it be used in different contexts and ways that are interesting?

Purchases such as touchable bubbles (bubbles that do not burst when they are touched or land on objects) are typical of an inexpensive resource that can be used to support creativity because the bubbles:

- do the unexpected and therefore challenge expectations;
- provide a stimulus for children to ask questions;
- offer opportunities for children to problem-solve;
- offer opportunities for children to participate in 'mind investigations'.

The role of language

Planning for creative teaching and learning in science must take account of the fact that language is central to science. Science requires different kinds of language, the language of:

- science – concepts, skills and processes;
- mathematics – metres, graphs, percentages, averages as well as positional language such as on, under;
- comparison – similarities and differences;
- awe and wonder, beauty, grace, horror, the unexpected and disgusting.

In order for children to share their ideas, solve problems, take risks and think the unthinkable, they need language to express themselves. That much is obvious. What is less obvious is the potential of children to be creative in communicating their science with humour and eloquence. Figure 26.1 gives examples from Feasey (2001), where children confidently combine scientific vocabulary and ideas with descriptive language creatively in their poems.

Encouraging creative use of language in science is not just about poetry, but about providing children with the tools to explore ideas, tackle problems, take risks with ideas and ways of working and collaborating – all those elements that are important to the development of creative potential in science.

This means that teachers should model the use of language not only in relation to scientific terminology, but also to describe and explore the emotions and the awe and wonder of science. How can this be done? Everyday objects when seen from a different perspective can be surprising. The digital microscope (every school in England was given an *Intel* digital microscope as part of Science Year 2001) is ideal for showing children fabric, leaves, flowers, jewellery, parts of the body such as hair, skin, the inside of the nose and ears, from a view that children cannot see with the naked eye. This is a WOW! factor in science, and children need to develop descriptive language in order to be able to talk about it and share their curiosity and wonder. The danger of prescriptive, concept-based national curricula is that the role of awe and wonder in science education is forgotten. Scientists across the centuries have been fascinated by nature, awed by its complexity and indeed its simplicity, its patterns and effects.

There are many ways to encourage children to learn and enjoy language in science, for example offering them opportunities to solve scientific word puzzles, matching words, word bingos, riddles, SPLAT games, charades. Equally

There was an old man called Fuse,
Who invented electric shoes,
He plugged in the laces,
Took a few paces,
and got on the Nine O'clock News.

Felix age 8

I watch the seed fly silently
Across the flower scattered
meadow
And as the seed hovers close to me
I see how it is carefully designed,
And aerodynamic, suited to fly
It is whisked away by the gentle
breeze.
Then other seeds come floating by
And each have the same qualities
As the other seed, now far away,
On the soft, rich soil of the
farmer's field.

Lizzie age 11

Meteorites are HUGE!
Meteorites are ZOOMING!
Flaming and flaring
Disturbing and destroying
Meteorites are GLOOMING
Meteorites came, dinosaurs go
Dinosaurs gone, people GROW!

Joseph and friends age 6 and 7

Now the storm is over
The sky is growing light
The rain has formed huge puddles
Sparkling deep and bright.

The sun begins to shine again
Warming all the land,
Sucking up the puddles
Like a straw held in a hand.

Peter age 11

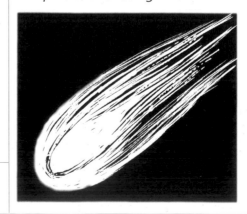

Figure 26.1 **Children's science poems**
(from Feasey, 2001).

important is to place the language of science around the classroom, including words associated with scientific concepts and scientific enquiry (e.g. graph, axis, conclusion, evaluation, table). Pictures from the digital microscope, such as a human hair, a piece of wool, a spider or a leaf, can be displayed with descriptive language around them, for example, *'Spiky spider's legs'*.

Use of ICT to develop creativity

Planned use of ICT has several important functions in developing children's creative potential in science, since ICT can:

- engage and motivate children;
- provide opportunities to collect and handle data that would not normally be available with standard scientific equipment (for example, collecting data over time, such as during the night);
- offer collaborative ways of working;
- offer new ways of using ICT in science;
- provide problem-solving opportunities;
- offer contexts that stretch the imagination;
- encourage creative ways of communicating science.

An example of creative use of ICT is the use of computer data-loggers in science. Once children are able to use data-loggers they can be challenged to ask questions that can be answered using a data-logger. Box 26.2 contains some examples of creative questioning prompted by the use of data-loggers.

Box 26.2

Which is the noisiest class in the school?

Why does the year 1 teacher always wear a jumper?

Where is it best to sit in the classroom if you want to stay warm?

Which is the coldest classroom in the school?

What happens in the school overnight?

How noisy are we in the dining room?

How can we make children be less noisy in the dining room?

Which teacher has the loudest voice?

Which teacher has the quietest voice?

Recognising creativity

So how do we know when children are thinking and behaving creatively? The QCA (see website) suggests that we will see children:

- questioning and challenging;
- making connections and seeing relationships;
- envisaging what might be;

- exploring ideas, keeping options open;
- reflecting critically on ideas, actions and outcomes.

Conclusion

The ultimate in creativity in science would be for teachers not to have to think of it as a discrete feature of provision, but for it to be second nature in terms of teaching and learning. Perhaps, though, each new generation of teachers needs to learn for itself the importance of aspects of teaching and learning. In the future, teachers will need to become risk-takers in their own thinking and practice and be prepared to try out new ideas and approaches. Importantly, schools must celebrate creativity and raise its profile in science by:

- involving children in discussion about what creativity is and in developing their own creative potential in science;
- inviting visitors into school who have links with science, from industry, universities, clinics, environment agencies;
- linking science with arts projects from music to sculpture, poets to drama;
- reconsidering resources to ensure teachers and children are stimulated by the resources and equipment available to them;
- offering regular 10-minute science sessions outside of the usual science lessons;
- developing children's higher-order skills linked with risk-taking and problem-solving;
- displaying science around the school;
- involving children, staff, parents/carers and visitors in science days, science weeks and fairs;
- celebrating children's achievements and creativity in science at every opportunity.

In all of this, an imperative for primary science will be to allow children time to think, to let ideas gestate and to explore and experience their world, so that they can be surprised, awed, shocked, angry and humbled, experiencing in science emotions ranging from humour and beauty to sadness and happiness. In order to develop creativity, children need to be given time to stand, stare, reflect, think and be surprised and awed by their world. Sometimes we don't need to do anything with that experience in science, the experience in itself will be enough to feed the creative mind, because sometimes:

Rainbows are just to look at, not really to understand.

(http:/www.juliantrubin.com/kidsquotes.html)

References

Feasey, R. ed. (2001) *Science is like a tub of ice cream – cool and fun! A collection of 100 science poems by primary and secondary school children.* Hatfield: Association for Science Education.

Feasey, R. (2005) *Creative science – achieving the WOW factor with 5–11 year olds.* London: David Fulton.

Keogh, B. and Naylor, S. (1997) *Starting points for science.* Sandbach, Cheshire: Millgate House.

NACCCE (National Advisory Committee on Creative and Cultural Education) (1999) *All our futures: creativity, culture and education*. London: DfEE.

Ofsted (2003) *Expecting the unexpected. Developing creativity in the primary school*. HMI document 1612. Available on: www.ofsted.gov.uk

Sternberg, J. ed. (1999) *Handbook of creativity*. Cambridge: Cambridge University Press.

Websites

QCA Creativity in the National Curriculum: www.ncaction.org.uk/creativity

Index